Special Voices

Special Voices

Cora Lee Five

HEINEMANN
Portsmouth, NH

Heinemann
A division of Reed Elsevier Inc.
361 Hanover Street Portsmouth, NH 03801-3912
Offices and agents throughout the world

To protect their identity, the names of the children in this book have been changed.

One chapter of this book appeared in *Toward Practical Theory: A State of Practice Assessment of Reading Comprehension Instruction*, a study funded by the U.S. Department of Education. A revised version is reprinted here by permission.

Library of Congress Cataloging-in-Publication Data

Five, Cora Lee.
Special voices / Cora Lee Five.
p. cm.
Includes bibliographical references.
ISBN 0-435-08594-8
1. Special education—New York (State)—Case studies. I. Title.
LC3982.N7F58 1992
371.9'09747—dc20 91-24709
CIP

Cover design by Thom Carter
Interior design by Jenny Jensen Greenleaf
Printed in the United States of America
99 10 9 8 7 6 5 4

To all my students
whose voices became special

Contents

Acknowledgments

In my wildest dreams, I never thought I could or would write a book, much less write anything. And then one summer I took a course with Nancie Atwell who taught me how to teach writing and more important, showed me that teachers can become learners who learn with and from their students. I am very grateful to Nancie. She changed my professional life dramatically as she led me into teacher research which made the classroom a rich and exciting place for me to grow and develop. As a result I began to write in order to share my experiences with other teachers.

I am grateful, too, to Jerry Harste, who taught me the importance of listening to children and learning from them. He enabled me to hear their special voices.

Glenda Bissex extended teacher research for me. I began to wonder, to question, to observe, and to treat problems as opportunities for learning. I appreciate her guidance and encouragement and suggestion that I turn my case studies into a book.

I was fortunate to study at Northeastern University's Institute on Writing and Teaching where I had some of the best workshop leaders in the field of writing and reading. They and my fellow participants created a stimulating environment and challenged my thinking and practices which led to continued growth and change.

I am grateful for the support and interest of friends and colleagues who wondered if and when I would ever surface again.

I am especially grateful and thankful for my principal whose trust and confidence allowed me to develop as a teacher. He gave me the freedom to learn and the needed words and gestures of encouragement when I was about to give up.

I appreciate the interest and suggestions from my class of 1990–91, writers who shared in the process of writing a book as I described each phase of its development to them.

I was most fortunate to have Toby Gordon as my editor. I appreciate her advice, guidance, gentle deadlines, needed support, and sense of humor which enabled me to complete this book. I am grateful too, to have Cheryl Kimball who took the book through production.

Most of all I am thankful for my colleague, fellow teacher researcher, and good friend, Marie Dionisio, who always listened, gave continued time, response, suggestions, encouragement, and emotional support. It has meant so much to me.

Last but not least I want to thank my family for their suggestions, understanding, and patience as I carried this manuscript with me on weekends, holidays, and vacations.

1

Cora

A teacher changes

THIS IS A book of stories, stories about a fifth-grade teacher and some very special students. It is a book about children with special educational needs whose voices have long gone unheard, children who have in the past struggled to experience success. These are the stories of children who discovered their own voices in a language-rich environment that respected and valued their ideas.

In order for you to understand the stories of the children that follow, I must tell my story first. It is a story that parallels those of my students. I, too, became a learner, found my own voice, and, as a result, was able to help students with special needs.

For years I tolerated, but never really taught, special students. I didn't know what to do with them. They might have been ESL (English as a Second Language) students, students with disruptive behavioral problems, or some of the increasing number of children who are today labeled "learning disabled." They sat in my classroom while I attended to the curriculum.

I left the decisions about their education to the various specialists who seemed to have the answers. The ESL teacher took over the teaching of students who did not speak English. Based on local and state guidelines, she determined the schedule and the amount of time she would work with these students, taking them from the room for long periods of time. The psychologist offered suggestions regarding behavior modification for children who were disruptive and took those with problems out of the room periodically to work with them individually or in small groups. And the skills teachers and the principal in conjunction with the Committee on Special Education determined the amount of aide time for individual instruction for children with learning disabilities, assigned aides to these children, and removed them from the class for specified intervals of time. The answer to the problems of the special student seemed to be removal from the classroom for instruction with the specialist.

For years I was content and relieved to let the selected people work with these students. I concentrated my efforts on the other members of my class and spent little time with the special children. Yet I felt uncomfortable with the fact that they returned to my room each day to work in workbooks provided by the specialists on isolated skills and that they seemed to make little progress. They were not involved in class activities and did not even seem to be part of the class. I did not do much about this situation for many years, until I began to grow and change as a teacher.

For me, learning and teaching started with Nancie Atwell. She taught me about the writing process, the workshop approach, and class management, but most important she enabled me to look at teaching and children in a new way. I began to observe "kids," to learn with and from students, and to take risks.

Atwell introduced me to "teacher research"; from the beginning she linked the study of writing to research. Atwell encouraged me to keep journals of what I observed. Journals allowed me to reflect on my teaching, and my reflections eventually led me into teacher research.

I began to think about children and how they become writers and learners. I discovered that I was doing less talking. I began to let my students make decisions about their writing. I began to trust them, granting them ownership. Writing became a fascinating subject to teach and the classroom became an exciting place to be, a vital place to learn and improve as a teacher.

My research allowed not only my students to flourish but me as well. As a teacher researcher I have become a continual learner who is committed to teaching. The classroom is now a constant source of discovery and excitement and I look forward to each day. Observing, listening, and learning with and from students are rewarding and satisfying experiences and powerful ways for teachers to learn about teaching. And I realize that as a teacher researcher I have the opportunity—and the power—to change things.

From my research, my philosophy of teaching and learning evolved. Central to this philosophy are letting go of the traditional curriculum and holding on to the child. The child and his or her learning process had to come first. I began to revise the hours I spent with my students.

As a result, I now give my students time to read, write, talk, listen, and especially think. My emphasis is not on how much I can teach them but on what they can learn for themselves. I provide many opportunities for collaborative learning, for responding to ideas, for testing and revising hypotheses. Throughout my students' learning experiences I try to inspire the kind of trust that allows them to experiment and take risks. I listen to them, respect their ideas, and try to make very few judgmental responses. I question and make suggestions to try to make them aware of a variety of learning styles and strategies so that they can grow and take responsibility for their own learning.

As a teacher researcher, I had to examine and question my own role in my students' learning. How did I affect what I was seeing in my students? As a result of my reading and my own experiences as a writer in writing courses, I knew I did not want to be "in charge" in the traditional sense. I did not want to take control and take away students' ideas with the "right answer." Such an approach in the past seemed only to lead to passive students, not active learners.

I wanted a classroom community that encouraged activity, where students could develop their own ideas without fear of failure or "being wrong." I wanted mistakes to be viewed as signs of learning in progress, not as failures. Bruner (1960) says that in order to solve problems on their own, students have to take chances and risks. If mistakes are treated as failures, children may not be able to take risks and discover their ideas.

My interest turned specifically to those students who did not learn in the same way. I felt many of these students were used to failure, and I wanted them to be part of this classroom community. Could they be active participants in class activities? In the past their lack of involvement in the regular classroom only encouraged their passivity and isolation. It became necessary to change things. These changes occurred at first through the process approach to writing and then spread slowly to other areas of the curriculum.

For my fifth graders and me the process approach to writing involves a cycle of brainstorming, drafting, revising, editing, and finally preparing a final copy or publishing. Conferences are a crucial part of the process and they occur often. They are essential because they provide feedback or response for the writer and can lead to revision. Conferences can be held with peers and/or the teacher to help the writer improve the quality of his or her piece. My students and I are listeners who respond honestly to student writing in conferences or in whole-group sharing sessions.

For the process approach to be truly effective in my classroom, it is necessary to have an environment that insures Mary Ellen Giacobbe's (1986) three basics; time, ownership, and response. These three elements have probably done more to change my teaching and my work with special students than anything else I have learned. The three factors create a special climate that fosters observing, questioning, wondering, investigating, and thinking. When I saw how my regular students responded to these ingredients—time, ownership, and response—I couldn't help but wonder if they would nurture the special child as well.

Time must be given on a frequent, regular basis for students to draft, confer, receive response, listen, think, reflect, revise, confer and revise again. I also provide time for the sharing of oral and written ideas. Setting aside time for all these activities underscores their value and also allows children to proceed at their own pace.

In the writing-process environment, students are encouraged to "own" their ideas. They are respected as individuals and they have choices. They select their own topics for writing, topics that are meaningful to them. Within that meaningful context, students can learn about writing and the skills involved in writing as they make decisions and take responsibility for improving their pieces. I try to make sure that students know they can have conferences and collaborate and still maintain ownership.

I work to establish a sense of community of writers that lets students respond to each others' ideas. As students write and share their work, they begin to realize that they are vulnerable and that response to writers should be supportive and constructive, feedback that helps them improve. In the classroom environment, writers must be able to take themselves seriously and be taken seriously by peers and me. Response also means that I listen to students to understand their special ways of learning, their conceptions and misconceptions. It involves my respecting their backgrounds and their ideas. And it also means being able to identify student strengths and build on them.

I spend the first month of the school year establishing what I believe to be an accepting, supportive environment. I model the writing process and I write with my students. I model conferences using my own writing to show children how questions, suggestions, and comments can help a writer. I ask for their feedback. I explain and demonstrate how negative comments can hurt and inhibit writing and all learning. In sharing sessions I encourage children to listen carefully for a chance to make positive remarks before they make suggestions. The work I do at the beginning of the year sets the tone for the classroom. Students seem to follow my model and support and encourage each other throughout the year.

As I evolved as a teacher of writing, I took specific steps to change my reading program. I gave up workbooks and modeled my reading program after the one developed by Atwell (1987). Time, ownership, and response continued to be the essential ingredients. I provided time each day for reading workshop and for reading aloud to my class. Students selected the books they wanted to read and responded to their reading in a variety of ways: whole-group sharing, letters to me and each other in reading journals, art work, and mapping. My students chose meaningful texts to read and wrote on topics that were significant to them. I hoped special students too would benefit from the shift from isolated skills drill to meaningful interaction with whole texts.

My classroom is arranged in a way that works to promote a sense of community. I changed the pattern of desks from isolated clusters of three or four desks to two semicircles of desks that face a small round table, the same height as the students' desks, which is at the front of the room. I abandoned my big desk and much of my teaching is done from the round table. It is close to the semicircles of desks and this arrangement seems to foster an open exchange of ideas between the students and me.

The round table is also the conference table during writing and reading workshops. Although I have individual conferences with students at their desks and pairs of students confer together in various parts of the room, writing conferences in my room are mainly group conferences of five or six students sitting around the conference table. These conferences, however, never seem to be limited to the group at the table. Because of the close proximity of the semicircles, all the children can be—and seem to be—involved in the conference. They respond from their seats at various times or they jump up and come to the table with a suggestion or an idea. They are all involved in each other's progress, and I think the very design of the room contributes to the creation of a supportive community.

As I made these changes in my classroom design and teaching approach, my interest in special children continued to grow. I began to question the special needs curriculum in the way I had questioned the traditional curriculum. Course work and discussions with Jerry Harste forced me to look closely at what was happening and to wonder if there was a "learning-disabled" curriculum rather than a learning-disabled child. Did recognizing that many learning-disabled children do not learn in the same ways as other students mean they were incapable of learning or participating in class activities? Perhaps they learned in different ways. I wondered what implications there were for working with various kinds of special students in a regular classroom. I extended my research to include ESL children and the many challenges the gifted present. I was curious to know whether the same conditions would nurture these children and provide an environment where they, too, could do their best.

Each year, for the next six years, I found one or two special students to observe and study—and learn from. The more involved I became in their progress, the more frustrated I became with state and local policies, pull-out programs, and standardized testing.

My state requires that every fifth grader take a writing test in May of each year. This test is divided into two parts given on two different days. Part 1 asks the student to write about an assigned topic that has to do with personal experience. Part 2 is another assigned topic but is more imaginative. Test scores are recorded on permanent records and the test results of each elementary school are printed in the local paper. There is pressure on principals to have their schools do well. This pressure is passed on to teachers and eventually to their students, who take a series of practice tests on assigned topics to prepare them for the real test.

As my special students became part of my community of writers and developed confidence in their abilities, my concern about their performance on this test increased. I knew how much they had improved but I was always nervous about whether one test would reveal the growth and progress they had made throughout the year. Fortunately my worries were unfounded. They approached the test with a positive attitude. They were far less nervous than I. When the results came in June I was always pleasantly surprised and gratified by their performance.

Angela, whose story is presented in chapter 2 changed dramatically during my first year of study. She stretched my thinking. What I learned about how she learned profoundly affected my attitude toward this type of child and made me rethink my methods of dealing with a different kind of learner. If I had not been a researcher studying Angela, I do not think I would have had the patience to struggle with the issues special students present. I would have been content to leave her school experiences to the specialists and aides as I had done for years in the past. I realized, too, another interesting aspect of teacher research. As I listened to and observed Angela, I also began to listen to and observe every other child in my room. I became curious about all of my students' learning processes. So even though I focused on one student, I learned from twenty-three. During the next five years when I had other children with learning disabilities; children with histories of emotional, behavioral, and learning problems; ESL children; and the gifted; I was able to use what I learned with Angela, apply it to these students, and continue to learn.

What follows in this book are the stories of these children, stories that paint a very different picture of the special student in the regular classroom. These students' stories consistently reveal that they can learn and flourish together with their peers in a language-rich classroom, in an environment that allows ownership, provides time, and values response. Their voices, once silent, were heard. I hope the stories of these students and my growth as a teacher will enable other teachers to work with and learn from the special children in their own classrooms.

2

Angela

A child with learning disabilities

WHEN ANGELA ENTERED my class in the beginning of September I thought she was hopeless. Over the course of the year, however, she changed dramatically. Ultimately I think it was Angela's involvement in a writing/reading process environment that enabled her to grow as a writer, a student, and most important, as a person who believed in herself.

Angela was eleven when she entered fifth grade, a year older than the other students. She was the youngest of two children in her family. Her mother spoke Spanish to the children at home as did the father, although he could speak some words and phrases in English. The parents maintained a very limited, restricted home environment. They took few trips and Angela was not allowed to play with other children after school. Her social contacts occurred in school.

At the end of Angela's kindergarten experience it was suggested that she repeat the year. She had not attended nursery school and had none of the preschool academic and social skills. She seemed to be immature and frightened. This recommendation was not accepted by the family and Angela was sent to a parochial school. At the end of first grade, retention was recommended. Her parents then brought her back to my school where she repeated first grade.

Angela was tested extensively in first grade by the skills teachers and the psychologist. The testing report noted many academic deficits and the results of an IQ test placed her below average. She was eventually declared learning disabled by the Committee on Special Education (CSE). There were many meetings between the family and the school in an attempt to place Angela in a special school for students with severe disabilities. When the parents continued to refuse, Angela was given an aide who worked with her for fifteen hours a week. She received this individualized instruction throughout her elementary school years.

I had heard from many of her previous teachers that Angela was a good quiet child who would sit in my room all year and do nothing. "Don't expect much," they warned. "It's not so bad. She comes with an aide who takes her out of the room most of the day so you really don't have to do anything." For the first month I believed them and didn't try to work with her. Her aide told me that Angela could do very little. "I'll work on the addition and subtraction facts and try to show her how to use money. Anything I can get her to do will be a miracle. She doesn't remember what I've taught so I have to go over and over it," she explained at the end of September.

Angela left my room at 9:00 each morning and returned for special classes, art, gym, and music. She didn't come back into my room until the afternoon and spent the last two hours of the day, when I usually had writing and either social studies or science, sitting at her desk working in the handwriting and phonics workbooks that the aide had given her to help her improve.

In the beginning of the year Angela was already taller than most of the other children. She was a slim, pale, pretty girl who rarely smiled. She had been placed in my room with her only friend, Amy, another girl with few friends. They had been together in fourth grade in an unstructured class environment. While their teacher was familiar with the writing process, the class did not write often. When they did write, Angela wrote with her aide who was not acquainted with the process. As a result, when Angela wrote, she either dictated to the aide or had her spelling and mechanical errors corrected immediately as she struggled to put her ideas on paper.

Since Angela was in my room without her aide in the afternoons when I taught writing, I decided to include her in my writing program. I had been involved in teaching the process approach to writing for three years and had also spent two years studying children's writing for my school district. I had seen other children flourish within the writing environment. As a teacher researcher, I wondered whether Angela could benefit from being included in our community

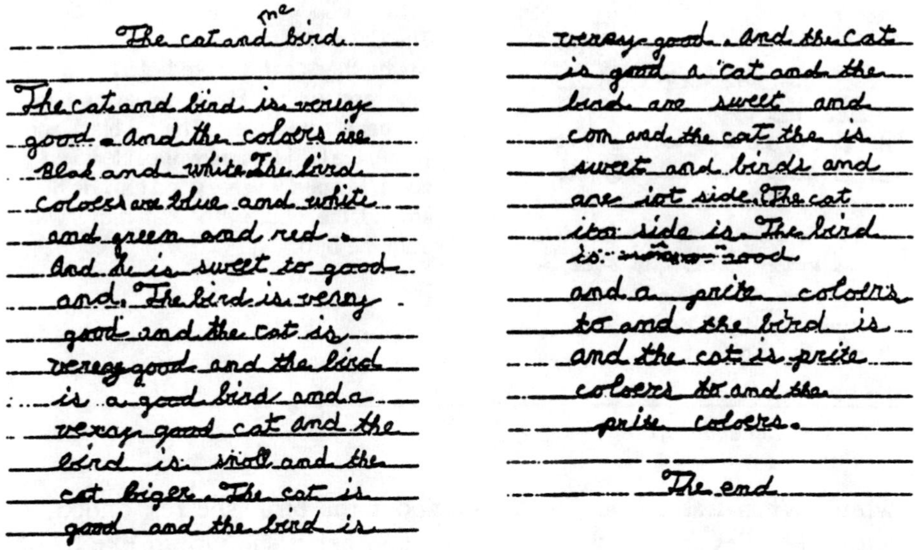

The cat and the bird
The cat and bird is verey good. And the coloers are Blak and white. The bird coloers are blue and white and green and red. And he is sweet to good and. The bird is verey good and the cat is verey good and the bird is a good bird and a very good cat and the bird is snoll and the cat biger. The cat is good and the bird is verey good. And the cat is good a cat and the bird are sweet and com and the cat the is sweet and birds and are iot side. The cat ito side is. The bird is very good. and a prite coloers to and the bird is and the cat is prite coloers to and the prite coloers.
The end

FIGURE 2.1 *Angela's journal entry*

of writers. I decided to observe and follow her progress. She became my first case study. I told her to put away the phonics and handwriting workbooks and write with the rest of the class.

For the first few weeks of fifth grade Angela wrote on her own. Often she wrote two or three words over and over again on a page (see Figure 2.1). Her journal entries and her class writing during September were about her family's cat and bird, topics she had used in fourth grade.

Toward the end of September she had a writing conference with me. She told me her piece was about her brother's cat and his bird. When I asked what the cat looked like she told me it was black and

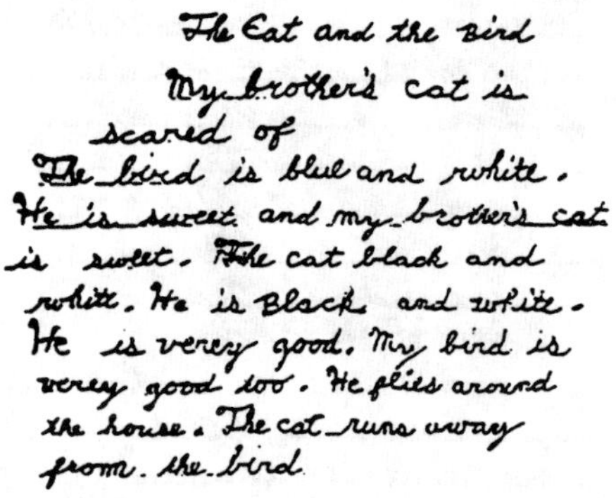

The Cat and the Bird
My brother's cat is scared of The bird is blue and white. He is sweet and my brother's cat is sweet. The cat black and white. He is Black and white. He is verey good. My bird is verey good too. He flies around the house. The cat runs away from the bird.

FIGURE 2.2 *The Cat and the Bird*

white. When I asked her to tell me about the bird, she responded with, "He flies around the house." I asked her if she would like to include these details in her piece. She said, "I don't know." I told her that she was the writer and she could decide what to put in her piece. She seemed confused and went back to her seat. She eventually included them. After an editing conference with me, she produced her first edited piece at the beginning of October, a result of her many journal entries (see Figure 2.2).

During October Angela continued to write in her journal. She described most things, animals, and people as "very good." She would not share these entries with me or her peers in conferences so I responded to them by writing back to her in her journal. Her journal writing seemed to be a vehicle for personal growth.

Toward the end of November she was writing longer entries and the topics were expanded. She wrote about playing in the park, about ice cream and other foods, and about her friend, Amy. She also began to express her feelings: "I love my brother to," "And I like you to Amy and my brother and my dad and my mom to."

Angela was reluctant to come for conferences but she sat near the conference table and seemed to be listening to other children confer together and with me. Gradually she began to talk to Amy, telling her about the topics of her journal pieces. Amy offered lots of advice, and sometimes Angela tried to include some of Amy's suggestions in her journal, usually at the end of her entry. I think this was an important first experience for Angela. Because she made some decisions about her writing based on Amy's response, it was the beginning of her developing a sense of ownership. It was also a start at interacting with and learning from another child.

Toward the middle of November I asked Angela if she would like to have a conference with me. Each day I asked every student to tell me what they planned to do during the writing period. Angela always answered, "First draft." She never requested a conference of any kind. This time however, she said yes and told me she was writing a piece about her duck.

During the conference, I asked her questions about her piece: "What parts do you like? What's the most important thing about your piece? What would you like the other kids to know about the duck?" She was eager to talk about the duck and wanted to include these details in her piece but appeared confused.

I thought perhaps it might be helpful if she added only one detail at a time. Each time she told me something about the duck, I asked her if she would like to add it to her piece. If she said yes, I would then ask her where she would like to put it. She would struggle to read her piece for she often had trouble reading her writing due to her difficulties in spelling. When she found a place she would rush back to her desk, write out a sentence, and tape it in the spot she chose. Then she'd come back to the conference table to tell me more, would again write out one sentence at her desk, and tape that in another place (Figure 2.3, page 14). This became a pattern for revision that continued for most of the year.

Her piece about the duck seemed to be a big breakthrough. It was the first time she had a sense of revision based on response. It was a new experience for her to rethink and add information to her piece to make it clearer and more interesting.

Another new experience for Angela was the importance of audience. She told me that the duck ate macaroni because that was what her mother cooked for the duck. She was somewhat perplexed when I laughed, but when I explained why I thought it was funny she laughed too. This was the first time I had seen any expression in her. She added to her piece: "He eats macaroni. My mother cooks macaroni for the duck. I think it is weird."

This story was a turning point for Angela. She was very proud of it. She knew she had worked hard on it and I think she sensed it was her own. She showed the piece to the skills teacher, her fourth-grade teacher, and her former aide (Figure 2.4, page 15). She would not

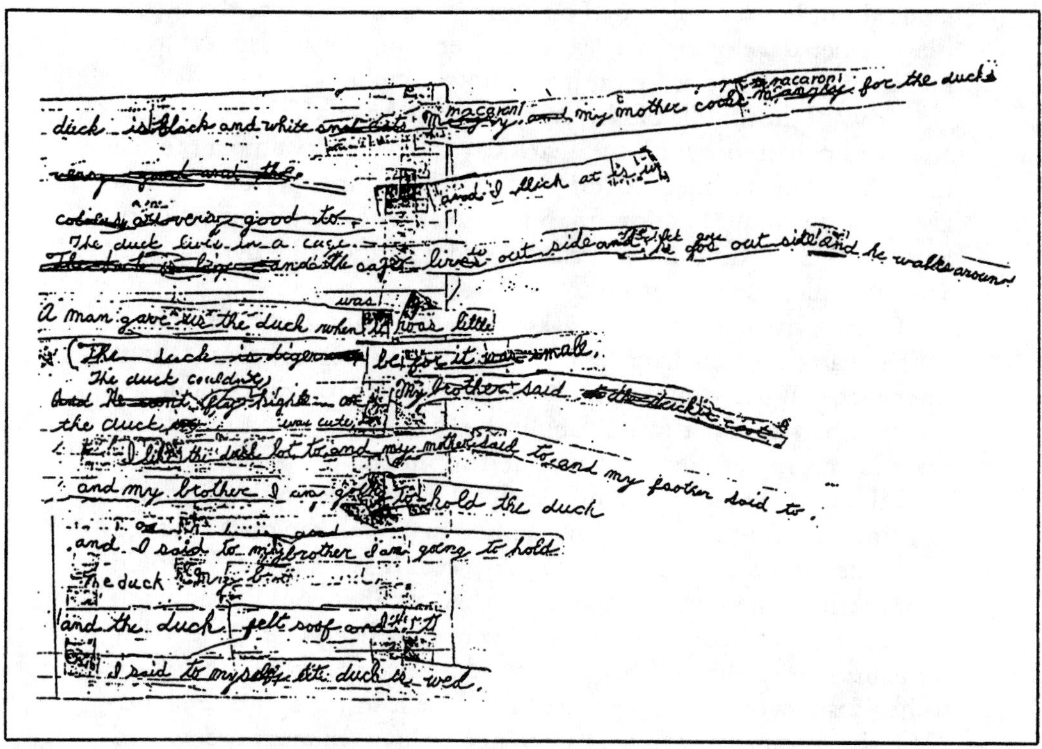

macaroni
The duck lives in a cage
A man gave us the duck when
and my brother
hold the duck
and I said to my brother I am going to hold
and the duck

FIGURE 2.3 *Angela's revision strategy*

share it with the class, but it remained her favorite piece throughout the year because "it was funny."

After the duck story Angela came for conferences often. She was most comfortable in expressing her ideas with me, but she talked often with Amy. I did not make any judgments about her writing but always asked for her opinion and thoughts. Amy, on the other hand, wanted to help Angela in any way possible and often wrote in sentences for her and told Angela what she should do to make her piece better. In group conferences Angela said very little but watched and listened and learned from the other children. Soon she was able to respond as they did. In a barely audible voice she would tell one thing she liked about another child's story. However, she would not discuss her own.

Her writing continued to improve and she took great pleasure in it. She began to ask each day, "Will I be here for writing?" She knew we always had writing in the afternoon when she was not with her

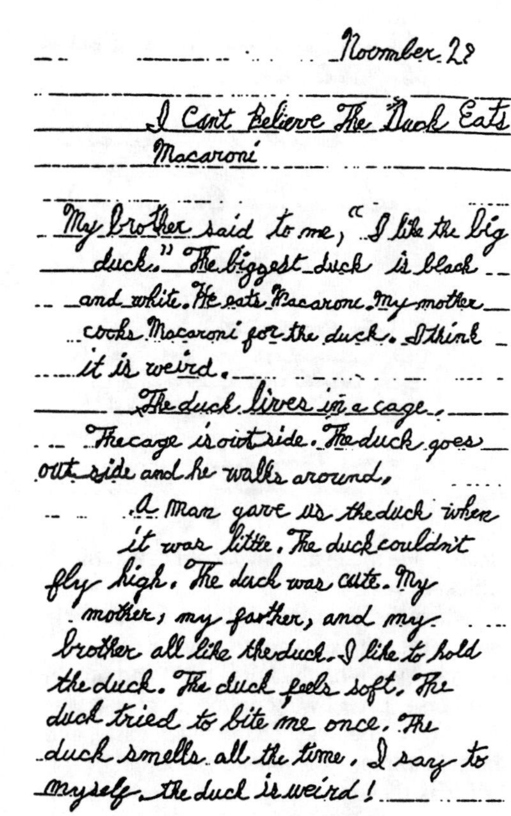

I Can't Believe The Duck Eats Macaroni

My brother said to me, "I like the big duck." The biggest duck is black and white. He eats Macaroni. My mother cooks Macaroni for the duck. I think it is weird.

The duck lives in a cage. The cage is outside. The duck goes outside and he walks around.

A man gave us the duck when it was little. The duck couldn't fly high. The duck was cute. My mother, my father, and my brother all like the duck. I like to hold the duck. The duck feels soft. The duck tried to bite me once. The duck smells all the time. I say to myself the duck is weird!

FIGURE 2.4 *Angela's duck story*

aide but she began to worry about the time she left the classroom once a week in the afternoon to work with the skills teachers. Often she did not want to go and occasionally she told the skills teacher that I would not let her leave the room that day.

In January Angela wrote a story about a trip to Playland, an amusement park. She talked about her first draft with me and two other children. She added details as a result of these conferences: "The boat was shaky. . . . The boat went through a maze. The maze was narrow. The boat hit the walls." She was pleased with this piece too but did not want to share it with the class (see Figure 2.5).

During the winter months, when the class was involved in the study of American history, Angela was exposed to additional

When I Went To Playland

It was my first time to go to Playland. I saw old red cars that were small. I also saw a boat ride and a horse on the Merry-go-round My brother and I went on the boat. The boat was shaky. Two people could go go on the boat. My brother sat in front of me. The boat went through a maze. The maze was narrow. The boat hit the walls.

In the middle of the maze my brother was scared. He made a funny face. I called him a chicken.

When the boat stopped, we got out. He said to me, "It was scary." I said, "It was fun."

Then I went on the horse and I had fun on the horse. Later I went on the dragon. It was fun. My brother went on the rollercoaster and he said to me, "It is time to go home!"

I was feeling very good. I was happy to have gone to Playland.

FIGURE 2.5 *Playland story*

strategies for learning: reading historical fiction, small group conferences, and simulations. The students participated in a game in which most of the class was treated unfairly by a small group given special power to rule. This was an attempt to have the students understand the sentiments and feelings of the colonists. Although Angela was a quiet participant, she was part of this group of learners. She was more actively involved when the class recreated the Constitutional Convention. The boys became delegates while the girls sat in the back of the room listening intently, angry at being excluded because of their sex. "It's not fair," she shouted with the rest of the girls.

Through these simulations and the sharing of ideas and feelings in group conferences, Angela seemed to realize that she too had ideas

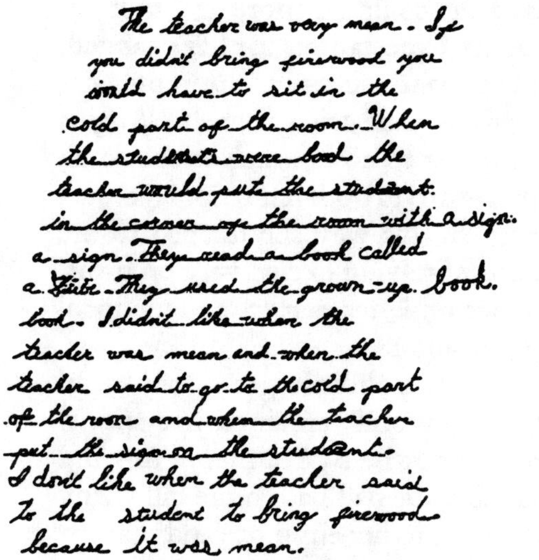

The teacher was very mean. If you didn't bring firewood you would have to sit in the cold part of the room. When the students were bad the teacher would put the student in the corner of the room with a sign. a sign. They read a book called a bibe. They used the grown-up book. book. I didn't like when the teacher was mean and when the teacher said to go to the cold part of the room and when the teacher put the sign on the student. I don't like when the teacher said to the student to bring firewood because it was mean.

FIGURE 2.6 *Colonial Times*

that she could express. She came to understand that her ideas were respected and taken seriously. She was also exposed to multiple perspectives from the other students.

As part of social studies, the class wrote reports about colonial times and the Civil War period. Before my students began writing the actual report, they spent weeks immersed in reading as preparation for writing. They selected books, nonfiction and historical fiction, that appealed to them. They also viewed filmstrips and films and listened to tapes. They discussed their ideas and findings with partners or in small groups. Angela was included in all of these activities.

Her first report, written in January, was about colonial schools. She read two short books, but since she had difficulty with reading, she relied heavily on the illustrations as a source of information. When she conferred with others who had the same topic she was able to explain what she learned through pictures from the books. She learned a lot from Amy and another child who had read extensively on the subject. In this context, Angela learned new strategies for acquiring information: the use of illustrations and discussions with peers. She incorporated this information into her report and added a section at the end describing her feelings (see Figure 2.6).

Angela was taking more and more risks. And so was I. I began to trust her and her abilities. I realized she could do more and more of her work with little help from me. My expectations for her changed. I noticed that she participated in many conferences and attempted her reports on her own. In fact, when the aide tried to help, Angela refused. It seemed to be important to her to do as much as she could by herself. She included many illustrations in both her colonial report and her report on Harriet Tubman. In this way she learned to use different forms of expression instead of relying exclusively on print, an area that, because of her insistence on letter-perfect conventional spelling, continued to cause her frustration.

As Angela's confidence in her writing abilities grew, her social relationships improved. Although Amy still remained her special friend, she began to socialize with other girls. By February Amy did not have the influence over Angela that she had had in the fall. Amy complained that Angela would not listen to her anymore and that she was even trying to boss her around.

Angela began to use the slang expressions that the other girls used, and seemed secretly pleased when the boys teased her as they did the other girls. She also started to dress the way the other children did. She wore the bracelets and necklaces that they wore and listened intently to all their talk about Madonna and the classes they had had in sex education. She didn't contribute often but seemed happy to be "one of the girls."

The classroom environment affected Angela in another way. As a writer Angela had begun to understand that she had options and choices and that there were opportunities to make decisions. My own growth as a teacher seemed to parallel hers. I realized that I, too, had options and opportunities to make decisions, decisions that could and would affect Angela's learning. I had allowed Angela to be removed from my room for long periods daily. Because I began to see the importance of having Angela in my classroom learning with and from her peers and doing the same activities her classmates did, I questioned the role of the aide and began to look for ways to change Angela's situation and keep her involved with other learners.

I realized too, the classroom environment gave Angela a sense of freedom she had not been exposed to before. Her past years had been spent obediently following the instructions given by her aide. In the early spring she became a "talker" and began to assert herself. In class, she began to talk, often disrupting the class at times with her newly developed confidence. Instead of leaving at 9:00 to meet her aide, she would look at the clock, look at me, and stay in the room to listen to the day's news team discuss news events. I never forced her to leave. I let her stay until her aide finally came to claim her.

Then Angela decided that she too, wanted to be on a news team. She and her aide selected a news article and she gave her news report. This was the first time she spoke in front of the class.

In the weeks that followed Angela raised her hand occasionally to answer questions. She also told me she wanted to stay in class and do the same math that the other children were doing. Again, the aide had to come to get her.

Angela also wanted to take the same practice writing tests for the state writing test that everyone else took. In the fall, I had decided that she would not participate in these practice tests because her score would not count due to her learning-disabled classification. However by the spring she was willing to experiment with the assigned topics I gave in preparation for the May test. She waited anxiously for me to return the practice tests so she could read the comments I wrote to her. If I held hers for a day or two to show other teachers, she demanded to have them and have a conference so she would know how to improve. After taking a number of the practice tests, Angela took the state test with the rest of her classmates and passed!

In May Angela and I convinced her father to let her go on a day-long trip to explore an 1830 restored village. She delighted in most of the things that she saw but was especially interested in the school and the schoolmaster. Here she related her prior knowledge of colonial schools to her impressions of this school.

School In Colonial Times

I saw in a Colonial School houes
that was old. The man expland
about the Colonial School houes he
replind about when the stunits.
Were bad the stunits on the hand.

And the stunit whould have
to bend down. And hold a nail up.
I thing that was not farner
and he.

Was bad because how he was talking
and he was mind and put a
book on or hand for an lower.

They at in woodn't chairs. And
they had a book in farnt of
the classroom!!

The Colonial School was small!!!

By late spring Angela became much more assertive and often refused to leave the class to work with her aide. She especially wanted to take part in our science study of bridges. The rest of the class had a good understanding of balance: the aide was positive that Angela could not understand the concept of balancing and would not work with her on it.

I began to work with Angela individually to help her understand. When I first mentioned the word "balance," Angela told me she had not heard of it. I took a piece of wood and a fulcrum from the science cart and made what she recognized as a seesaw. We moved the board around on the fulcrum until it remained level. I told her it was balanced. Then I took a block and placed it on one end of the board and asked her how I could make the board balanced again without removing the block.

At first she didn't know and didn't seem to have any ideas or strategies for discovering an answer. I suggested she look at the materials on the science cart to see if anything there might help her. She selected a few blocks of different sizes and finally placed three of various sizes on the other side of the board and looked to see what had happened to the board. It was not level and I told her it was not balanced. She then began to experiment by removing blocks one at a time. When the board still did not balance she began to examine the block I had placed on the board. She found a block that was the same size and shape and placed it on the other end of the board. However, she did not place it as close to the end as I had so the board was not exactly level. This dissonance caused her to look again at my block. She then adjusted her block so it was in the same place as mine, and the board was balanced.

Angela spent the next half hour balancing blocks of various sizes on the ends of the board. She discovered that she could balance three small blocks with my one block. Then she decided to investigate her idea of balance with other things. She balanced her pencil and eraser

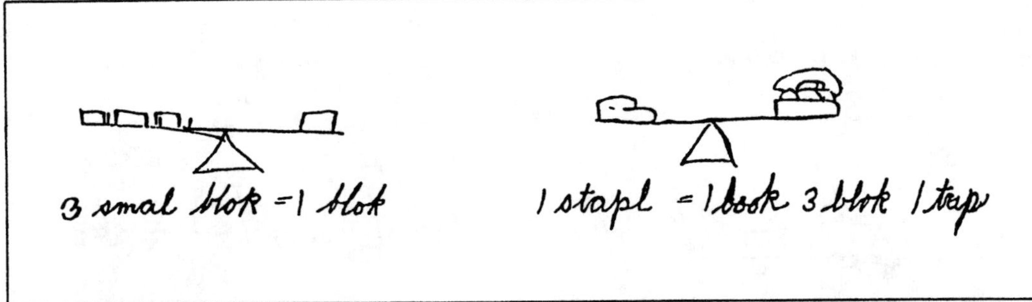

FIGURE 2.7 *Journal entry: balance*

with a small block; the stapler with her math book, three blocks, and a roll of tape. After a while I asked her to record her work in her science journal and she drew diagrams showing the board with the various items balanced. I told her she could express her ideas in another way. She could use the equals sign. She tried this way too (see Figure 2.7).

Angela continued to enjoy the concept of balancing. She began to move the items to various places on the board and still had them balanced. She learned that it made a difference where the objects were on the board. She continued to record in her own way, mainly through pictures.

Angela eventually went on to apply her understanding of balance to various structures and to her final project, a bridge, built out of 250 plastic straws, tape, and straight pins. She selected cues from many sources—books, pictures, discussions—and built a strong, well-balanced bridge. Her creativity was expressed in the design of her bridge and structures. She continued to rely on drawings as she recorded her progress in her journal (see Figure 2.8).

Throughout the unit on structures, the children did much brainstorming. Often they did more talking than building as they discussed ideas and experimented with materials. They tried many different ways of making a bridge that would hold a lot and would not collapse. They wanted response and were very accepting of suggestions as they revised their bridges by adding triangles and squares to make them stronger. They tore down and reconstructed their bridges many times. They conferred, researched, and revised again. Each time, the bridges improved. Angela was part of this process. She learned from her peers through conferences. She revised her bridge many times and was delighted with the finished product.

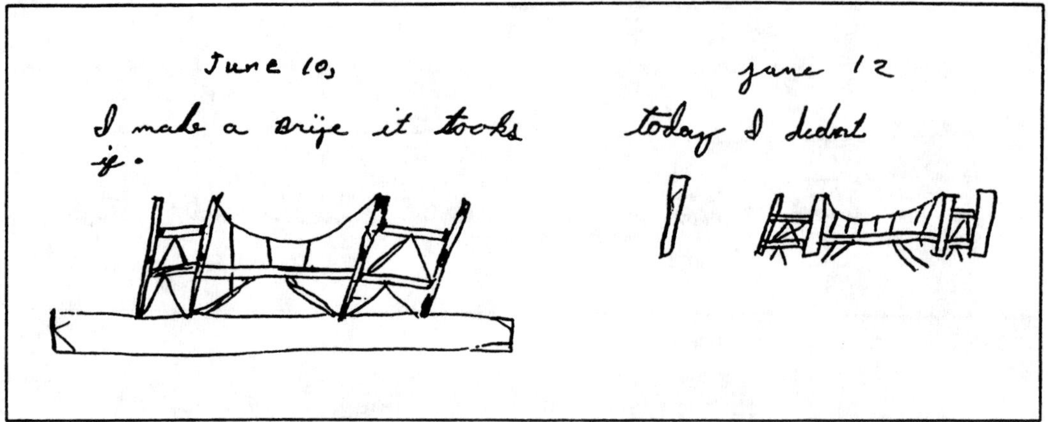

FIGURE 2.8 *Journal entry: bridge building*

By the end of the year Angela had blossomed into an enthusiastic girl, who raced across the playground eager to get to school. She was animated and playful, full of affectionate gestures for those she liked. Her last writing project involved writing a fictional story based on her first-grade partner. The fifth graders in my room had been paired with first-grade partners in September. They worked together weekly on various activities. Angela had worked with Jennifer all year helping her as best she could with reading, writing, and math. In June she had her interview with Jennifer. She used the information from the interview to write her story.

Angela initially put all the information she gathered into her draft. When she came for a conference John said to her, "That doesn't sound like a story. It sounds sort of like a report."

Angela was confused and told us she didn't know how to write a story. Finally another student asked what Jennifer liked best and Angela told us, "Spaghetti and meatballs!"

Michael suggested that Angela have Jennifer go to Spaghetti Land. "How can I do that?" Angela responded. She appeared to think about it as she listened to other children's stories. Later, she discussed her ideas with Amy and Kathy. Eventually she had the first draft of a story about Spaghetti Land and Jennifer's adventures in the land of pasta.

Angela continued to add details as a result of conferences. The details were imaginative: "She looked on the ground and she saw green spaghetti that was grass." "She played with a jump rope that was spaghetti." "Jennifer looked up and she said, 'It is snowing! I

She saw flowers that were spaghetti and meatballs. She played with a jump rope that was spaghetti. Jennifer looked up and she said, "It is snowing! I can't believe it! It is cheese!" She tasted it. It was cheese! She exclaimed, "OK. Right now, I can have all the spaghetti and meatballs that I want." She ate the spaghetti and meatballs. "That was good.

FIGURE 2.9 *Spaghetti land story*

can't believe it! It is cheese!' She tasted it. It was cheese!" In this final writing piece she included dialogue, humor, and, for the first time, imagination (Figure 2.9). What a long way from "The cat and bird is very good"!

At one point she was stuck on an ending. I told her to keep thinking about it and to try some different endings and see which she liked best. Two days later she came racing to school with a crumpled piece of paper in her hand. "Here is the ending!" she shouted. "I thought of it on the way home and wrote it down. . . . I know just where to put it." She grabbed her folder and taped on the ending.

Angela went on to make a hardcover book for her story. She carefully illustrated it and included a section called "About the

Author," in which she wrote: "Angela likes basketball, ice cream, school, and Miss Five. Angela likes gym, writing, and reading."

I worried what was going to happen when she finished her book. All the other students had read their books to their first graders in front of the first-grade class and my other fifth graders. Angela still had not read any of her writing pieces to the class. But when I asked her if she would like to read it to her first grader alone or in front of the class, she surprised me by saying, "I'll read it to the whole class because I love the ending."

She thought the ending was very funny because after spending a day playing with spaghetti jump ropes, looking at trees and flowers made out of spaghetti, and eating all the spaghetti she could eat, Jennifer arrived home to find out she was having spaghetti for dinner! This time Angela was aware of the humor and appreciated it herself, often laughing as she read it to herself.

While Angela took another risk, I sat in the back of the room praying that she would be able to read her story without embarrassment. She read confidently and beamed when everyone clapped. I didn't hear the comments from her classmates about the parts they liked best. I sat marveling at the changes that had occurred in this child and wondering what had allowed them to take place.

Was it the environment that enabled Angela to grow and change over time as a writer, a learner, a person? What part did I play in helping these changes occur? When I reflected on Angela's progress, I discovered my own. I had realized the importance of a supportive classroom environment and had worked hard to preserve and sustain it. I became aware of the importance of trusting the student to take responsibility for her learning and letting go of the control. Seemingly my instructional approach helped Angela develop some self-confidence and independence. It also provided her with many opportunities to read and write, and to see demonstrated and to come to value a variety of strategies for effective communication. This environment gave her options and allowed her to take risks. There were expectations set for her and she developed some for herself. She was part of many communities of learners and experienced the flow of ideas through prolific reading, writing, listening, and talking.

For years, isolated with an aide, Angela had attempted to learn by herself, practicing number facts and working in handwriting, spelling, and phonics books. This year she learned with and from others. She became aware of her ideas and her ideas were valued. She learned to express those ideas through art, discussions, simulations, manipulation, reading, and writing.

Angela's aide that year did not allow her to take risks. There was no opportunity for experimenting and exploring. Instead the curriculum for students like Angela focused on very specific skill-oriented goals. The emphasis was on what the students could not do and what they did not know. It did not seem to build on prior experience or abilities. It did not seem to engage students in different strategies for learning. The curriculum for these special children—these Angelas—let them be learning disabled, and perhaps kept them disabled.

A literate, supportive environment seemed to let Angela be a successful learner. This type of environment built on what she could do and respected her as an individual. It encouraged ownership of ideas and responsibility for learning. From this sense of authority or control over her learning came the independence that Angela developed. In her final writing evaluation conference of the year Angela told me the best thing about her Harriet Tubman report and her book for her first grader was "that I did them myself."

Angela changed dramatically during the year. The shy, dependent child who had no confidence and no real connection to her classmates and to learning turned into an animated, involved girl who thought of herself as a learner. She was able to participate in all activities, not just art, gym, and music, as in the past. And she raised her hand to voice her opinions. She was accepted socially and developed friendships with the other girls. She was no longer an outcast.

The sparkle in Angela's eyes and her enthusiasm came, I believe, from her inclusion and acceptance as a member of the learning community. She no longer felt different. She could do what the other learners did, on her own level, at her own pace, and her efforts, her own process, and the results were supported by her peers and by me. This was a new experience for Angela and for me. At the beginning I think we were both unsure of the outcome, but we took risks, we took small steps together, and we grew.

Angela taught me a lot that year. What I learned about how she learned profoundly affected my attitude about teaching and made me rethink my methods of dealing with a different kind of learner. Like Angela, I needed time and space to evolve, examine, explore, and experiment with alternate strategies for learning. I developed as a teacher as Angela developed as a student.

3

Mark and Peter

Problem learners in contrast

THE FOLLOWING YEAR, I had Mark and Peter in my classroom. These two boys were viewed as children with problems, but their situations were quite different. Mark's progress had been followed since kindergarten; in second grade it was determined he was a child with learning disabilities. Peter came to my school in fourth grade and was not thought to have any outstanding difficulties. When he entered fifth grade, I noted obvious problems and enlisted the support of the skills teachers and the psychologist. Although these people were willing to meet to discuss Peter, there was a reluctance to identify him as a special student and provide him with extra support.

Mark was the youngest child in his family. He seemed to have academic problems from the beginning even though he was older than most of the other children in his grade. When he entered kindergarten, it was noted that his speech and verbal expression were below average. During kindergarten he made some progress in reading readiness skills but he was still below average for his age when he went to first grade. In first grade he received skills help three times a week and also worked with the speech therapist. This individual instruction did not help Mark develop his reading skills at the expected rate and he eventually was referred for a psychological evaluation. He was given a battery of tests and scored well above average on IQ tests.

In his early years in school Mark was seen as shy and uncommunicative. He would not ask for help even when he did not understand.

Those who worked with him felt his reluctance to communicate was due to articulation problems. He said "cuddles" for "colors," "togebba" for "together." He also used words such as "tooken" and "eated." Mark's written work showed letter reversals and he did not or could not use phonics for decoding. From the beginning Mark wanted to succeed. Achievement was important to him and he was embarrassed by his academic difficulties. He dealt with his insecurity by remaining quiet and passive in the classroom.

The specialists felt that Mark's language and perceptual problems would make it difficult for him to learn through conventional instructional methods. They recommended that, in addition to individual help from the skills and speech teachers, Mark receive individual assistance within the classroom. An aide, Anne, was assigned to Mark in second grade and she continued to work with him through third, fourth, and fifth grade. In fourth grade there was some discussion as to his continued need for an aide but Mark's mother preferred to have the aide's help because she thought it would help Mark develop greater self-confidence.

Peter came to my school in the spring of fourth grade. In his previous school he had had behavioral problems since kindergarten. Some testing done in the fourth grade indicated that Peter's IQ was below average. The testing also uncovered emotional as well as cognitive problems. These problems appeared to affect his reasoning skills, social judgments, and verbal comprehension. It was found that Peter had a language disorder that affected his ability to remember verbal information and his ability to sequence events. These problems made it difficult for him to organize his work. Peter showed low self-esteem, fears, and anger. He also had a tendency to act out. The behavior problems Peter experienced in school seemed to be related to his sense of insecurity.

When the school psychologist saw and tested Peter in November at my request, she found gaps in his learning and negative feelings about his ability to learn. It was recommended that he receive help from skills teachers to fill in the gaps.

Peter, too, was the youngest in his family. Some of his siblings also had difficulties in school. The parents were very concerned about all the children and communicated with me and the school at regular intervals.

From the beginning Peter was the opposite of Mark. He did everything quickly. He worked fast and carelessly whereas Mark worked slowly and methodically. Peter moved with speed, never able to stay in the same spot for very long. His attention span was short and he was unable to focus on a given task. Mark, on the other hand, labored over his work. While Mark struggled with oral and written expression, Peter expressed himself constantly, usually orally at inappropriate times, but often in writing. Mark absorbed what went on around him; Peter was distracted by everything around him. Mark worked well in a group; Peter could only work in a one-to-one situation. Mark was quiet and calm; Peter was loud and demanding. Mark's lack of confidence was evident; Peter boasted about how much he knew in a desperate attempt to cover up his inadequacies.

I became especially interested in the two boys because they both had problems in language development. I wondered if a writing and reading workshop approach would help. I hoped to apply what I had learned from my study of Angela to these special kinds of learners. I was also intrigued by their different temperaments and attitudes. Would they respond in a similar way to the same environment? Would they, could they, both become part of the classroom learning community?

Mark

When Mark entered my room in September, he spent the first few weeks doing very little on his own. He was a passive learner with very limited oral and written language. He had great difficulty expressing feelings, ideas, and opinions. He was usually quiet, said little to me, and never volunteered to speak in any class discussions. If consulted, he was content to agree with whatever idea or opinion was presented. He appeared to be very dependent on his aide, Anne, who had worked with him since second grade. I remembered this dependency had also been true of Angela. Each day Mark waited for Anne to come before he would begin his work. She was assigned to him for two and a half hours each day. She felt it was her responsibility to work with him on an individual basis in social studies, but primarily in language skills; vocabulary, spelling, reading, and writing. Mark's math skills were strong.

Anne took over Mark's writing and reading activities in the early days of fifth grade. I had noticed that he worked and responded slowly to everything. However, she nudged and badgered him to talk, to write, and to work in a reading skills workbook, thus fostering the dependency I felt already existed. I used to wince when I heard her forcing words out of him when he did not answer right away. When he finally came out with something and then wrote it on his paper, I would hear her say, "No, I don't like that. Let's write it this way." She had been in charge of his writing in fourth grade and seemed to continue the pattern during the first two weeks of fifth grade. Slowly I began to realize that Anne would pose a problem for me. Her method of dealing with children differed drastically from my own, and it had a negative effect on the environment I was trying to create.

When Anne was not around during writing time, Mark did not write. He sat with an empty piece of paper on his desk and often talked to his friends, Bob or Peter. He was easily distracted by these two. When I encouraged him to start his work, at times he made flip remarks to me under his breath. He did not come for conferences but seemed to listen to the conversation at group conferences because his seat was close to my conference table. Again I was reminded of Angela. She too had spent the first month sitting at her desk doing what appeared to be nothing. Yet I was aware that she too listened to the conferences around her.

After the first few weeks of school I told Anne that I did not want her to work with Mark on his writing. She gave him less help but seemed to hover in the background, at times reading over his shoulder, at other times reading other students' writing pieces and telling them what they should change and what she liked about their pieces. I could see that she was a force to be reckoned with.

During the third week of school, I noticed that Mark had written a two-page piece about a trip to Vermont (see Figure 3.1). I asked him to join us at the conference table. He listened to others share their writing but did not volunteer to read his work. The next day I asked him to come again and this time I asked him to read his writing. The class had been working on focusing on one topic. Mark did not read his piece but he told us about it briefly.

Some of the students at the table told him they thought he had more than one topic. I asked him what he thought. He answered with a response that was to be typical of him for the next few weeks, "I

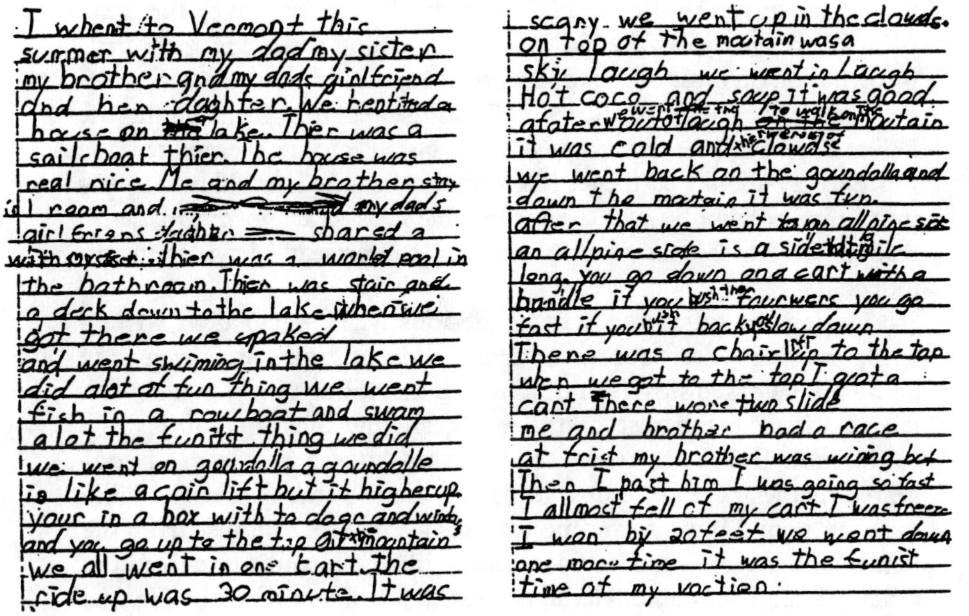

I whent to Vermont this summer with my dad my sister my brother and my dads girlfriend and her daghter. We rentited a house on a lake. Thier was a sailboat thier. The house was real nice. Me and my brother stay in 1 room and——my dads girlfriens daghter shared a with my sister. Thier was a world pool in the bathroom. Thier was stair and a deck down to the lake. When we got there we upaked and went swiming in the lake we did alot of fun thing we went fish in a rowboat and swam alot. the funitst thing we did we went on goundolla a goundolle is like a cair lift but it higherup. your in a box with to door and windows and you go up to the top of the mountain we all went in one kart. the ride up was 30 minute. It was scary we went up in the clowds. on top of the mountain was a sky laugh we went in Laugh Hot coco and soup it was good afater we went out of the laugh to walk on the mountain it was cold and their were lots of clowds we went back on the goundolla and down the moutain it was fun. after that we went to an allpine side an allpine side is a side that a mile long. you go down on a cart with a handle if you bush the fourwers you go fast if you bush it back you slow down There was a chair lift up to the top when we got to the top I got a cart. There wore two slide me and brother had a race at frist my brother was wining but Then I past him I was going so fast I allmost fell of my cart I was freeze I won by 20 feet. we went down one more time it was the funist time of my vacation.

FIGURE 3.1 *Mark's writing sample: Trip to Vermont*

don't know." I suggested that perhaps he would like to decide on one topic. He shrugged. We questioned him about the topics in his piece, where he stayed in Vermont, what the house was like, the lake, fishing, the gondola, the ski lodge, the alpine slide. He gave little information on most of the topics but seemed slightly animated when discussing the alpine slide. A peer suggested that he thought the alpine slide might be a good possibility because Mark seemed to have more to say about that topic. Mark again shrugged. I told him it was up to him because he was the writer. He looked at me and made no response. "At least he participated in a conference!" I wrote in my journal.

During the following writing periods Mark decided to write a completely new draft about the alpine slide. It took him a long time because he worked slowly and, if he had the opportunity, talked with friends. It took the rest of the week and he did not come for a conference. The next week we discussed and shared leads. I suggested that Mark try two new leads and come to the conference table to share them. He did come and read his leads. The response from the students at the table was divided. Some liked one and some liked the other, a situation I could tell did not make Mark comfortable. He was not used to making choices. He would have been far happier if his friends had told him which one to choose. I asked him which one he liked and he responded with his usual "I don't know." Again I told him he was the writer and it was up to him. With another shrug, he returned to his seat.

A few days later Mark came to the group conference on his own. He read his leads again and told us he wondered if he could combine them. He had heard other children do that. He read his leads together, one after the other. I asked, "Would you like to combine them that way?" Mark said, "Yes." This was the first time he had made a decision about any of his work since he had entered fifth grade. Mark again returned to his seat to tape on his lead. He also added on an ending. He did both of these things by himself. It was October and I felt Mark had made a big step; he had become part of the community of writers in my room. Anne hovered in the background as usual but I would not let her help or interfere with his process.

Mark returned to confer about his piece in the next two weeks. He added details to make his piece clearer. He also changed some words and put in periods. His last conference on this piece was about a title. I had asked him to write down some possible titles and share them with us. He did that but was pleased when others suggested titles he could put on his list. His final title, "Race for Victory," which he liked very much, was a result of his collaboration with his peers.

Even though Mark was pleased with his finished piece (see Figure 3.2), he would not share it with the class. In fact, it would be a long time, not until March, before he felt confident enough to share his writing with the class. Even then it was at my request rather than his own desire.

Because my students express their ideas both orally and in writing in all areas of the curriculum, I could not distinguish Mark's behavior and progress during writing periods from his work in other areas. He demonstrated the same type of behavior in reading, social studies, and science. At first, he kept himself on the fringes of class activities; he participated, but with minimal involvement.

Mark had been tested by the skills teacher and had been found to be reading below grade level at the beginning of the year. He was scheduled to go to skills twice a week for twenty minutes. The skills teacher gave Anne a phonics and vocabulary book to work in with Mark. During the class reading period Mark had to select a book he wanted to read. Even though we had spent some time discussing selecting and abandoning books, Mark was not able to select his first book on his own. He finally did pick a book that one of his friends, Bob, was also reading. When I came to him for his daily conference and asked him how it was going, he would always answer, "Good." When I would ask him to tell me about his book, he would say, "I don't know. It's good." Early responses in his literature journal were a few sentences about the book (see Figure 3.3, page 35).

Mark's difficulties with oral and written expression were not as great when it came to social studies and science. Perhaps because he was writing in a journal and knew he did not have to share it with anyone, he was able to write about his ideas. Furthermore, in these subjects he was given a topic and did not have to think of one himself; he was also not personally involved in the topic and could therefore express some ideas without putting in his feelings. In our very first unit, Who Discovered America, the class was asked to write in their history journal who they thought discovered America. Each day they

Race For Victory

My dad told me that we were going to go on an alpine slide today. I was so excited! I could hardly wait.

When we got to the slide, I begged my dad if we could go on it two times.

An alpine slide is like a paved chute that fits one person. There were lots of turns and bumps. We bought tickets first.

Then we went up the mountain on a chair lift. I went on the chair lift with my brother. When we got to the top we jumped off and grabbed a cart. The cart has a handle in the middle. If you pushed the handle forward you went fast. If you pulled it back you slowed down. My brother, David, and I ran to the slides. There were two slides the same, close together. My brother asked me if I wanted to have a race. "Ok," I said. We gave the lady out tickets. We both put our carts on the slide. "Go," the lady said, I went speeding down the slide. David was in the lead. I gripped the handle tighter and pushed forward. I sped up. I was going so fast! I almost fell off my cart. But I passed my brother. I was freezing cold. I won by 20 feet. I was happy.

We went down one one more time with out having a race. It was more fun to have a race. That was the best alpine slide that I had been on because it had lots of turns and bumps. It was the best time of my vacation.

FIGURE 3.2 *Mark's writing sample: "Race for Victory"*

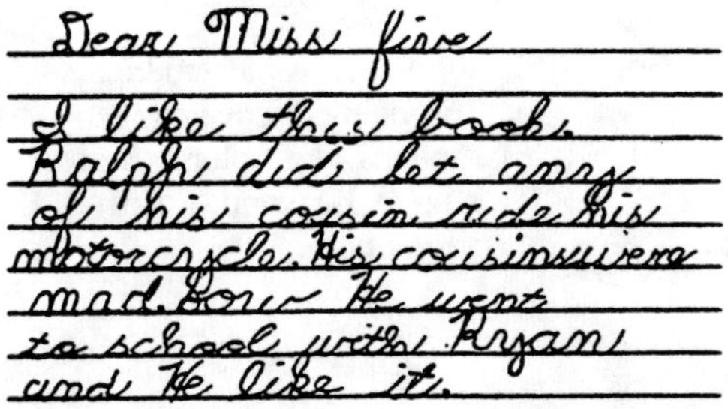

Dear Miss Five
I like this book.
Ralph did let any
of his cousin ride his
motorcycle. His cousins were
mad. Sow He went
to school with Ryan
and He liked it.

FIGURE 3.3 *Literature response journal entry: Mark*

were presented with new kinds of historical evidence about Columbus, the Vikings, the Indians, the Chinese, and the Egyptians. Mark began to write his thoughts in his journal in a very limited way (see Figure 3.4). After examining evidence on all the groups over a period of two weeks, he even attempted a generalization (see Figure 3.5).

I began to notice that in contrast to Mark's reluctance to speak to me or contribute to class discussions, he talked with friends, at times disrupting the class. It was then that I decided to involve Mark in more opportunities for collaborative learning. Once again I remembered the success I had had with Angela when she was involved in learning with her peers. I taught science and history increasingly through a collaborative approach. Mark was already involved in group conferences in writing and now seemed able to express more ideas within a small group of friends.

By November Mark seemed to feel more comfortable within the classroom. His self-confidence increased and he began to initiate more work on his own, although he still worked slowly. He wrote a piece on a ride he took at an amusement park. He came for conferences on his own, listened, and participated to some extent. He was able to draft, make some revisions, and do some proofreading on his own. I noticed that he began to use new vocabulary words such as "rushing," "suddenly," and "huge." Since one of Mark's disabilities involved his limited vocabulary, I was pleased to see him trying out new words. With this piece Mark made most of the decisions with some help from his friend Bob. He did not receive any advice from Anne or any other adult.

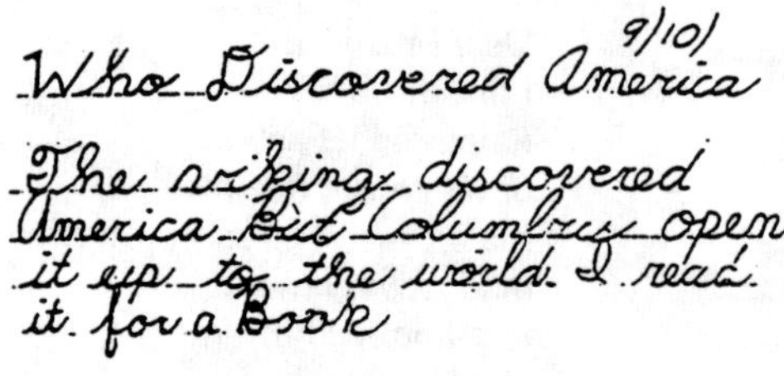

Who Discovered America
The viking discovered
America. But Columbus open
it up to the world. I read
it for a book

FIGURE 3.4 *Mark's journal entry for "Who Discovered America"*

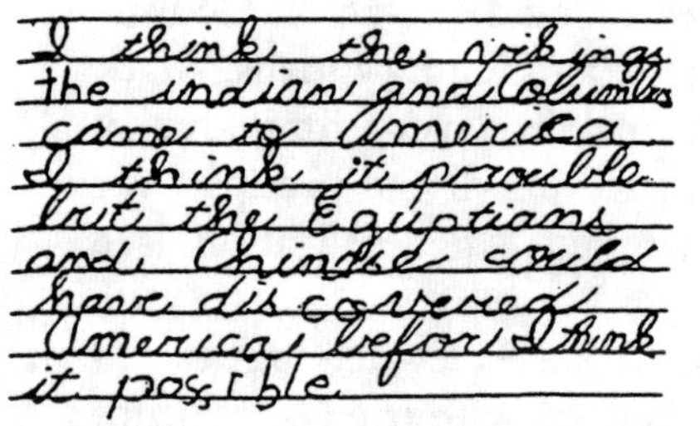

I think the vikings
the indian and Columbus
came to America.
I think it prouble
but the Eguptians
and Chinese could
have discovered
America befor I think
it possible

FIGURE 3.5 *Mark's later journal entry for "Who Discovered America"*

When I had my writing evaluation conference with Mark at the end of November before his report card, we discussed his answers to the evaluation form (as recommended in Atwell 1982). He told me he liked "Race For Victory," his first piece, best because "it was exciting and I had fun writing it." That was the first writing piece he had made decisions about and completed on his own. I think he was beginning to develop a sense of ownership or authority over his work.

We filled out the writing section of his report card together. He was able to tell me what he thought he deserved for grades. Gone was "I don't know." He had finished two pieces; I had expected three. He set a goal for himself to work harder and finish four new pieces by the end of March when the second report card came out. He also set a goal of learning how to use quotation marks because "I want to have people talking," an interesting goal for a child who didn't speak very much himself. The piece he started after our conference, "Summer Skiing," was his first attempt to use conversation and thus quotation marks. It was his longest piece to date and his revisions were much more extensive. Mark was beginning to take risks (see Figure 3.6).

Mark began to make bigger strides in December. He worked together with Bob and Peter gathering information for a history test. They discussed the ideas presented and searched for information to support their ideas. It was Mark who looked up various terms, discussed them with his group, and eventually came up with the correct answers. I was amazed at how verbal Mark was in this small group. He went over and over several points to show his classmates the meaning of words. This was very different from the Mark who had said "I don't know" to questions about his writing or his reading. Mark went on to get the only 100 on the test, which involved writing his thoughts on various issues. I was again convinced of the value of collaborative learning. In this case it allowed Mark to become a leader as he helped his friends understand.

By the middle of December Mark began raising his hand in class. At first, it was to answer a math question. Then he moved into the area of our daily news discussion. He sat near me and would lean over and talk mainly to me in a low voice telling me of a news event. I'd repeat what he said by saying, "Mark said . . ." From the news reports, he began to make some comments to the whole class about science activities. An interesting thought began to occur to me. During math, news, science, and social studies, Anne was not in the room. These were the times that Mark began to speak.

During December I discovered Mark had a very good memory and realized that he seemed to absorb everything that happened around him even though he couldn't always express himself. Gradually he began to take more risks with oral expression. He started to participate more often in class discussions, at first by summarizing a book I read to the class. Then he reviewed why the French came to the New World. At the same time he was making longer entries in his science and history journals. Not only was Mark's oral ability improving, his written expression was too.

I felt that Mark had become part of the community of learners within my classroom. He was no longer on the edge. He had become part of the writing community early in the year. I was exhilarated at his participation in other activities. His biggest step came when I presented a map of the thirteen colonies to the class. We located

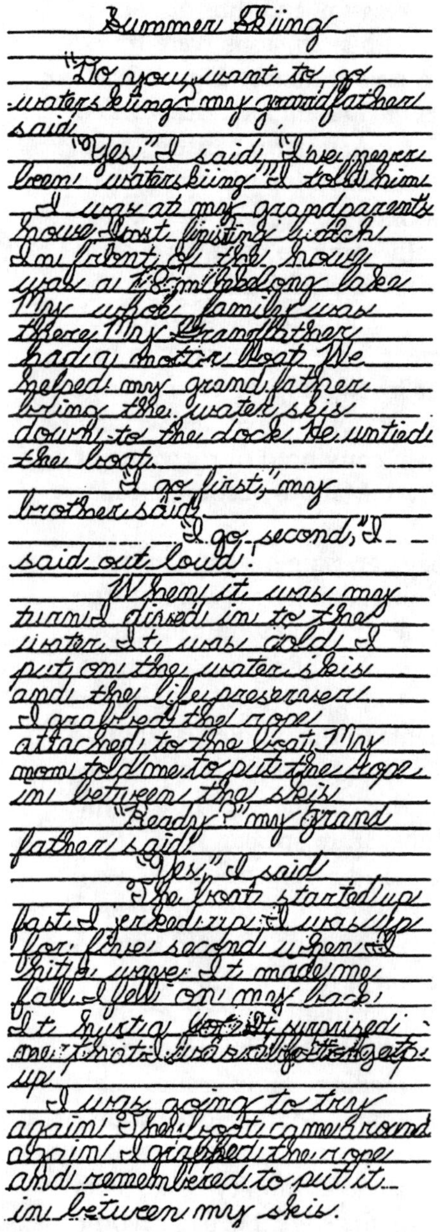

Summer Skiing

"Do you want to go waterskiing?" my grandfather said.

"Yes," I said, "I've never been waterskiing." I told him.

I was at my grandparents house, Just finishing lunch. In front of the house was a 18 mile long lake. My whole family was there. My Grandfather had a motor boat. We helped my grand father bring the water skis down to the dock. He untied the boat.

"I go first," my brother said.

"I go second," I said out loud!

When it was my turn I dived in to the water. It was cold. I put on the water skis and the life preserver. I grabbed the rope attached to the boat. My mom told me to put the rope in between the skis.

"Ready?" my grand father said,

"Yes," I said.

The boat started up fast. I jerked up. I was up for five second when I hit a wave It made me fall. I fell on my back. It hurt a lot. It surprised me that I was able to get up.

I was going to try again. The boat came around again. I grabbed the rope and remembered to put it in between my skis.

FIGURE 3.6 *Mark's story: "Summer skiing"* *(continued on page 39)*

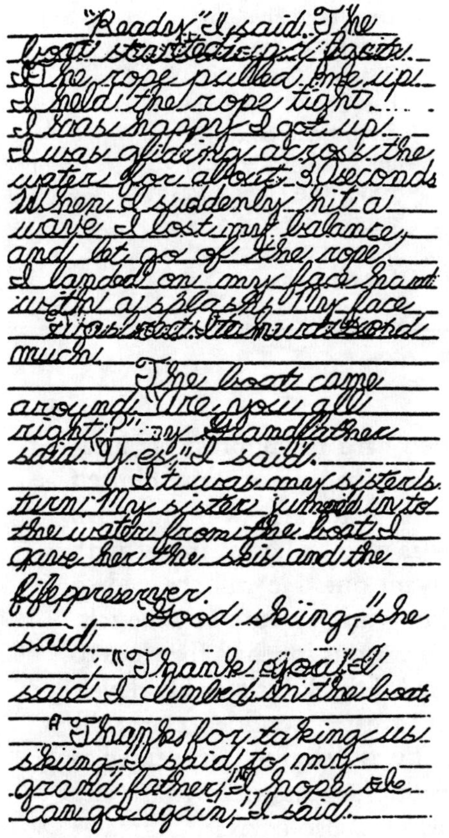

"Ready," I said. The boat started up faster. The rope pulled me up. I held the rope tight. I was happy I got up.I was gliding across the water for about 30 seconds When I suddenly hit a wave. I lost my balance and let go of the rope. I landed on my face hard with a splash. My face was red. It hurt so much.

The boat came around. "Are you all right?" my Grandfather said. "Yes," I said.

It was my sister's turn. My sister jumped into the water from the boat. I gave her the skis and the lifepreserver.

"Good skiing," she said.

"Thank you," I said. I climbed on the boat.

"Thanks for taking us skiing," I said to my grandfather, "I hope I can go again," I said.

FIGURE 3.6 *Mark's story: "Summer skiing" (continued from page 38)*

Philadelphia, Boston, New York, and Charleston as major cities. I asked why they might have become important cities. No one answered. I waited. They looked at their maps. I continued to wait as they thought about the question. Mark raised his hand. I smiled and nodded at him to respond. He looked at me, at his map again, and said, "Never mind."

I encouraged him and, despite his reluctance, he said, "The cities are all on the coast, so they are near water. That means they can trade, so they can send things to England, and England and Africa can send things back. That's why they are important cities. They are trading centers." The other students began to chime in, in agreement with

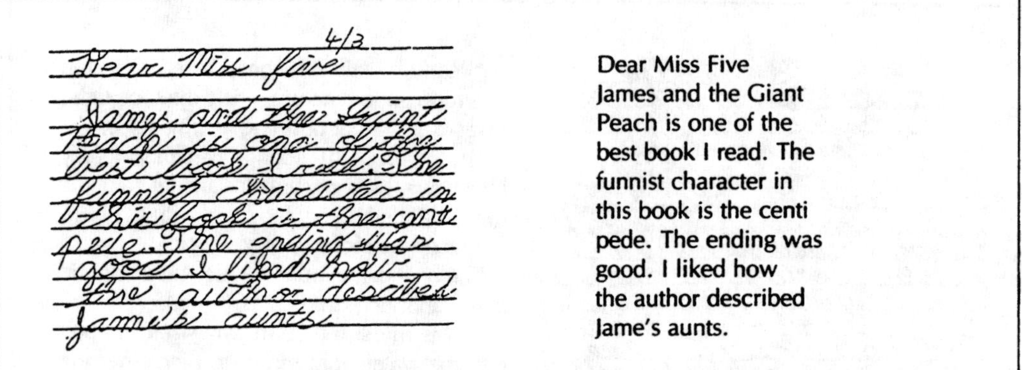

Dear Miss Five
James and the Giant
Peach is one of the
best book I read. The
funnist character in
this book is the centi
pede. The ending was
good. I liked how
the author described
Jame's aunts.

FIGURE 3.7 *Mark's response to James and the Giant Peach*

and response to Mark's idea. Mark tried hard to suppress his pleasure. I realized after this episode that Mark would not allow himself to smile if he felt pleased with his efforts. After school I told Mark what a good theory he had and that I was glad he had shared it with the class. He said, "Thank you" and went out. He still showed so little expression that I had no way of knowing for sure how he felt.

I returned again and again to Mark's various journals for clues to his feelings about the subjects we covered. I think his steadily developing confidence in writing gave him greater confidence in self-expression in social studies and science. I was delighted. It seemed as though the ownership aspect of the writing process freed Mark and gave him a sense of independence. Mark was also exercising greater authority over his reading. He was selecting books on his own and when he found an author he liked, such as James Howe or Roald Dahl, he read many books by that person. His responses in the form of letters to me were longer and seemed to express more of his opinions (see Figure 3.7).

During December I had a conference with Mark's mother. I told her he was making very good progress and I didn't think he needed as much individual instruction per week from the aide. She told me she thought he was bright, but she didn't want to remove the support of Anne just yet: "This year he can take risks and flounder and if he needs help, she'll be there for him." She mentioned that she was surprised one day when Mark announced, "Miss Five is the best teacher I've had. She's a good teacher." She was shocked because "Mark doesn't usually express any opinions."

Even though Mark's mother did not see a need to remove Anne, I did. I did not think Mark needed her and I was having serious problems with her. Her instructions as an aide were to follow my directions and to help me help Mark. She seemed to be more and more unwilling to follow my directions and instead did exactly what she wanted to do with regard to Mark and my other students. Often she told me what she thought I should be doing!

Anne had been an aide in my school for many years. In the past she had been allowed to take over many of the teaching responsibilities in the classrooms in which she worked. She gave and corrected spelling tests, read books to the whole class, discussed the news, organized various classrooms, and taught small groups of children. She had been given, and was used to, control. She had difficulty adjusting to my class environment, which was a community of learners rather than a teacher-centered classroom. She had an even more difficult time accepting my philosophy of teaching and thus my suggestions to her for working with Mark.

It soon became an intolerable situation, with Anne and I battling for control of *my* classroom. The environment I had tried so hard to establish—one of trust, compassion, and respect for each individual—was at stake. My theories about working with special learners like Mark and my philosophy of teaching were being compromised and I began to feel very uncomfortable in my own room, a place I usually love. I tried many strategies to work out the problem. In my talks with her regarding Mark she would agree to do as I asked, but would continue to do as she pleased. Meetings with the skills teachers didn't help either. Finally when I was convinced that she was using Mark and the other children in this power struggle and that they were suffering because most of my energies were directed toward dealing with Anne instead of teaching them, I went to my principal for help. After some thought he reduced the number of hours she worked with Mark to thirty minutes a day, much to my relief. I wondered how Mark would fare without her for most of the day.

In January Anne started her thirty-minute sessions with Mark. We agreed she would work in the phonics/vocabulary book only. She worked with him and left abruptly at the end of her time. There was very little contact between the other children and Anne, nor did she speak to me at any length. The situation continued in this manner for the remainder of the year. I felt guilty and inadequate because I hadn't been able to solve the problem in a better way. And I felt very

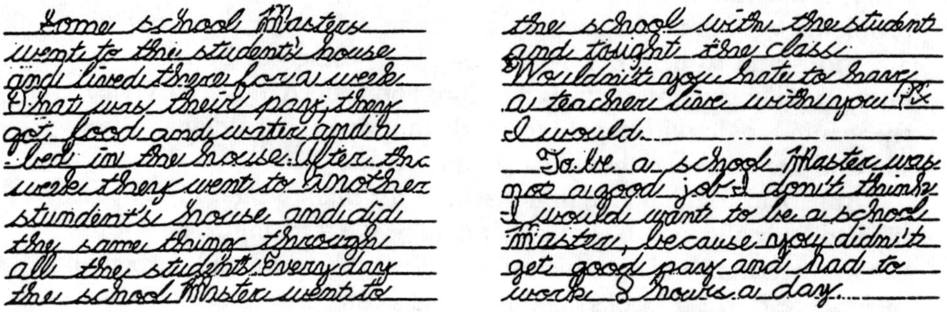

Some school masters went to the students' house and lived there for a week. That was their pay, they got food and water and a bed in the house. After that week they went to another stundent's house and did the same thing through all the students. Every day the school Master went to the school with student and taught the class. Wouldn't you hate to have a teacher live with you? I would.

To be a school master was not a good job. I don't think I would want to be a school master, because you didn't get good pay and had to work 8 hours a day.

FIGURE 3.8 *Mark's report*

uncomfortable around the other teachers who thought Anne was wonderful. At least, however, I had regained control of my classroom and from then on my main responsibility was to my students. I could finally teach in the environment that I felt was conducive to learning. I hoped Mark would benefit, too.

Mark made good progress throughout the winter. His confidence continued to increase and he began to take more risks in writing, reading, and expressing his ideas in front of his peers. He did not seem to need Anne. In January he did much reading about colonial times in preparation for a report he would write. He read at least six books and then decided to do his report on colonial schools. He was involved in the topic and was able to express his thoughts in his report (Figure 3.8).

Even though Mark was involved in his report, he began to express his dislike for work and especially homework. He continued to work slowly and this often put him behind. I think it was because it took him so long to do his work that he complained about it and tried to do the minimum. His verbal expressions and excuses were a delight to hear, in a way, because at least he was talking and expressing himself, something he had not done in the fall.

Despite his complaints he made steady progress, and by March was beginning to put more effort into assignments. He and Bob became better friends and sat together for two or three months. Mark would help Bob with his math, Bob would help Mark with spelling and vocabulary, and they learned from each other. They both discussed the books they read, often reading sections aloud and usually recommending books they had just finished to each other. These two nonreading fourth graders were gradually turning into fifth-grade readers who liked books. Often they would not leave at noon for lunch because they were finishing a chapter. Mark's responses in his literature journal became longer and he expressed more of his opinions rather than retelling the story.

During the early spring I gave the class the series of practice tests for the state writing test. During the practice tests there were no opportunities for conferences and no help with proofreading. Mark started out with short pieces but began to write more with each test. He had difficulty with spelling and adding endings to words when he had to write without the benefit of proofreading conferences. However, as he did more tests, I noticed that he took more risks, especially with vocabulary and the use of conversation. He did not take the safe way and use words he could spell. "Incredible," "approached," "believe," and "flipped" appeared in his stories. With each practice test, he seemed to have an easier time completing it independently.

It was at this time that I asked him to share a practice test he had just completed with the class. He was reluctant at first, but as I held my breath, he read his piece and received much praise from the group. His smile, which he could not suppress this time, was worth the wait.

Mark did well on the state test when he took it in May (see Figure 3.9). He focused on the two topics, included details, and used conversation. During one of the tests he came up to me and said, "I want to use the word *uninhabited* in my piece. I know it means the same thing as deserted, but can I say an 'uninhabited building'? I think I can." I was very surprised to hear him consider the two words, which would not have been in his vocabulary two months before. I was even more pleased that he was experimenting with their use on this important test. He had heard many other students share their writing pieces during the year and he was aware that these students tried to use different words. Now Mark too had developed enough confidence to part 2 Superman

I was flying over New York City to see if anyone needed help. I was Superman.

I saw my friends Batman and Robin's car outside of that uninhabited building. I smelled trouble. I use my x-ray vision to see what was in the building. It was Batman and Robin tied up hanging by a rope over a big pot of lava. A candle was burning the rope. It looked like they were just about to fall. It was the Joker, my worst enemy. He was laughing.

"Help!" Batman and Robin screamed! I rammed right through the building and caught Batman and Robin in midair. Then I put them down.

"Thanks Superman," Batman and Robin said. Then I went after the Joker.

"You can't catch me Superman!" the Joker laugh.

"Oh yes I can!" I shouted. Then the Joker climbed up a forty foot rope hanging from the ceiling. Batman and Robin came over to help me.

"We have you corner Joker!" I shouted at him. Batman shot his spiderweb at the Joker.

"Nice work Batman," I said. "We got him trapped."

"All get you next time, you'll see!" the Joker laugh.

"Batman bring the Joker to jail," I instucted.

"O.K.," Batman answerd.

"By Batman and Robin," I said.

"By Superman," they said to me.

As I was flying home I was glad nobody needed any more help to day.

"Help," I heard in the distance.

I spoke too soon.

Superman

I was flying over New York City to see if anyone needed help. I was Superman.

I saw my friends Batman and Robin's car outside of that uninhabited building. I smelled trouble. I use my x-ray vision to see what was in the building. It was Batman and Robin tied up hanging by a rope over a big pot of lava. A candle was burning the rope. It looked like they were just about to fall. It was the Joker, my worst enemy. He was laughing.

"Help!" Batman and Robin screamed! I rammed right through the building and caught Batman and Robin in midair. Then I put them down.

"Thanks Superman," Batman and Robin said. Then I went after the Joker.

"You can't catch me Superman!" the Joker laugh.

"Oh yes I can!" I shouted. Then the Joker climbed up a forty foot rope hanging from the ceiling. Batman and Robin came over to help me.

"We have you corner Joker!" I shouted at him. Batman shot his spiderweb at the Joker.

"Nice work Batman," I said. "We got him trapped."

"All get you next time, you'll see!" the Joker laugh.

"Batman bring the Joker to jail," I instructed.

"O.K.," Batman answered.

"By Batman and Robin," I said.

"By Superman," they said to me.

"As I was flying home I was glad nobody needed any more help to day.

"Help," I heard in the distance.

I spoke too soon.

Figure 3.9 *Mark's state test*

take risks, to stretch and extend his ideas through the use of new words. This was especially significant in light of Mark's initial disability, his limited oral and written language.

Mark's reading also improved. He continued to read slowly but made significant gains in comprehension. On the Gates McGinitie reading test that I gave, he went from a fourth-grade reading level in comprehension in September to a seventh-grade level on a timed test in March. Untimed, he scored at the eleventh-grade level. By the end of May Mark had completed twenty-three books and his responses to reading showed greater depth. During a conference with him, he told me that reading was his favorite subject, "then comes writing." After some thought he added, "Oh, there's history too. I forgot about that."

More important, Mark spent the month of May expressing more of his ideas to his peers and to me. He seemed to be developing a sense of humor; he would share little jokes with Bob, and I could kid with him. He laughed often. He continued to raise his hand tentatively to answer some questions and when I would call on him, he would still hesitate, often saying, "No, it's probably wrong." I would smile at him and say, "Come on take a risk. Try it." He would then give his answer and actually smile when he realized that it was correct. He became more assertive and also found it easier to make decisions. He seemed to feel very much a part of the classroom community and was able to function as well, and in some cases, better than many of my other students.

It was Mark's continued success in fifth grade that led the skills teachers and me to recommend that Mark enter sixth grade without authorized aide time. He had developed into a student who was able to function with greater independence and who could take more responsibility for his own learning.

Peter

Peter's year in the same class was not as successful. And I spent much time wondering why. Was it due to his erratic behavior, his learning problems, his self-image?

Peter was a presence from the moment he entered my room. He was a good-looking boy with brown hair and a wonderful smile.

He was charming one minute and fresh the next, often boasting about his ability to scare teachers. He was outgoing and appeared to be well liked. On the playground he was a leader among his peers and a threat to younger children. In the classroom he was the center of attention at the beginning of the school year; the other children laughed at his antics. He was restless, easily distracted, and had trouble following directions. He seemed to be unable to initiate much of his work.

I realized that in order for Peter to be able to do some work on his own, he needed a very structured situation with my attention as often as possible. This condition usually occurred in the morning. The one-hour writing period in the afternoon was a very difficult time for him. He viewed it as unstructured time and spent the hour walking around the classroom, talking, and distracting other students. Even though I would ask each child what he or she would do during writing time, Peter would forget what he planned to do within two or three minutes. During the first few weeks of school Peter wrote nothing and disturbed everyone.

Toward the end of September Peter wrote a one-page draft about his trip to a floating restaurant. It was a true "bed-to-bed" story and included all the events of the day, the car trip to the dock, the activities at the dock, the boat ride to the restaurant, what each member of his family ate, the fish they saw in the water, the trip back to the dock, and so on. He brought his draft to me and said, "I'm finished." I realized that he had had no experience with the process approach to writing. My immediate task was to involve him in each stage of the process with as much guidance as possible. I hoped to include him in conferences each day.

His first group conference was a disaster. He talked to everyone and listened to no one. When he read his draft, others pointed out to him that he had many topics. They asked questions to help him focus. He made jokes out of every question and then announced again that he was finished and he liked his story the way it was. He was not going to change it. The children at the conference accepted his decision.

The next day I included him in a conference again. Some students read their drafts to show Peter how they had focused on one idea. He told us it was too much work to do his draft over again. The children showed him their strategies for revision. He seemed taken with the idea of adding flaps and cutting out parts. With my help he cut out sections that he thought did not have to do with the restaurant. During the next week, he added five thin strips with parts of sentences to his draft that was now held together with scotch tape. Again he announced with a sigh that he was finished. When I explained editing and proofreading to him, he told me once more that it was too hard. Somehow over the following few days he did some proofreading. His inability to focus prevented him from doing much self-correcting. I worked with him, helping him punctuate and mark paragraphs, and he was finally ready to copy his piece in pen. Again his problems with concentration got in the way. He copied his piece all in one paragraph not bothering to spell the words we had corrected the right way. He was very upset when he had to copy it over again. He finally finished "The Floating Restaurant" at the beginning of October (see Figure 3.10).

I spent the fall trying many strategies to involve Peter in our community of writers. His problems in concentration seemed to stand in the way of all his learning, not only his writing. I realized that he could not remember what he had been taught fifteen minutes earlier. I discovered gaps in his background in many areas. In math, he had little understanding of place value and did not know basic number facts. His vocabulary was weak and his general knowledge of the world and history was limited. He had either never been exposed to or had never mastered certain very elementary concepts. His reading was below grade level. Because he read so fast, he understood very little. His main objective during the first four months of school was to complete whatever he had to do as fast as possible, whether it was correct or not.

I wondered and worried about him. He seemed to need extra assistance more than Mark did. Could he have learning disabilities? I decided to read about learning-disabled children and found that the description of the symptoms of a child with learning disabilities seemed to fit. Peter had poor self-control. He was hyperactive. He seemed to have behavior and thought disorders: short attention span, distractibility, memory difficulties, emotional instability, and disorganization. I asked the school psychologist for advice. She tested Peter and after meeting with the skills teacher and me, said that perhaps there were possible learning problems. The parents met with us and were willing to follow any suggestions we had. I spoke with them at regular intervals throughout the year, reporting both progress and setbacks.

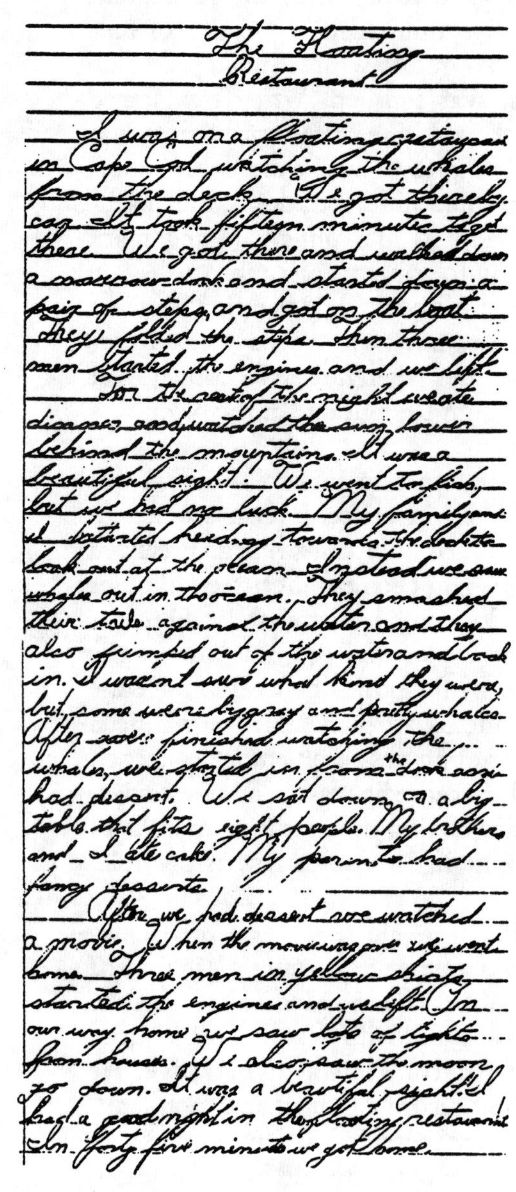

The Floating Restaurant

I was on a floating restaurant in Cape Cod watching the whales from the deck. We got there by car. It took fifteen minutes to get there. We got there and walked down a narrow dock and started down a pair of steps and got in the boat. They folded the steps. Then three men started the engine and we left.

For the rest of the night we ate dinner and watched the sun lower behind the mountains. It was a beautiful sight! We went to fish, but we had no luck. My family and I started heading towards the dock to look out at the ocean. Instead we saw whales out in the ocean. They smashed their tails against the water and they also jumped out of the water and back in. I wasn't sure what kind they were but some were big gray and pretty whales. Aftert we finished watching the whales, we started in from the dock and had dessert. We sat down on a big table that fits eight people. My brothers and I ate cake. My parents had fancy desserts.

After we had dessert we watched a movie. When the movie was over we went home. Three men in yellow shirts started the engines and we left. On our way home we saw lots of lights from houses. We also saw the moon go down. It was a beautiful sight! I had a good night in the floating restaurant. In forty five minutes we got home.

FIGURE 3.10 *Peter's final version of "The Floating Restaurant"*

The school psychologist preferred not to recommend specific aide time for Peter. The skills teacher questioned if he might do better in another fifth grade where there might be more structure. And I wondered how I was going to help this child become part of my community of learners.

It was agreed that Peter would go for skills help in reading and math four times a week. Meanwhile I would give him as much individual attention as possible. I had plenty of time to do that because he was sent out of every special class he had due to his disruptive behavior, back to the classroom where I would work with him.

Peter was a true challenge. He had been the "bad boy" at home and at school since he entered nursery school. This was his perception of himself and it seemed he had given up trying to be anything else. He had no confidence in his academic abilities, despite his bravado at the beginning of the year, and would tell me all the time that he was stupid and that he couldn't do his work because it was too hard. I realized that I had to try to change his self-image as best I could.

I spent the fall reassuring Peter over and over again that he could do all the things he thought he couldn't do. I think I provided an environment where there were expectations for him, where there was support for him when he needed it, and where his ideas—if and when he expressed them—were respected. Gradually I began to see some progress, but his behavior was erratic. He was able to concentrate for longer periods of time and was not as easily distracted for days in a row. Then I would find him walking on desks, knocking everything off a shelf, and refusing to work. Any work he completed he either lost or almost destroyed by stuffing it in the back of his desk. His standard response to his behavior was "I don't care."

Writing period remained a problem for him. He could not work on his own. Finally I decided to have a conference with him every day and include him in all the group conferences. At least in this way his attention was focused on his own writing or what the other students were reading or discussing. At times he continued to joke, but the children who were at the conference seemed to disregard his behavior and responded to his writing instead. I found this interesting because once he was back at his seat, his behavior was disturbing enough for them to complain to me and ask to have their desks moved away from him.

In November he wrote his second piece. This was a focused piece about a ride he had taken on a roller coaster. He had heard other pieces about amusement park rides and I think this helped him focus his own piece. "The Heat Seeker" was shorter than his first piece, but he had worked harder on it, had shared it during conferences, and used the feedback he remembered to revise it (Figure 3.11).

He read this piece to the whole class during sharing time and seemed to enjoy the positive comments he received. I marvelled that the class could respond well to his writing but express annoyance at his behavior.

During the fall and winter I tried to include Peter in collaborative learning situations but he saw group work as an opportunity for play. However, he did take part in the many simulations the class did in social studies. Although he participated, he could not understand the involvement and passion of his friends as they took the roles of various delegates to the Constitutional Convention or expressed their views as colonists against unfair taxes. He remained puzzled, shook his head often, and kept himself on the fringes of class activities. At least he was a participant, I thought.

By February Peter began to change. Suddenly there was little evidence of his previous poor behavior and his outbursts. It appeared that he wanted to learn and he began to try to complete his work. He began to participate in group work and discovered he could learn from other children. He looked to them for help when he did not know what to do. He formed a good partnership with John who helped him figure out strategies to solve math problems and often gave him suggestions in writing. Peter, in turn, included John in recess games. He came to me often to "start me off so I can do it right." I was very excited about his progress and realized once again the importance of giving children time to grow. During this time I often speculated on the reasons for his change. Did he feel more confident about his abilities? Did he feel more comfortable in the classroom environment? Was he caught up in the academic activities of his friends?

Peter attended writing conferences on his own and was able to listen to others and give responses that were helpful. His writing improved as he made more extensive revisions based on the feedback he received (see Figure 3.12). He still needed reassurance at various points in the writing process but was developing greater independence as a writer. He told me: "I love writing. It's my favorite

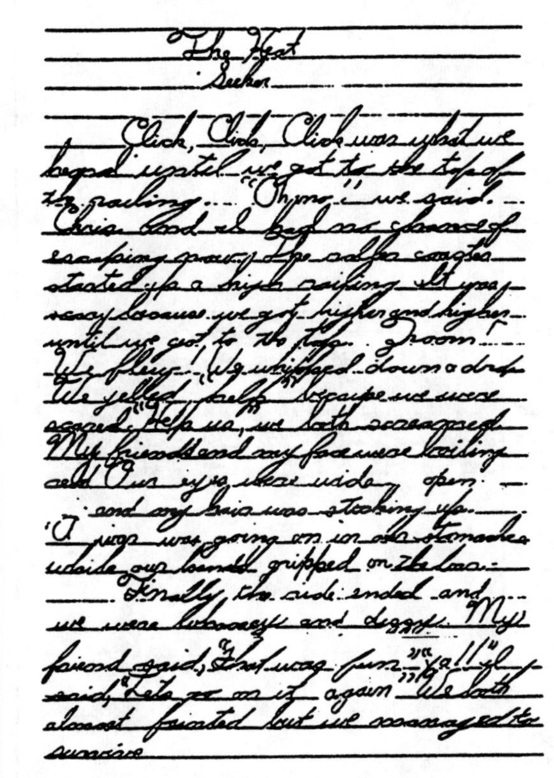

The Heat Seeker

Click, click, click was what we heard until we got to the top of the railing. "Oh no," we said. Chris and I had no chance of escaping now. The roller coaster started up a high railing. It was scary because we got higher and higher until we got to the top. Zoom! We flew! We whipped down a drop. We yelled "help" because we were scared. "Help us," we both screamed. My friends' and my face were boiling red. Our eyes were wide open and my hair was sticking up. A war was going on in our stomaches while our hands gripped on the bar.

Finally the ride ended and we were whoosy and dizzy. My friend said, "That was fun." "Ya!!" I said, "Lets go on it again" We both almost fainted but we managed to survive.

FIGURE 3.11 *Peter's second writing piece*

subject." I continued to praise all his efforts and he seemed pleased with his progress. At this time he began to show an interest in me. He asked questions about my life and began to talk to me about his interests. Often he came to school early or stayed after school for a few minutes to tell me about a particular incident. And he showed genuine concern when I came to school with a bad cold for a week. He was very worried the class might have a substitute.

Peter continued to make progress during February and March. He was working on his colonial report and wanted to do as well as his peers. However, his expectations and the report became sources of frustration for him. He had a difficult time sustaining his effort on his report over a long period of time. He became upset and often gave up. Some of his previous behavior surfaced. There were frequent

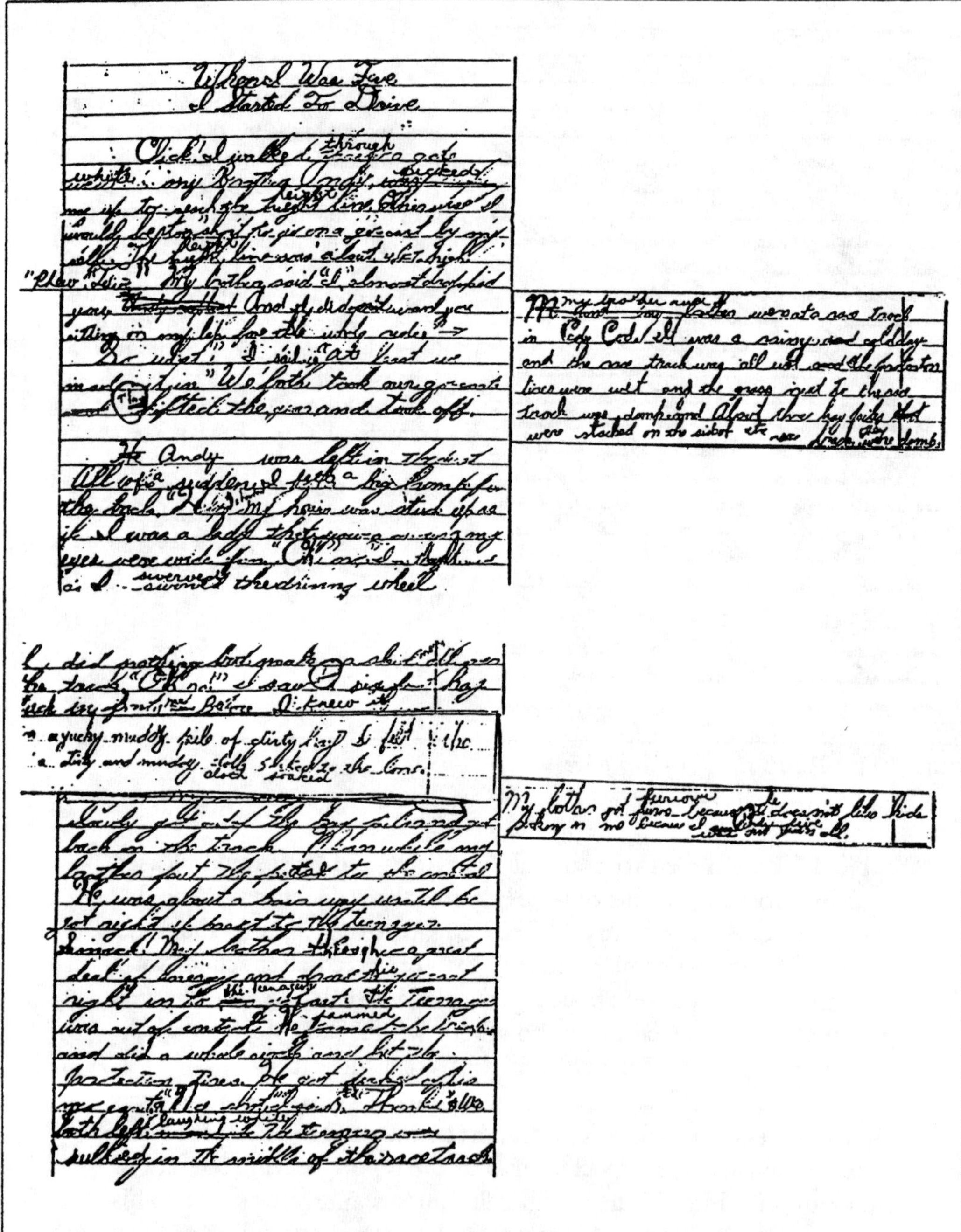

FIGURE 3.12 *Peter's revision strategies*

outbursts where he would tear up his papers and tell me he didn't care. He would add or change one thing and then come back to me announcing in a loud voice, "O.K., I'm finished!" Often when he went back to his seat, he fooled around. When I went over to his desk, he would inform me, "I can't do this!" I would try to reassure him. When I moved him to a quiet corner of the room, he was able to finish his revisions in five or ten minutes. He would come for individual conferences and we would discuss the information in the books he had read about colonial times. At times he appeared not to be paying attention when I reviewed the material discussed. Yet when I asked him what he would like to include in his report, he remembered every detail. I thought back to the September when it was indicated that he could not remember information. Was the report accurate or had he changed?

Peter finally completed his report, but he left out illustrations and refused to make a cover. However, when he saw the reports of his friends, he changed his mind and worked hard on both. Like Mark's, his report was on colonial schools and he too included his feelings (Figure 3.13).

After Peter had written his colonial report, he seemed to be more interested in writing again and came for conferences often. He helped children with leads for their reports and looked to them for response to his writing. I felt he was finally a part of the community of writers.

In the spring Peter's new interest in writing seemed to extend to reading. He had been unable to concentrate on reading for the first half of fifth grade and his letters to me were brief (Figure 3.14).

However, in the middle of March a friend recommended *James and the Giant Peach* and Peter became a reader. He could not put the book down and went on to read other books by Dahl. Then, in April, he discovered picture books, because I suggested that the whole class read books about animals, many of which were picture books. Peter discovered books about bears. He had never read picture books before. He told me he had not read in first and second grade, he had "just watched TV." His letters to me expressed his joy in finding wonderful books (Figure 3.15).

During the spring Peter's attitude toward school and learning continued to improve. He showed greater interest in his work and seemed to enjoy the classroom. He came to school in a happy state and did not want to leave the class for any reason. He began to resent they wrote on birch bark. Birch bark came from chipping the bark of a birch tree. And charcoal comes from burning branches and leaves. After they burned the leaves and branches all that was left was charcoal.

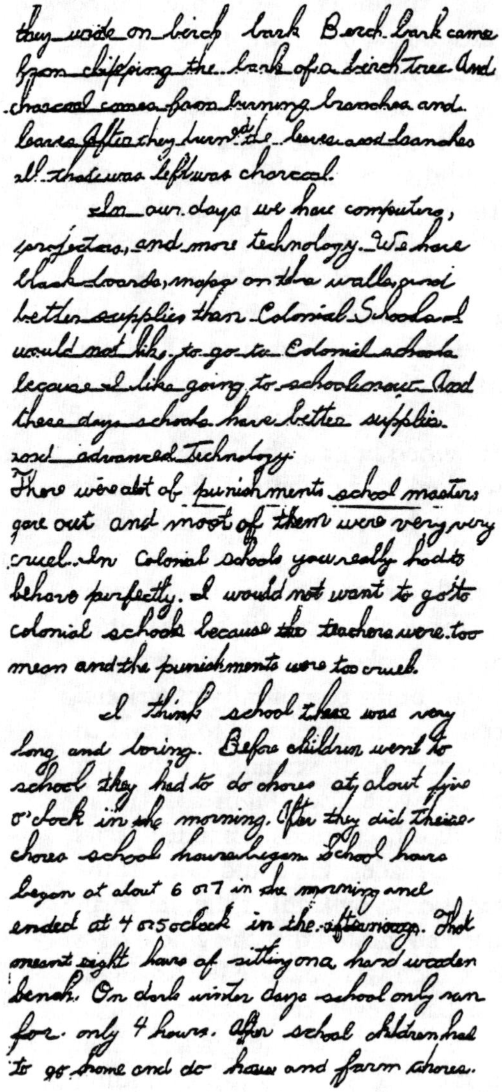

In our days we have computers, projectors, and more technology. We have blackboards, maps on the walls, and better supplies than Colonial Schools. I would not like to go to Colonial schools because I like going to school now. And these days schools have better supplies and advanced technology.

There were alot of punishments school masters gave out and most of them were very very cruel in Colonial schools you really had to behave perfectly. I would not want to go to colonial schools because the teachers were too mean and the punishments were too cruel.

I think school there was very long and boring. Befor children went to school they had to do chores at about five o'clock in the morning. After they did theire chores school hours began. School hours began at about 6 or 7 in the morning and ended at 4 or 5 o'clock in the afternoon. That meant eight hours of sitting on a hard wooden bench. On dark winter days school only ran for only 4 hours. After school children had to go home and do house and farm chores.

FIGURE 3.13 *Peter's report*

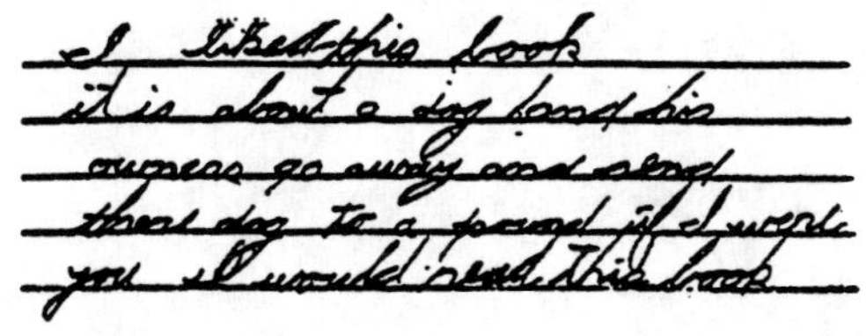

I liked this book
it is about a dog and his
owners go away and send
there dog to a pound if I were
you I would read this book

FIGURE 3.14 *Peter's letter*

his skills sessions. For one week I found notes like the one in Figure 3.16 all over the room—in my desk, on my desk, on my message board, and in my briefcase.

I think Peter finally felt included in the learning community. He participated in social studies and science activities and seemed to be truly involved. There was very little play when he worked with his friends. He began to be more attentive in class discussions and often contributed his ideas. He was able to listen when I read to the class each day. Previously he had drawn, played with items in his desk, or

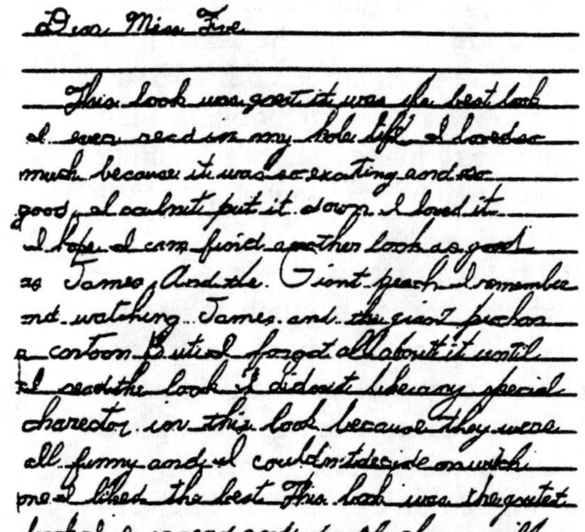

Dear Miss Five

This book was great it was the best book I ever read in my hole life. I loved so much because it was so exciting and so good I coulnt put it down. I loved it. I hope I can find another book as good as James And the Giant peach. I remember and watching James and the giant peachon a cartoon. But I forgot all about it until I read the book. I didnt like any special charectar in this book because they were all funny and I couldn't decide on witch one I liked the best. This book was the greatest book I ever read and proply always will be my favorite. I hope to find another book like this one.

FIGURE 3.15 *Peter's response to James and the Giant Peach*

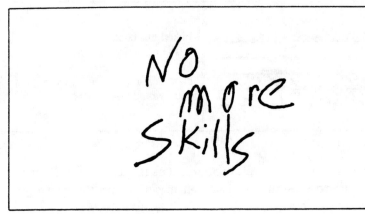

FIGURE 3.16 *Peter's plea*

had to be removed from the room because of his attempts to "whisper" to friends who sat across the room.

For some time, we had been working on word processing as a class. I realized that the computer might be a good tool to focus Peter's attention. And I was right. He loved it and was able to work for longer periods of time on his writing. He revised without any complaints and now made good use of the writing time. In fact he came to school early to write on the computer. Once he asked if he could use it during reading time but then he remembered his "bear" books and told me, "Oh no, I want to read my bear books." I felt pleased at Peter's progress. He was going to make it; he was making gains in all areas. I felt confident and gratified. However, my contentment did not last.

Suddenly in May, Peter seemed to be in trouble everywhere—in music where he distracted the whole chorus, at lunch where he talked back to lunch aides, on the playground where he fought and disobeyed rules, and in the classroom where he behaved as he had in the fall. He knocked over a desk and threw things. He picked on other children. Everything in class became a chore for him and he often refused to do his work, saying "I don't care". He had very few days where he could work without becoming distracted and disruptive.

I don't know whether my patience had run out or whether Peter's behavior was worse than it had ever been. I felt I did not have the resources left to deal with him. I had made a commitment to Peter somewhere along the way and had given so much time to him that I felt I had shortchanged other students in my class. When his behavior had improved, I was able to devote more time and energy to the others. Had I taken away too much attention from him? What had happened?

The end of May was a disaster. My principal clamped down on Peter for his behavior by keeping him after school. He was sent to the office frequently by other teachers and often by me. I felt as though I had exhausted all my strategies for dealing with him. I also felt the pressure of a heavy testing schedule and wondered how I would help Peter focus on the writing test. I prayed that the testing dates would be on two of his "good" days.

Peter took the writing test in May. The first part of the test was writing about learning to do something for the first time. Peter was calm and decided to write about learning to jump off the high dive. He concentrated on his draft and I saw him revising various parts. He included interesting details, dialogue, and good vocabulary (see Figure 3.17).

The second part of the test was in direct contrast. It seemed that the two parts of the test were a true reflection of Peter himself. The topic was to pretend to be someone else for the day—a difficult topic for many children. Peter was stumped. "I can't do this," he muttered at the beginning of the test. Then he began to play with items in his desk. I came over to him after an hour and said, "Peter, you have to try to do this test." He shook his head and told me he couldn't imagine being anyone else. I asked him if he had any heros or favorite television stars he could "become." He shook his head and asked me what would happen if he didn't write anything at all. I told him that he would probably fail the test. He sat thinking and I moved away. Eventually I saw him writing. He was bent over his paper and writing quickly. When I passed by he told me that he had decided to be a baseball player he admired and had once met. I said, "Good idea. I knew you could do it."

An hour later he was finishing copying his test in pen. Suddenly he sighed and said, "I hate this topic." He then took his nearly completed test and ripped it up. I almost collapsed. It was nearly 3:00 and I had to collect the tests. I knew Peter had improved in writing and I felt I could not let him fail the test due to his own frustrations. He sat at his desk and looked at me and for a few moments I didn't trust myself to move or speak. I just stood and stared at him. Finally I went over to him and said, "I know you don't like the topic but I also know you have turned into a very good writer. I am not going

High Dive Phobia

Maybe today I would learn how to jump off the high dive. I always wanted to do it.

"We are here," my friend John said.

"OH great," I thought to myself. John and I quickly got out of our car.

"Let's go to the main pool, then the diving pool," John said.

"Ya sure," I exclaimed. We sat down under a big tree that looked like a big brown bear on its hind legs. We took off our shirts and shoes and charged the main pool like a herd of buffalos being run off a cliff by Indians. "Wee," John yelled as he dropped into the pool. I followed and jumped in after him. We were splashing all over the place. We probably looked like two wild dogs."

"Let's go two the diving pool," John said. We slowly got out of the pool. I slowly staggerd to the diving pool. I finally got there.

"Come on," John said.

"Let's go to the high dive."

"I am going to watch you for a little while," I mumbled. I sat in complete fear hoping John wouldn't ask me to go on the high dive. As I watched John was getting higher and higher every time. Just when I thought it was safe to lie down on the bench, What do you know?

"Are you ready to jump off the high dive, chicken?" John threatenid.

"AH, AH, AH, AH, Ya." I said not meaning to. I slowly walked towards the ladder and went up it slowly. I stood there on the top diving board and shook in fear. My legs were trembling and my teeth were chattering. I was stiff and scared. I walked to the end of the diving board and thought to myself "I cant wait until I complete this mision and go

FIGURE 3.17 *Peter's writing test (continued on page 59)*

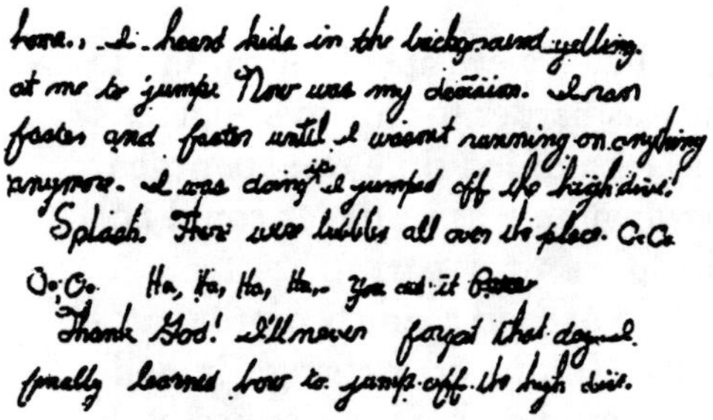

home." I heard the kids in the background yelling at me to jump. Now was my decision. I ran faster and faster until I wasn't running on anything anymore. I was doing it. I jumped off the high dive!

Splash. There were bubbles all over the place. Oo, Oo, Oo, Oo Ha, Ha, Ha, Ha, You did it Pete.

Thank God! I'll never forget that day. I finally learned how to jump off the high dive.

FIGURE 3.17 *Peter's writing test (continued from page 58)*

to let you fail this test. You are going to copy your draft over again and I am going to sit next to you until you finish it. I don't care if it takes the rest of the day!" The class left at 3:00 and I sat with Peter while he copied and sighed and muttered. He finally finished his test at 4:00. His score on both parts of the writing test was a 15 out of a possible 16.

The beginning of June brought no happy finale for me and my efforts with Peter. He had returned to the "bad boy." I wanted desperately to restore his growing positive image of himself as a learner and as a person before he left fifth grade and went on to a departmentalized sixth grade.

The last few weeks of school rushed by filled with tension and hope. I kept thinking I still had more time. And Peter looked forward to the end of the time, the end of the school year. The last day of school Peter stood in line waiting to receive his report card and be dismissed. When he came to the doorway, he took his envelope, smiled, and said, "Thanks a lot."

I wanted to shout, "Wait, come back! I could have done more."

The story of Mark and Peter did not end for me on the last day of school. I continued to think about them both long after school was over.

I was amazed to find similarities between Mark and Peter given all their differences. Both boys came into fifth grade easily distracted and not very interested in learning. Both talked to whoever sat close by and the talk was initially unproductive. Both wanted to do as little work as possible and felt insecure about their academic abilities. They had no confidence in their ideas, in fact they weren't sure they had ideas.

It turned out that both Mark and Peter were able to learn in the classroom environment, although it was harder for me to see Peter's progress. Both boys needed time. Mark needed time to experiment and take risks and it had to happen when he was ready. It could not occur according to any planned schedule on my part.

Peter too began to take risks but he needed a much more structured setting. His risk taking involved more of a change in self-image. He began to believe that he too could do well academically. It was at these times that he was able to concentrate for longer periods of time, complete assignments, and become involved in class activities. His improved image seemed to cause conflicts for him. He often wavered between his negative past and more positive present. Often I think he felt more comfortable with his former image and behavior.

Both boys developed self-confidence through their growth in writing, which eventually affected their work in other areas of the curriculum. Mark began to express his ideas earlier than Peter, but both were able to participate through journal writing and class discussions. As the year went on Mark and Peter achieved greater independence as learners and tried more of their work on their own, Mark to a greater extent than Peter.

Collaboration with peers seemed to be very important for these two boys. Working with other children helped bring both boys into my community of learners, although Peter often remained on the edge. As the boys developed academically, they also changed socially—again, Mark much more so than Peter. Both boys were well liked. At the beginning of the year, classmates laughed at Peter's antics, but still admired him. Later on, there was some resentment. No one wanted to sit with him because of his disruptive behavior. The class as a whole, however, was supportive and accepted his erratic behavior. As Mark and Peter began to take themselves more seriously, Mark even began to develop increased leadership potential, and Peter during the middle of the year became somewhat more responsible for his behavior.

On the whole it appeared as though the year was a successful one. But I did not feel it at first. I knew Mark had flourished but Peter was a different story. I had focused on his behavior and his setback at the end of the year remained a puzzle to me. What could I have done to help him? What caused it? Perhaps it was Peter's realization that it was the end of the year. Perhaps it was the only way he could deal with leaving an environment where he had met with some success.

As I read and reread his journals and writing pieces and my own journal notes on him, however, I became aware of the vivid detail, the voice, and imagery of his writing. And I realized he had turned into a good writer. He had also discovered reading and had become involved in learning. I was certain that despite earlier reports and test results this was not a child with a below-average IQ. His behavior during the last few months of school had prevented me from recognizing his achievement. I didn't see his true progress until I had enough time to think about his growth throughout the year. Once again I became aware of the value of reflection on the part of teachers and the need for time for looking back and learning from what happens in the classroom. I needed the time the summer provided to reflect on Peter's and Mark's growth as learners as well as my own continuing development as a teacher.

4

Karen

A student with complex needs

THE YEAR I had Karen in my classroom, I purposefully did not drink coffee on the first day of school. I wanted to make sure I would be calm and prepared when I encountered her. I had heard the worst for years, yet had no idea what to expect. My principal had told me last year, "She's one of the most difficult students I've seen in my twenty years of being a principal." My fourth-grade colleague who had her in class had moaned and complained about her, calling her "impossible" and telling me I'd better hope I didn't get her in fifth grade. In June I learned that she had been placed in my class for the following year, and all summer I wondered about her.

I had heard about Karen since she had entered school. She had been disruptive in kindergarten and first grade. By the end of first grade, she had been labeled a "discipline problem" by the teachers in the school and tales of her difficulties and antics filled the teachers' room for the next three years. During fourth grade the situation worsened when Karen was placed in the room of a teacher who was very structured and firm. The two clashed from the beginning. Karen did very little work and spent much of her time in fourth grade getting the attention of her peers through inappropriate behavior. She was often sent out in the hall or to the office. She was once again declared "uncontrollable" and "impossible" and I was told again, "You'll be lucky if you don't get her next year."

At this point my interest was aroused. She seemed like the perfect student for me. From previous studies of children with special needs,

I had learned that many of their learning and behavioral problems could be solved within the classroom context. I thought Karen would be a good child to observe.

I was nervous the first day of school. I waited at the door for Karen, not sure I knew who she was or what she looked like. Students filed in. I greeted them and told them to take any seat. All of a sudden she appeared before me. She entered my room and I waited for chaos. Her looks defied her reputation. She was small and had long dark brown hair which accentuated her beautiful dark eyes and lashes. When she smiled, she could have been a model. She wore a brightly colored T-shirt and a denim skirt. She took a seat next to some of the other girls and for most of the morning, while I expected the worst, she sat and listened attentively and even contributed to our discussions by trying very hard to remember to raise her hand.

At recess, she sat next to me on the wall while I watched the seventy-five fifth graders get to know each other all over again after their summer vacation. She told me about her clothes, how she liked to wear dresses and skirts and didn't like to wear pants. She also told me that she had few friends and spent most of her time with her family. I remembered my students from last year. They had told me that she had no friends because, as they saw it, "She doesn't dress and look the way the other kids do."

Karen spent the day doing all the activities the other students did. There were no outbursts and no inappropriate behavior. At the end of the day, she introduced me to her mother who told me she thought Karen would have a very good year. Karen said she was very worried about spelling. And then they were gone. I was left feeling quite puzzled. Nothing serious had happened. She had behaved very much like the other fifth graders, in fact better than some boys who I had spotted as potential behavior problems. Could she have changed so much over the summer? What exactly were her problems?

Karen's previous history

Karen had academic and interpersonal difficulties since her entrance in school. Attention problems and poor social skills were discovered when she was tested in fourth grade. It was felt Karen would benefit from one-to-one assistance and monitoring. Test results showed that Karen was well above average in IQ and was reading above grade level. Her understanding of math concepts was good but she had difficulty with forming numbers on paper, putting them in sequence, and writing math examples properly. These same problems showed up in her written communication, where writing and language skills were below grade level. Her writing and spelling were impaired due to her decoding difficulties, sequencing problems, and her handwriting. She had trouble listening, spoke in a babyish voice, and was disorganized in her oral and written communication. She also had difficulty recognizing relationships and making inferences. Her social development was poor. She made demands on other children and was dependent on adults. She had poor fine motor skills and was restless and easily distracted. She lacked self-control and needed constant attention to complete her work.

In child study group meetings, it was recommended that she be given extended time to work and that her assignments in math, social studies, and writing be abbreviated. Goals set to be accomplished during the academic year were to improve organizational and listening skills, and writing, spelling, and punctuation skills. It was suggested that she learn to explain instructions in her own words, and dictate her responses to an aide. Goals were also set for her behavioral and social improvement. They were to improve her self-esteem, self-control, independence, responsibility, and social relationships. Help was to be given to remind her to raise her hand to answer and to take her turn when working with classmates.

Karen lived with her mother and her father. Her aunts were frequent visitors at the house. Karen spent much time with her mother and her aunts who seemed to treat her like a much younger child. Karen and her mother were involved in many activities after school and on the weekends.

Karen spent little time with other children. Perhaps this was due to her schedule. She often ate dinner at 4:30 or 5:00 and went to bed by 7:00. Her mother told me that Karen got very tired in the afternoon, usually could not concentrate, and needed to go to bed early.

The family thought of Karen as their little girl and were very protective of her. She dressed like a little girl, wearing short skirts and dresses to school each day. She was not given the same independence as other ten-year-olds. Her mother told me at the beginning of the year that she was worried about her spelling and her handwriting and she would appear at my door at 3:00 often during the first few

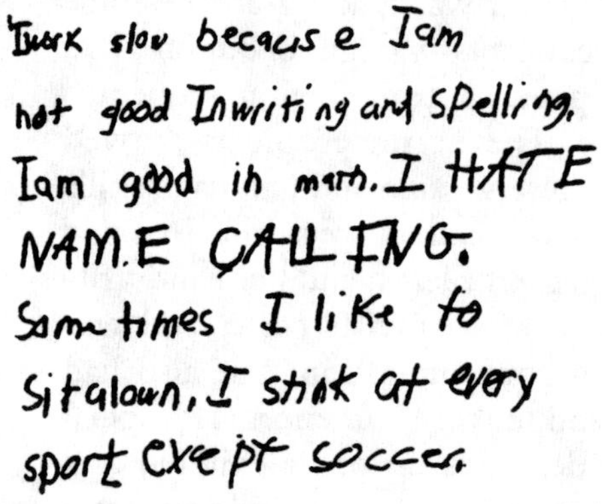

I work slow because I am
not good Inwriting and spelling.
I am good in math. I HATE
NAME CALLING.
Sometimes I like to
sit alown. I stink at every
sport exept soccer.

FIGURE 4.1 *Karen's response*

weeks of school. She told me frequently about Karen's terrible fourth-grade experience and how she hoped fifth grade would be a positive step before junior high.

The first few months of school

At the beginning of the school year I asked the children to write something about themselves for me. I told them I wanted to know more about their strengths and weaknesses, what they liked and didn't like, so I could make them feel more comfortable in the classroom. Karen's response is shown in figure 4.1.

Her concern for spelling also showed up in the Burke Reading Interview I gave her in the fall (see Figure 4.2, question 9).

Her writing survey, given the third day of school, gave me a clue to some of her language problems. Her answer to "What is the hardest part of writing for you?" was "gett my thoughts down." For the questions "What is the easiest?" and "What kinds of changes do you make when you revise?" she answered, "I don't know"—a response that I received often from her during the first four months of school.

During the very first writing period each year, I begin by modeling the writing process. I brainstorm for topics on the overhead

Burke Reading Interview

Name ______ age 10 Date Nov 9

1. When you are reading and you come to something you don't know, what do you do? [illegible] out. figer it out.

Do you ever do anything else? No !!!

2. Do you think that your teacher is a good reader? Yes.
Who is a good reader that you know? I don't know anybody.

3. What makes her/him a good reader? finish books at [illegible] and knows a lot about the book

4. Do you think that she/he ever comes to something she/he doesn't know when she/he is reading? yes

5. Yes What does she/he do about it? trys to figure it out.
No If she/he had trouble what would she/he do? ______

6. If you knew that someone was having difficulty reading how would you help that person? help them sound out the [illegible]

7. How would a teacher help that person? teach them how to reconize words

8. How did you learn to read? [illegible] me read to me and helped me

Burke Reading Interview p. 2

learn. my teacher help pronounce words and read them

9. What would you like to do better as a reader? Spell things [illegible] because if [illegible] come across a word you [illegible] reconise words [illegible].
How would you do that? paying [illegible] to the spelling. learning it from your spelling book

10. Do you think that you are a good reader? yes
How do you know that? I read with a [illegible] I read fast. know every thing about the book

FIGURE 4.2 *Burke Reading Interview*

projector with the class listing all the possible topics I could write about. I then tell them something about each topic and have them help me decide which topic would be the most interesting. Then I ask the students to think of topics, list them, and discuss their topics with a partner. After the students have sufficient time for this brainstorming conference, they return to their desks and begin a draft. I write my own draft as they write theirs.

It was at this point that Karen came up to me and said, "I have so many topics to write about, I can't choose." I asked if her conference with her partner had helped. She told me in a loud voice, "No!" I suggested that she pick one of the topics she had on her list and try it out. She returned to her seat and sat. The next day, she came to me again to tell me she couldn't decide on a topic. We discussed her list of topics again and she was able to choose one to try out in a draft. She went back to her seat and wrote three pages about an experience she had at the pool on Labor Day. She printed the words and skipped a space between each line (see Figure 4.3).

During the week I modeled a conference, reading from my draft. I usually include sentences that are out of sequence and ones that don't have much to do with the topic. I have found in the past that most fifth graders can write about a topic but tend to include information that distracts from the topic and information that might be more appropriate if it were placed in a different part of the piece.

After I read my piece I ask for their comments. I tell them that I want comments that will help me make my writing piece better. I also explain that I hope the comments will still make me feel good as a writer. I explain the difference between a positive suggestion or comment and a negative one. As the class responds to my piece, I show them how a comment can be phrased that will help me as a writer. They tell me that some of my sentences are not necessary. For example, on one occasion, Ken said, "It doesn't really matter what you had for breakfast that day. You don't even need the part about breakfast if you want to tell about when you got the kittens." I asked the class if they understood his suggestion and if they agreed. Generally, I explain to them that I am listening very carefully to their suggestions, but since it is my writing piece, I will decide what to do. Usually I agree with them and then I show them ways that I could revise my piece. I cut out a part and move it some place else. Or I cut out a part and put it in my folder and know I will not use it in the piece. I show them how I can add information by adding flaps or by using

labor day
On labor day at the pool
I won free stile and
the kick bord races
The Pool alaso had
A penny hunt I collected
arond 50 pennys Then
the pool had a
Questeain about
walt dinsey
I got them all
right so I got
a cool Teeshirt with
micky mouse an it
at night he is waring
a grey coat with
brown shoes and
he has blere pants
on with a star
behin him To topp
it all off I won
chel cafe I had
a supper exelant
terriffick nice
day that made
glad and grinning
plus I had my friend
Candy and I am
truly great ful for
it was so good
I wich it would happen
again I also was
In the weekender
of the [illegible] news
and I was in the [illegible]
[illegible] and
I'm truly happy I am
alive.

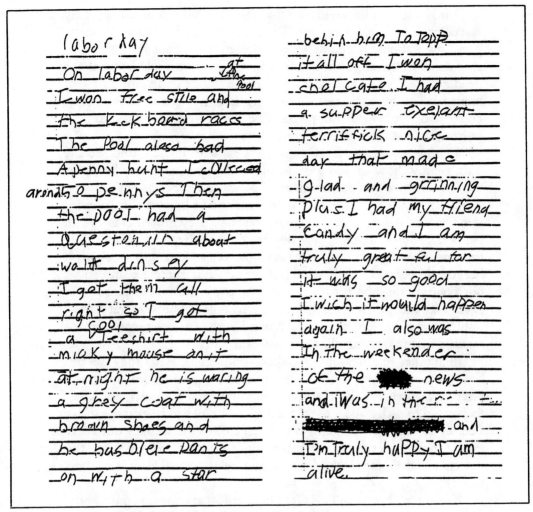

FIGURE 4.3 *First draft of Labor Day piece*

carats within the piece. These revision strategies are presented in various mini-lessons throughout the week. As children finish writing their drafts they come to the conference table to read and discuss their drafts.

When Karen had completed her first draft, she came to the conference table to read it. She began to read in a loud babyish voice with exaggerated expression. I realized she had gotten the attention of not only the students at the conference table, but the whole class. I noticed that some of the children were embarrassed and some were annoyed. Children looked at each other and made faces.

I told the conference group that their job was to listen and help Karen make her piece better. When she finished there were some good suggestions. Karen listened and then said in her babyish voice that she didn't want to change anything. The group told her that she needed to add some information to make things clear. She listened, went back to her seat, and sat smiling as she began chewing on an eraser and spitting out the pieces. She then started to make strange noises that disturbed the other students.

During the next writing period she came to me and told me she didn't know how to add any details. I showed her how she could write a sentence on another piece of paper and attach it with tape in the right spot. For the rest of the week she had great difficulty with this idea and did very little writing. Instead, she chewed erasers and paper clips and continued to annoy the class with strange noises. She told me often that she couldn't revise her piece. I tried to work with her to help her add information but she was not interested and could not concentrate. She finally decided to copy the whole piece over again and add the information as she recopied. She was very frustrated by the whole experience. When I looked at her second draft I realized that it was exactly the same as the first one.

In another mini-lesson we talked about leads, what they do and how important they are. I experimented with some leads for my piece and asked for the children's opinions and suggestions. They responded to each lead and I told them how they had helped me select a better lead than my original one. Then I asked them to try out a few leads for their piece and we shared the results. In conferences, the students helped each other revise and select good leads for their stories.

Karen read her three leads (see Figure 4.4) at a group conference, again in her baby voice, and the kids told her how much they liked the third one. She decided she would use it and then became confused as to how she would put it in her piece. I suggested that she cut it and tape it over her original lead. She told me she couldn't revise that way, "It's too confusing." I remembered her sequencing problems and suggested she use a big piece of white construction paper. I explained this would make it easier to cut and add details. She said she'd try, but not before she copied the lead onto a new piece of paper. She began to add more information as she copied again.

Then she was ready for the bigger paper. She taped her piece on it and began to add flaps. I showed her how she could draw lines to

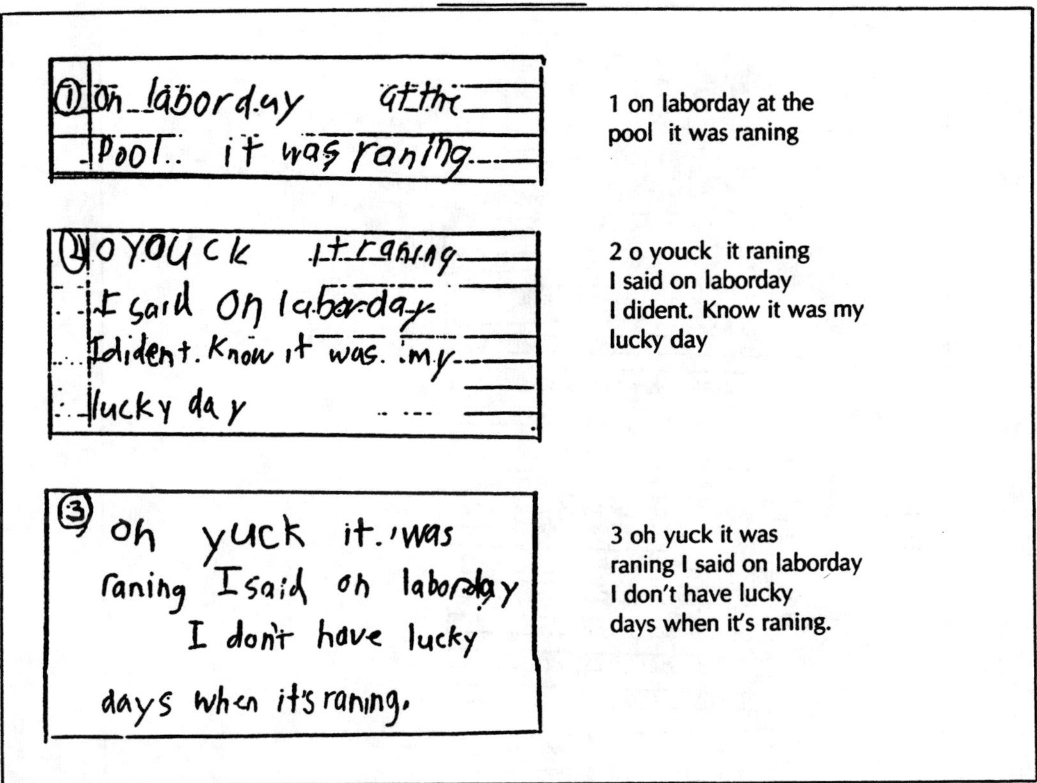

1 on laborday at the
pool it was raning
2 o youck it raning
I said on laborday
I dident. Know it was my
lucky day
3 oh yuck it was
raning I said on laborday
I don't have lucky
days when it's raning.

FIGURE 4.4 *Karen's three leads*

sentences that she wanted to come next. She enjoyed this activity and was pleased with her progress. Her revised draft included flaps where she added information, parts she taped at the end of each page, and lines to delete words and add sentences (Figure 4.5).

During the first few weeks of school, Karen was very much a baby. She talked in her babyish voice, often accompanied by whining. I asked her each time she said anything in her baby voice to repeat it in her "fifth-grade" voice, which she often tried to do. After an assembly in September, she watched the kindergartners walking out of the gym and then began to walk like a toddler, pigeon-toed with slow, faltering steps, talking her baby talk! I asked her to walk in her "fifth-grade" walk and she experimented with a few kinds of walks and finally decided on what her fifth-grade walk was. Her handwriting, too, was very immature. She wrote in large letters that often took up more than one full space. She skipped a space between each line and always printed. Her papers looked

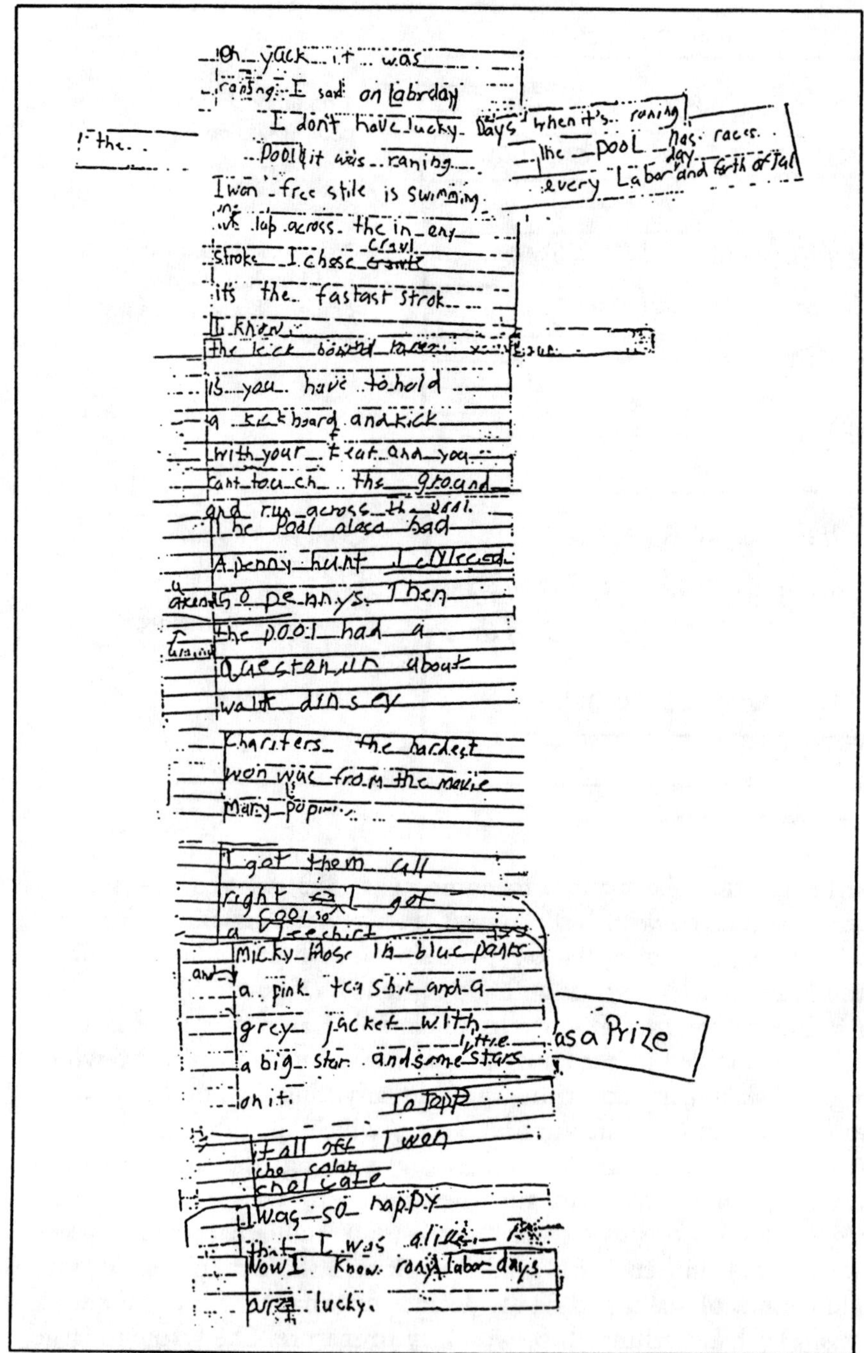

Oh yack it was
raning I sad on labrday
I don't have lucky Days when it's raning
the pool has races
the pool it was raning every Labor day and forth of Jul
I won free stile is swimming
one lap across the in-eny
stroke I chose crawl
its the fastast strok
I know
the kick board races
is you have to hold
a kick board and kick
with your feat and you
cant touch the ground
and run across the pool.
The pool alsa had
A penny hunt I collected
around 50 pennys. Then
the pool had a
Questenair about
walt dinsey
Charaters the hardest
won was from the movie
mary popins
I got them all
right so I got
a Teeshirt cool so
Micky Mose in blue pants
and a pink teashirt and a
grey jacket with
a big star and some little stars
on it. To topp
it all off I won
the chocolate
I was so happy
that I was alive
Now I know rany labor days
are lucky.
as a Prize

FIGURE 4.5 *Karen's revision of Labor Day piece*

very similar to first-and second-grade papers. When I told her that in fifth grade I expected her to write in script like all the other fifth graders, she at first told me that she couldn't. But then she started to try out different letters and began to write in script, although she had trouble with the formation of the letters and still needed to skip spaces.

The first two weeks of school went well. Karen seemed to respond to my suggestions and, despite the chewing and the noises, was trying hard. By the third week, however, more of her problems became obvious. She had days when she was easily distracted, whined, wouldn't write in script, and handed in sloppy work. During writing period and at times when the class was involved in discussions, she would get up from her seat and walk around the room explaining to me that she was restless and couldn't sit still. At other times she had outbursts of loud laughing for no discernible reason causing some of the boys to imitate her. At times she attempted to become part of our discussions by raising her hand and laughing when I called on her. She talked in her baby voice and would say something totally unrelated to the topic. Then she would smile and giggle and look around the classroom to see the response she received. Many children were annoyed and angry. Some whispered to each other about her and others said out loud to me, "Can't you make her stop!" I explained that Karen was learning how to be part of the group and that I hoped we could all help and support her. The class was not pleased with this answer. They wanted her removal from the class. This was the course of action her teachers had taken in the past.

After a short unit on the Constitution I asked the class to write about the Constitution. Karen could not or would not write: "I have nothing to write. I have no ideas." When I asked her what she thought the Constitution was, what she knew about it or what meaning it might have for her, she smiled, shrugged, and said in her baby voice, "I don't know." This was to be a common response for the first part of fifth grade and I was reminded of Mark who had responded in the same way. Perhaps these children had never been given the opportunity to have ideas. Perhaps teachers' expectations had been low and children with special needs had not been given the time to think and respond. Perhaps their ideas were not valued. Often aides had provided the answers, the ideas. I wondered if this was the case with Karen.

After much time reviewing what we had learned in class and encouraging her to talk to me first about her ideas, she finally wrote in her journal: "The constion is a groop of laws. The constion means alot tome and everybody. It makes us have a better life."

As September turned to October, I became acutely aware that Karen's most difficult times were in the afternoon. She resorted to her loud, high-pitched baby voice all the time and had outbursts of laughing for no apparent reason. The worst time was the last hour of the day. Her mother said she got tired in the afternoon. I realized that the afternoons appeared less structured than the mornings because in the afternoon we had writing every day and either science or social studies. These three subjects involved more group work, discussion, and physical movement within the classroom than the subjects I taught in the morning. Another factor was the absence of the class aide in the afternoons. The aide was in the classroom every morning from nine to twelve. Karen often went to her before beginning any assignment. In the afternoon she had to initiate work on her own.

Karen's desk was near the conference table and she often sat and listened to the conferences taking place. She began to come to the table each day. She read her pieces in a very loud voice and would laugh loudly at parts, causing the other kids at the conference and in the rest of the room to look puzzled. I was perplexed myself, wondering at times what anyone entering my room and hearing her constant loud laughing and baby talk and observing her chewing, spitting, and restless behavior might think. Often the class complained that they could not concentrate due to her behavior. They began to remind her to talk in her "fifth-grade" voice and then pinned notes to me on the Message Board (a special bulletin board on which students write notes to each other and to me) pleading for help. David and Jeb were particularly upset. Jeb's letter seemed to express the feelings of the class:

> Dear Miss Five,
>
> Im realy trying to be paicient but now its gone to far. Would you please move me as far away as possible from Karen. She throws things at me, yells at me and I'm speaking for all, well atleast most of the class here. She realy gets on my nerves.
>
> from Jeb
>
> P.S. she makes messes write next to me.

Despite her behavior, there were brief periods during the daily writing time when Karen was completely absorbed in her work. This usually occurred after a conference with me or the group. She told me she liked writing and wanted her piece about Labor Day and the pool to be a good one. She was proud of the changes she had made. When we proofread it together, she was anxious to copy it in script and she worked very hard to copy in her neatest handwriting. She also put much effort into drawing her cover.

In the middle of October, Karen read her first writing piece about Labor Day and the pool to the class.

Lucky Lucky
Labor Day

"Oh yuck! It is raining," I said on Labor Day. I don't have luck days when its raining. At the pool it was raining.

The pool has races every Labor Day and Fourth of July. I entered the freestyle race even though I don't swim very fast. I won the freestyle in swimming one lap across the pool in any stroke. I chose the crawl. It's the fastest stroke I know. Next was the kick-board race. You have to hold a kickboard and kick with your feet and you can't touch the ground and run across the pool. The pool also had a penny hunt. I collected around 50 pennies. Then the pool had a questionnaire about Walt Disney characters. The hardest question was from the movie Mary Poppins. I got them all right so as a prize I got a cool T-shirt with Micky Mouse in blue pants and a pink T-shirt and a grey jacket with a big star and some little stars on it.

To top it all off, I won chocolate. I was so happy I was alive. Now I know rainy Labor Days are lucky.

She sat in front of the class and read with great expression. The class seemed to ignore the manner in which she read and focused on her piece. They gave her very positive feedback pointing out specific words and parts that they liked. She was very pleased with her piece and the comments she received.

Karen's next writing piece was easier for her. She had five possible topics and wanted to come to the conference table to discuss them. She again had difficulty making a decision. As she waited for her turn, she listened to the other children read their drafts and then began to make suggestions that at first were dismissed by the other children. However, after I asked them to listen carefully, they began to see the validity of Karen's points. Some of the children agreed with her. I could tell she was pleased. When it was her turn, she discussed her topics and listened to their response. This was the first time I felt she was beginning to realize the value of response. She followed their suggestions when she went back to her seat and instead of chewing or laughing, she began to write.

Her next conference showed increased progress. She was not distracted but listened intently and offered more suggestions. I noticed, too, that when she came for a conference, she began to speak in her "fifth-grade" voice. When she read her draft, she experimented with different tones of voice, often reading in a soft low voice. She paid greater attention to the response she received from the other children. It made revision easier for her. She would return to her desk and follow one or two of the suggestions made, as many as she could remember, and return to the table to read her revised piece. Feedback had a special meaning to her now. I don't think she was aware that she was learning from them, but soon conferences became very important to her and she came every day if not to read, just to listen and participate.

As I observed Karen begin to interact with her peers in conferences, I remembered previous studies I had done on other children who had special needs. I remembered the importance of response for Angela and for Mark and Peter. These three students had benefited from discussions with and response from peers. Through collaboration, they discovered they had ideas and choices about topics. The response they received helped them make their own decisions about revision. The ownership and authority they developed through selecting their own topics and making decisions about revision led to greater self-confidence and eventually affected their work in all areas of the curriculum. I felt that this result was possible for Karen too.

As Karen began the draft of her second piece, I noticed she was involved with her writing for at least thirty to forty minutes. She was able to sit at her seat and write. Every now and then she stopped and sat very still thinking and then would start writing again. During these times she did not get up and wander around the room. There was no loud laughing, no chewing, spitting, and strange noises. She did not come to me for help. She was completely absorbed.

She came to the conference table when her draft was finished and read it in her "fifth-grade" voice. It is interesting to note that it was during the writing period when she first stopped using her baby voice, although she continued to revert to it in other areas. It was at the end of October when she told me often that she liked writing and I suspect that for the first time in her school career, she was taking a subject seriously, a subject that had meaning for her and was important to her. Her focus was on her writing and not on her behavior. She wanted the response of the other children and not necessarily their attention.

Her second piece was about a time she went to a restaurant called Gene's with a friend. It was through this piece that I became aware of her sense of humor and her interest in words. She made a play on the word *Gene's,* thinking of *jeans,* and wrote in her piece, "The food must be blue!" She added that her friend said, "And it has little pieces of denim in it." She enjoyed writing this piece very much. She titled it "Eew Its Blue."

> "I think we'll never eat," I said to myself. I was starved. "When will eat? I'm hungry," I said in the car.
>
> I was at Laura's summer home and in the car.
>
> We were driving and found our goal. It was Gene's, a restaurant. I said "The food must be blue!" Laura's grand father agreed with me and said, "It's blue."
>
> "Oh yuck" I said.
>
> Laura said, "And it has little pieces of denim in it."
>
> I said, "Double oh yuck! "Pleease ," I begged "don't go there. Please, please, with sugar and ice cream on top."
>
> Every one in the car started laughing like crazy excapt the driver. He screamed and yelled "STOP IT!!!"
>
> But anyhow we went to Gene's. We were going to play video games but I was having a hard time deciding what game to play. Just when I thought I knew what game to play, Laura cried, "My favorite game is broken so let's go to the table."
>
> We waited and waited. Then finally the food came. I pigged out. I had all my hambuger paddy and french fries and had extra ketchup so I took Laura's french fries and ate them too. When the desset came I was full so I ate a little bit of my ice cream. "Let's leave. I'm tired and full," I am going to burst. I said. Blue jeans should be worn but not eaten.

It remained her favorite piece throughout the year.

In this second piece she was able to make revisions on the original draft without copying it over and without using large paper. She crossed out words and drew lines to show additions. She experimented with leads, read them to the conference table group, and

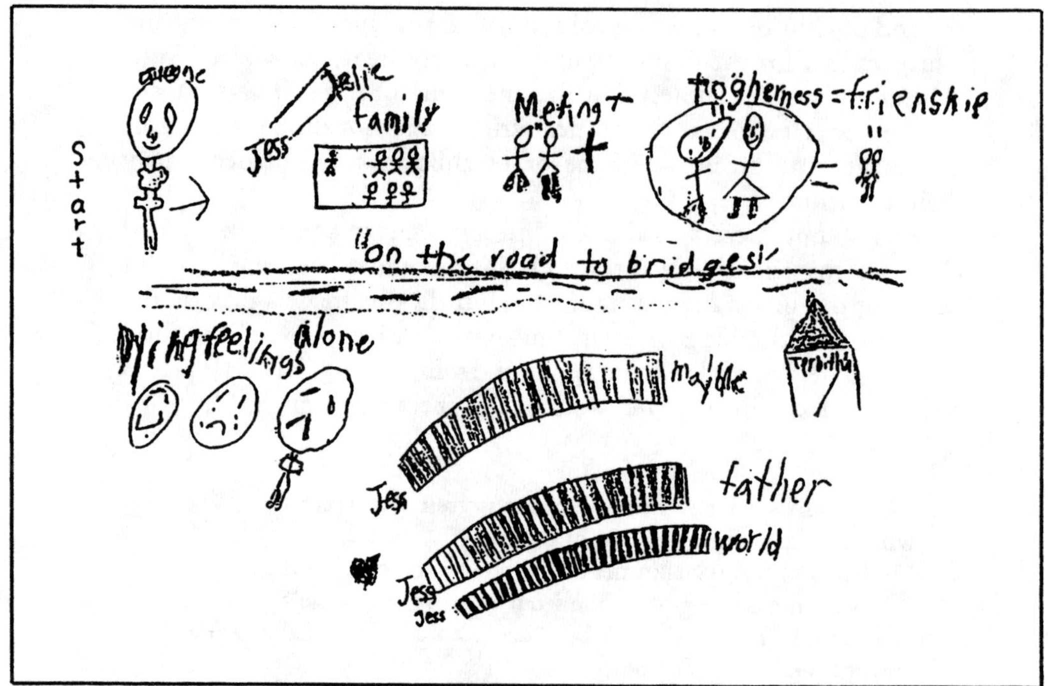

FIGURE 4.6 *Karen's response to Bridge to Terabithia*

taped the new one over the original. She discussed her ending with the group and was very pleased when, with the help of another student, she wrote, "Blue jeans should be worn but not eaten." It was her work on this piece and response from her peers that brought out her sense of humor and her ability to "play" with words.

At this time I had finished reading *Bridge to Terabithia* (Paterson 1977) to the class. Aside from loving this book personally, I use this book to teach character development and to have the children experiment with looking beyond the story line. Karen could respond in depth orally to this book. She began to present many ideas in her grown-up voice, a voice that made the other kids stop making faces as soon as she spoke and begin to listen. When we were discussing the meaning of the title, Karen said about Jess, the main character: "He made bridges to Leslie, his father, and the world. He respected the world and the world respected him." Her response surprised me. She had not been able to respond in such depth when writing about the books she read. Up to this point Karen's written responses were usually limited to naming the book and telling me whether she liked the book or not.

My students also respond to their reading in other ways—through mapping, for instance (Five 1986). The children draw or diagram significant events or characters from a book and connect them in a way that is meaningful to them. Karen was able to include her oral response to Paterson's book in her map (Figure 4.6).

When I asked her to write about these ideas in her reading journal, at first she had trouble. She sat at her desk with her journal open but could write nothing. She told me she couldn't remember what she had said or thought. However, when I sat with her, she was able to express some of her ideas. She told me a few things and then wrote in her journal. She'd tell me more and then begin to write again. She seemed to need to discuss her ideas first in order to write in depth. Her final journal entry on *Bridge to Terabithia* appears below:

> Dear Mrs. Five
> At first Jess was a little country boy, all alone then leslie stepped in and when she went away he made a bridge with May Belle and brought her in to Terabithia and taught her the magic. then he made a bridge with his dad because he was having a hard time dealing with the fact Leslie was dead so his dad picked him up and twirled him around like he wanted to do for ever so long. as long as all this happens he mades a bridge between the world before he had know wone his age to look up at for help, then leslie came and to terabithia and taught him about the world wich helped him under stand life and the world wich he lived on. he respected the world and it respected him

Her difficulties with writing her ideas in journals were not limited to reading and history. In November I noticed that Karen was using her "fifth-grade" voice when she discussed the experiments we were doing in science. I was also aware of her wonderful ideas. She was able to form hypotheses and reach conclusions before any of the other children, which seemed to contradict her so-called inability to see relationships and make inferences. At first the class disregarded her opinions but soon they saw the validity of her ideas. However, when it came to recording her observations, predictions, hypotheses, and conclusions, she could not do it with the same depth she was able to express orally. Perhaps her problems with handwriting and spelling prevented her from writing more than the minimum.

In November, despite Karen's problems with journal writing, there was continued progress in her personal writing. Her third piece was about her desire for a new bicycle. For the first time she knew what the topic would be and needed no help on topic selection from me or the group. As soon as she finished her second piece, she told me she was going to write about getting a new bike. Her draft was easier to write. I had a sense that because she knew we had writing every day, she had been rehearsing possible topics in her mind. The consistency of writing workshop seemed to provide a context for her ideas. She felt sure of what she wanted to write and became very involved in writing her draft. Her revisions were again made on the original draft, only this time she taped on additions at the end of her pages. She seemed better able to deal with the confusion or messiness of the revised draft.

Another significant event was the inclusion of her vocabulary words in her piece. My vocabulary program consists of each child selecting one word a day from anything they have read. They choose a word that they want to learn and do not already know well. They write their word in a journal, including the definition, a synonym and antonym if possible, and the sentence using the word from the dictionary. They also use the word in a sentence of their own. All the children had been very interested in words by October and many were using their words and class words—words selected by the class to put on the walls around the room—in their writing pieces. Karen decided to experiment with her words in her third piece. She wrote, "My mom gave me an evasive answer. 'Stop giving me evasive answers!' I screamed." In another part, she wrote, "I was elated and delighted. I was jumping up and down with joy." She was very proud of her use of her words "evasive," "elated," and "delighted."

An additional change that accompanied her bicycle piece was her ability to come for a conference and ask for help in a specific area. Instead of reading her whole draft and waiting for response, she told the group, "I'm going to read part of my draft because I need help on the lead." At another conference, she read her draft and said, "I don't know what else I should include to make it clear."

Karen was taking herself and her writing seriously. She realized that the class was listening to her ideas and that they seemed to respect what she had to say and write. She realized, too, the importance of response for revision. I think she felt very much a part of the community of writers that existed in my room. She realized she was able to help others with her suggestions and she benefited from the response of her peers. This reciprocity made her feel needed and important. The writing period was the one time during the day that she was more accepted as part of the group. This was the first time she had been included academically and socially since she entered school in kindergarten.

Her acceptance as part of the community of writers led her to continue to explore her ideas and take risks in other areas. She started to take other subjects more seriously. She listened to discussions and began to experiment with her ideas orally, often astounding me with the astuteness of her comments. When presenting her ideas on the characters in a science series, she said to the horror of the rest of the class, "I think Captain Granville deserves to get wet [he had almost died of hypothermia after nearly drowning] because C. T. [his grandson] will get to know him better and they'll care more about each other." She turned out to be right.

During a history discussion, she again shocked the class. We were discussing whether we value freedom. Most of the class said yes and gave various reasons. Karen said, "No!" The response of "Oh, Karen" was accompanied by sighs of exasperation and eyes rolled to the ceiling. She went on to explain: "I think we take it for granted. We're so used to having it, we don't think about it so we don't really value it." The other kids listened and could see her point of view. Many of them began to agree with her, citing their own examples and extending her ideas.

When asked to write these ideas in her science and history journals, she again had trouble. She pushed her chair out, coughed, cleared her throat loudly, causing the other students to look up from their own writing and ask her to be quiet. She finally came to me and told me she couldn't do it. I expressed confidence in her ability and discussed and repeated her ideas with her. She settled down and wrote, stopping often to think and to put her head on her desk. She was not able to record all her ideas but did include phrases.

At the beginning of December, Karen and I had a writing evaluation conference. I have a conference with each child before sending home the report card. Each child fills out a writing evaluation form based on Nancie Atwell's (1987) evaluation sheet. In a conference we discuss the child's responses, look at samples of his or her writing, and together we mark the report card and establish goals for the next four months. Karen was eager for her conference. We discussed her responses to her writing evaluation form. In answer to the question "What do you have to do to be a good writer?" She told me, "Learn to spell." The hardest part of writing for her was "getting my thoughts down." The easiest was making the cover. Her favorite piece was "Gene's" because "I put in a few jokes." When asked about the kinds of changes she made when she revised, she answered, "Put in details."

When we looked at the report card, we both agreed that a mark of satisfactory was appropriate for "Uses Mechanics Correctly." She told me she gets mixed up with quotation marks. She called them "66" and "99." She said, too, that she didn't always know when to put in a period and a capital. "If I knew where to put a period, I'd know the next letter should be a capital." Then we discussed the next two categories, "Drafts and Revises" and "Applies Qualities of Good Writing." She expressed confidence in both of those areas. We also talked about establishing goals for the next four-month marking period. She told me she would finish four or five pieces because she "liked writing and it is easier now." She also set other goals for herself. One was "to get better at spelling." Spelling continued to be a source of frustration for her. Her second goal provided insight into her difficulty with journal writing: "I want to get my thoughts down 'cause my hand and my brain aren't exactly together. My brain goes faster." She went on to explain when I questioned her: "My hand writes something else. I'm thinking about something and when I come to write it, I don't exactly put it down on paper." This was upsetting to her. I suggested using the tape recorder to help her record her thoughts for journal writing. She could then listen to the tape and write her ideas in her journal, stopping the tape as she wrote. She said she was willing to try. She was pleased with her progress in writing, telling me that it was her favorite subject.

I was pleased with Karen's progress too. I had tried to establish the same supportive environment within the classroom that I had created in past years. From my work with other special students I knew the importance of an environment that accepts, respects, and emphasizes the *ideas* of students rather than their skills. If skills are stressed, the consequences of their creative attempts might be failure. If I focused on Karen's weaknesses, she would continue to be concerned about spelling and handwriting, and her good ideas might be lost. Karen was able to take risks with her ideas orally in reading, science, and social studies within the classroom environment. She experimented with her ideas, her sense of humor, and her vocabulary in writing. Things were going well.

In the middle of December, Karen went through a series of difficult times. I saw a different side of her, one I had been denying to the other teachers in the school. I termed these difficult periods her "days of deviousness." It seemed to happen quite suddenly. She disobeyed, she lied, she ran out of school early, she "took" candy, and she did no homework and very little class work. She provoked other children and disappointed her news team by not bringing in news, causing them to lose a star. She continued to provoke the whole class by telling them that she would not bring in a gift for the holiday grab bag. Throughout all of this she smiled and grinned and answered "I don't know" to questions about her behavior, apparently enjoying the reaction she was getting from the other students and from me. She was completely helpless when it came to doing her work. She came to me all the time for help . And then withdrew from me and spoke to me as little as possible. I was at a loss as to what had happened. Were there problems at home? Were there difficulties with classmates that I didn't recognize? Did she feel more comfortable with her previous behavior and former image? Had I changed the classroom conditions, my expectations, my attitude? I could not figure it out and she could not tell me anything.

In an attempt to bring Karen back into the classroom community, I decided to try to help her record more of her ideas in her journals. Since she was having difficulties with her peers, sharing her ideas with a partner did not seem to be the answer. I decided to use the tape recorder. I thought something different might interest her. I asked the classroom aide to take her aside and tape a discussion of the book Karen had finished. I hoped Karen would then be able to play back the discussion and write her ideas about her book in her reading journal. She could stop the tape when she needed time to write. Karen loved talking into the tape recorder. However, the task of copying her ideas in her journal proved tedious and she soon gave up.

And suddenly her "bad days" were over and she appeared one day dressed like all the other fifth-grade girls, wearing a long shirt over pants. During the week before the Christmas holiday, she wore pants and a long shirt frequently. I told her often how wonderful she looked.

She wore this type of outfit once or twice a week during January and February and then would return to her former mode of dress. It was as if she was experimenting with this new image. It reminded me of her first tentative steps into the writing community. During this time there was another change. She seemed to be involved with the girls at recess and at lunch time. She did not make excuses to stay inside at recess but went out and played jump rope with the other fifth graders.

During this same time Karen began to take a more mature part in class activities. Each year as part of our study of American history, my students are involved in a simulation where most of the class was treated unfairly by a small group given special power to rule, in an attempt to have them understand the feelings of the colonists. Karen was part of the majority who felt the rules were unfair. She worked within her group to try to change the rules. In another simulation she and other girls were angry when they could not be delegates at the Constitutional Convention because of their gender. In both these activities, she was involved and voiced her thoughts well. She received positive response instead of the negative feedback she got for her inappropriate behavior.

In January I started to read poetry to my class. Each day I read a poem. Some were humorous, some rhymed, some told stories, some described feelings. Soon some of the students were reading books of poetry. I saw the connection between reading and writing when Karen came rushing into school one day to tell me she had written three poems. She couldn't wait to read them to the class. She read her favorite first, a rhyming poem, and received very positive response. Many of the boys said they wanted to write a poem "like Karen's." And they did. Their poems rhymed too. I became very interested. I had not had many children who had turned to poetry in the past. Why did they like to write rhyming poems? I began to wonder if rhyme seemed to be an easier, safer way for these ten-year-olds to write poetry. Perhaps it provided a structure or perhaps it seemed more natural to them for poetry to have a rhythm or a beat. Whatever the reason, they were having fun with their rhyming verse, and their enthusiasm was infectious.

A week later Karen tried out her other two poems. The class told her that she was just rhyming words and that the words together had no meaning. She agreed and explained her writing process: "I looked for words that rhymed and listed all the words that rhymed and then I tried to put them together." This led to a discussion of poetry and whether poems had to rhyme. For me it meant reading lots of poems to the class that did not rhyme.

I introduced similes and for days the students described everything in similes. They even used their vocabulary words in similes: "as ecstatic as the Mets winning the World Series" wrote John; "as conspicuous as a bear in the desert," said Libbi. And Karen, intrigued, wrote her own: "as isolated as a house on a hill"; "as conspicuous as a funny clown"; "as nocturnal as a raccoon." She spotted similes in everything I read to the class.

Then I showed them metaphors and they were off again! They discovered metaphors in the books they read and the books I read aloud. Karen, too, was caught up in the excitement of experimenting with similes and metaphors. She began another poem about snow: "The snow is a white angel flying from the sky. then eyeing the ground she flew down and landed. As it hits the trees wings form, icles when the sun shines on them are halos. Snow is like white butterflys flying by and by in the sky and then the butterflys land on the angel."

For the next few weeks, many students worked on poems. They wrote story poems and gradually moved to poems that expressed their feelings, their fears, and their thoughts. Karen continued to work on her first poem. She changed some words as a result of suggestions made at a group conference. Jeb, one of her fiercest critics at the beginning of the year, was very interested in her poem and helped her add better words. Greg read a poem at a conference and said he had written a poem "like Karen's." Karen was the first student to write a poem and had now become not only accepted but respected by the writing community. She copied her revised poem as neatly as she could. In fact, she moved to a desk in a far corner of the room away from the circle of desks to copy it, telling me, "I have to concentrate and I can do it better here." For the remainder of the year, she would return to that desk whenever she felt she needed a quiet place. She made a cover for her poem and shared the final version with the class. She beamed with pride at the response she received and told me that her poem was now her "best piece but 'EEw It's Blue' [the piece about Gene's/jeans] is my favorite." I continued to wonder about poetry and why it clicked. Was it an easier form of expression? It seemed to be for Karen. Thoughts flowed with fewer words.

When Karen became aware that many of the students were working on fiction stories, she decided that she would write one, too. "I'm going to write about a boy who has trouble making friends," she announced one day at the conference table. She discussed that idea and went back to her seat. The next day she had another idea: "I'm going to write about a girl who finds a fifty-dollar bill and thinks of all the things she could buy with it." She told the group at the conference table about this idea and said, "I don't know how to start." We discussed some possible strategies and she went back to her seat.

During her fiction writing, she returned to the conference table often. This was an exciting time for me because I realized she knew what she wanted to accomplish and where she needed help. She wanted to share her lead one day because she didn't know what to do next. She told us, "I want to get suspense and tension into my story but I'm not sure how to do it." Karen was thinking of herself as a writer!

Melissa asked, "Do you want to focus on finding the money or on spending it?"

Karen answered, "I think on spending it because that would be more interesting. There's not a lot that's exciting about just finding it sticking out of the sand."

"Then don't spend too long on having her find the money. Maybe you could have her find it at the beginning in your lead and then go on," suggested Michael.

Karen agreed with this idea and returned to her seat to rewrite her lead.

She worked on her fiction story for the next week. She became very interested in writing in this genre. Suddenly, it seemed, she made more of a connection between the books she read and those I read aloud, and her own writing pieces. Her interest prompted her to write to Katherine Paterson. It seemed to me that she was writing as one writer to another (Figure 4.7).

Although Karen never finished her fiction story, she made progress as a writer through it. She learned with the help of her peers that she could combine two of her leads to make a stronger one. "Now," she sighed with pleasure, "the main character has found the bill in one paragraph." She came to the conference table constantly for help and reassurance and I noticed most of her revision took place at the table. She began to number sections of her story and used the numbers to put the sections in the correct order. This was a big step for a child who has difficulty with sequencing and a giant leap for Karen, who had not been able to reorder, much less revise, at the beginning of the year. Her new revision strategies were all on her draft (Figure 4.8).

Karen became more accepted by the other girls during this time. She dressed as they did and even wore her hair back in a barrette the

Dear Katherine Paterson,
I'm writing
fiction. Im wondering
how you got the
topic. Please give me
tips for fiction.
from
Karen
P.S. I loved Bridge to
terabitha I loved lesle.
There were lots of
bridges between Jess.
and the world.

FIGURE 4.7 *Karen's letter to Katherine Paterson*

way they did. She was always in a rush to get out for recess to play with them. In a jazz assembly she sat with the girls, instead of me, smiling and singing. She looked truly happy.

Difficult days

Then in February, Karen went through another difficult time, during which she did very little work. She pretended she did homework when none was done. She blatantly ate candy in class and chewed gum. She provoked the other students by making noises and taking things out of their desks. She reverted to her baby talk, her whiny voice, and she walked like a toddler. She was constantly loud and experimented with "dirty words" and gestures, enjoying the negative attention she received from the class.

At this time I started two new topics in writing. I gave the class a practice test for the state writing test. The state test and the practice

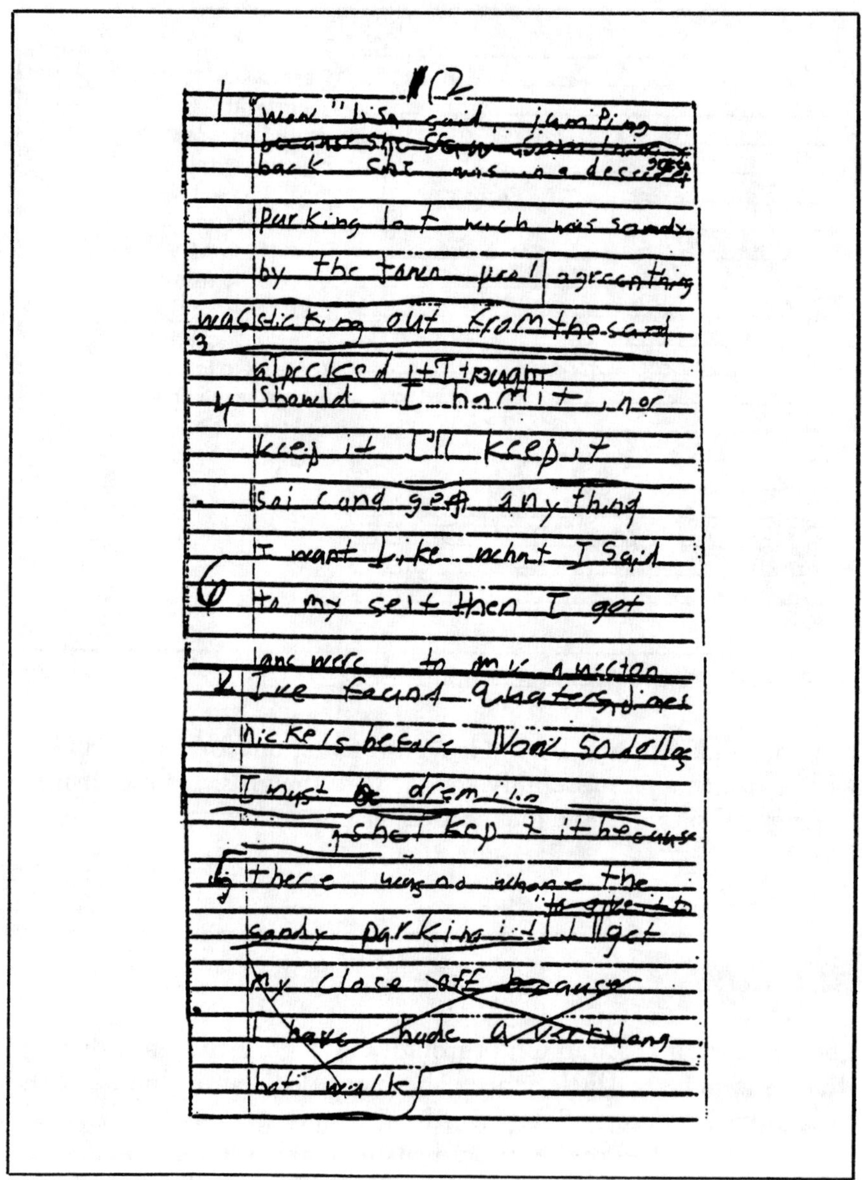
#12
1 "wow" lisa said, jumping
because she saw something
back she was in a desert
parking lot which was sandy
by the farm pool a green thing
was sticking out from the sand
3 I picked it I tought
4 should I hand it, or
keep it I'll keep it
so i cand get any thing
I want like what I said
6 to my self then I got
one were to my
I've found quaters, dimes
nickels because I won 50 dollars
I must be dreming
I shal kep it it because
there was no where the
sandy parking it I'll get
my close off because
I have hude a
bat walk

FIGURE 4.8 *Karen's numbered draft*

tests are always a source of frustration for me because they are the complete opposite of the writing workshop environment. During the test students must write independently without the benefit of conferences and they must write on assigned topics. I feel students need practice especially in dealing with assigned topics since they select their own topics during the daily writing period. At the same time I introduced content writing to the class through reports about colonial times.

Karen had a difficult time with both. She could not write about the practice test topic of helping someone do something. And I did not give her any help. I wanted to see what she could do on her own. She was very upset and ended up writing about a recipe. She told me she had helped her mother make the recipe but she was only able to write about the ingredients. She had more trouble with her colonial report. Even though she had been reading both historical fiction and nonfiction for the past month on her topic in preparation for writing her report (Five 1985), she could not remember anything and decided to copy pages out of a book.

The month of February was a hard time for me too. I had to rethink my strategies for teaching Karen. I knew a supportive environment had been created within the classroom. I also knew the value of collaborative learning. I had built that into my program three years ago and had been increasing the amount of time children could learn from each other. I knew kids needed time to think, to wonder, to reflect, and to grow at their own pace.

I realized as I returned to the works of Atwell (1982, 1988); Graves (1983); Harste, Woodward, and Burke (1984); and Stires (1983, 1988) that perhaps I had expected too much of Karen too soon. I had been determined to have her achieve independence as a writer and as a learner. In my desire to accomplish my goal, I had not listened to Karen's needs. I had interpreted her progress in writing and in her other academic subjects as a signal that she was ready to take responsibility for her learning. I had not continued my individual help and support when she started her practice tests and I had assumed she could integrate her reading about colonial life and organize her report. And while she had made great strides, she was not ready for complete independence. She obviously still needed my support and individual attention, which I had withdrawn too soon. The amount of support and the length of time it is needed, I realized, depends on each individual child and that child's special needs.

I decided to work with Karen in the mornings before school started. She told me she could come early because her mother would drop her at school on her way to work. She came at 8:00 and we talked and worked on her practice test. Or we talked and we worked on her report. She needed to discuss her ideas before she could write.

Before she wrote her second practice test, Karen discussed her ideas with me. The topic was an adventure with a magic carpet. She explained her ideas and told me she was going to put in "a lot of good words." She came to me often for reassurance that she was writing about the topic and was pleased when I told her she was. She talked to me about her ideas and sat near me as much as possible as she worked on proofreading her draft. She wanted the spelling to be correct and consulted the dictionary frequently (she had not been as concerned about spelling since the beginning of the year). She was particularly pleased with the vocabulary words she used, such as *camouflage, vanish, mysteriously, curiously, bellowed.* However, by 2:00, she was restless and couldn't concentrate. She had been working on the test since 9:30 because we tried to simulate test conditions. (The children are given the test in the morning and have all day to finish it.) She began making noises, chewing on erasers and paper, spitting, and moving her desk around the room to sit next to others and disturb them. Finally she started yelling, "I hate practice tests!" I told the other students that she was tired and we all stopped. She left at 3:00 very angry, telling me, "When I get mad, I can't concentrate. I'm just mad!"

Surprisingly, her third practice test given two weeks later was much easier for her. The topic was to describe how the writer learned to do something. Karen remembered an earlier piece she had written about learning to dive off the high dive. She decided to write her practice test based on this piece. She had no difficulty with this piece and sat absorbed in it for hours. She completed it and enjoyed sharing "Finally Diving" with the class.

Finally Diving

"Karen, you have to dive before the school year starts." my mom bellowed. I was very reluctant. I wanted to jump so I could get wet. My mom finally bet me jump off the divingboard.

After I jumped and climbed out of the pool, I was burning even though I was wet. I went up to the board. I tried to dive but I ended up like a frog. I swam to the wall with a heavy heart and body. When I got out of the pool every step felt heavy.

I felt isolated because everybody was diving.

While I was walking I knew diving is a catastrophe. My aspiration was to dive and then . . . I rembered what my swimming teacher did to me. He held my feet so I could get the feeling and I

> did. Now I'm still trying to dive. So I went up to the board with a heavy heart and body. Every step felt heavy. Then I went up to the board, bent down. hope was rising in my soul. Kapoom. I had finally dived by myself.

She was particularly pleased with her use of vocabulary words such as *bellowed, isolated, catastrophe,* and *aspiration*. When questioned by the class on her repeated use of the word *heavy*, she explained that she repeated the word so "people would really know how heavy I felt." Like Karen, I also felt "hope rising in my soul"—soaring might be a better word—as I realized that she was able to initiate and complete her writing test on her own!

Karen showed greater improvement as she became involved in her colonial report. During conferences on content writing, she was brilliant. She asked all the right questions to help other students make their reports clear. She became very interested in the ideas discussed at the table and spent most of the writing period at the conference table listening or participating in discussions of ideas about witchcraft, colonial schoolmasters and punishments, the Boston Tea Party and Paul Revere. She did little work on her report but learned a lot about colonial times from her peers.

She worked on her report in our early 8:00 sessions. She had selected colonial women's crafts for her topic but quickly became very confused with what seemed like the enormity of the topic. As we discussed the crafts, she was able to narrow her topic to candle-making and soapmaking. Her sequencing problems emerged as she tried to describe the steps involved in these two processes. However, she had spent a day making candles and as she related her experiences, we began to write them down in the order they occurred in the process. She reviewed these steps with the class aide later on in the morning to be sure she had them in an order that made sense.

I was encouraged to see that she was organizing the pages of her draft. She began numbering the pages and then taped revised sections in the correct place. At conferences she revised and self-corrected as she read her draft aloud. At one point, she needed my help to go from the lead to her report to her introduction to candlemaking. Again through talking it through, she was able to figure out a transition (Figure 4.9).

She had difficulty with ending her first chapter and making it lead into her second chapter. Again we talked and experimented with

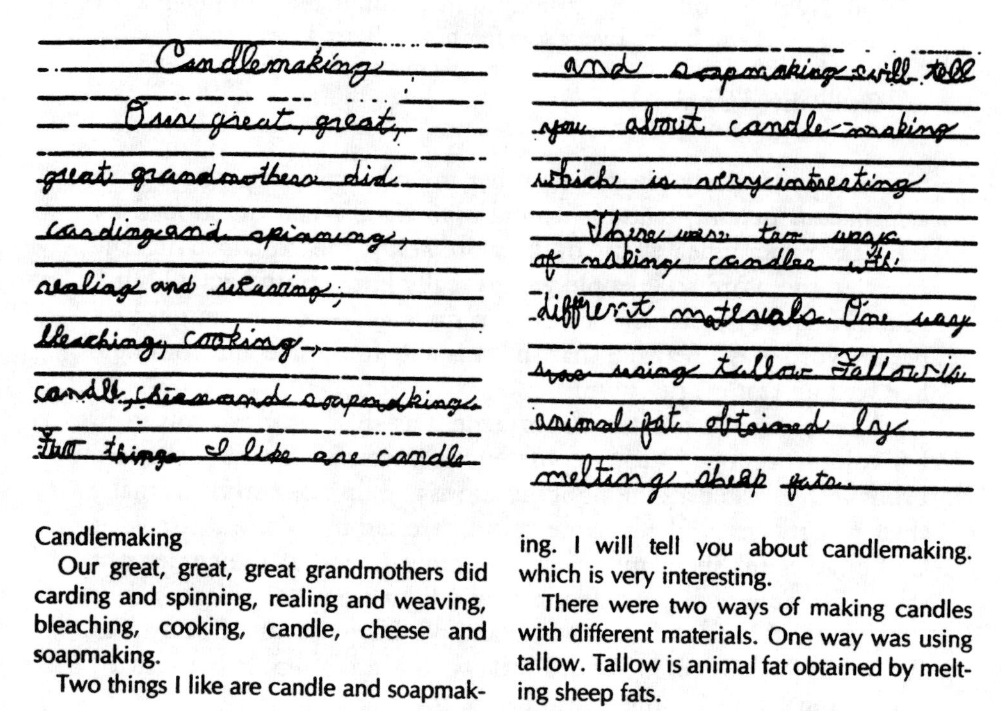

Candlemaking

Our great, great, great grandmothers did carding and spinning, realing and weaving, bleaching, cooking, candle, cheese and soapmaking.

Two things I like are candle and soapmaking. I will tell you about candlemaking. which is very interesting.

There were two ways of making candles with different materials. One way was using tallow. Tallow is animal fat obtained by melting sheep fats.

Figure 4.9 *The beginning of the candlemaking section of Karen's report*

different strategies. She told me how much fun she had had making candles. I asked her if she had ever made soap. She said she hadn't and since she knew how it was made, she didn't think she'd want to. "It wouldn't be much fun," she told me. I suggested that she could end her chapter with her thoughts about candlemaking and soapmaking. When she seemed confused, I repeated what she had told me: "You said you had so much fun making candles and then you told me you didn't think you'd like to make soap. That might be an ending and a way to lead to your next chapter." She realized what I was suggesting and was delighted. She ended her first chapter with "I have made candles before and I think candlemaking must be easier and more fun than soapmaking. But colonial women had to make soap too."

Once Karen got started on her report, she was able to work on it without constant help from me. She required assistance on the first chapter but seemed to have acquired enough confidence from doing

FIGURE 4.10 *Cover of Karen's candle-and-soapmaking report*

the first chapter to enable her to write most of the second chapter on her own. She still wanted the help the writing group conference could provide and came to read parts of her chapter often. She was able to work for longer stretches of time at proofreading her draft during the class writing period. However, she saved copying it in script for our morning times. She was trying very hard to write in her best handwriting because she wanted her report "to look like the others." Her painstaking work to copy her report in small neat script was slow but she kept at it. She drew her illustrations with care and worked hard to make sure her bibliography was correct. The report had taken on a special meaning for her. She wanted it to be excellent and I had not seen her put so much effort into any other projects. I imagine she noticed how hard the other students were working on their reports. She knew my expectations for the reports and realized, I think, that I had the same expectations for her. She was proud and pleased with her completed report (Figure 4.10) and could not wait to

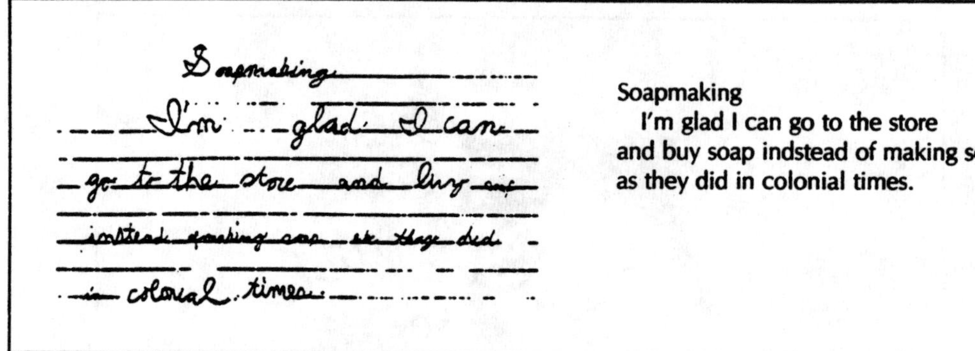

Soapmaking
I'm glad I can go to the store and buy soap indstead of making soap as they did in colonial times.

FIGURE 4.11 *Karen's soapmaking lead*

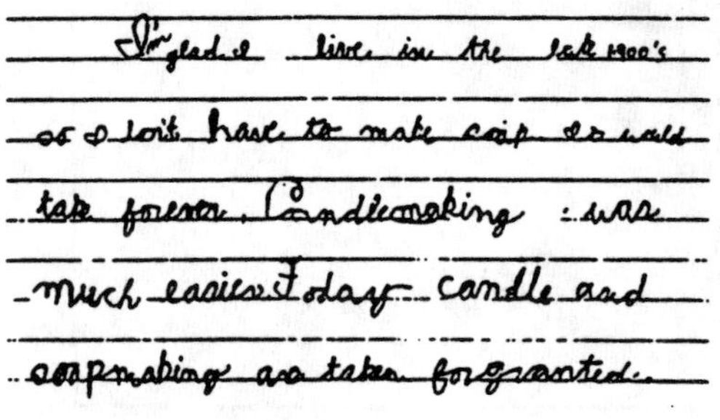

I'm glad I live in the late 1900's so I don't have to make soap. It would take forever. Candlemaking was much easier. Today candle and soapmaking are taken forgranted.

FIGURE 4.12 *End of Karen's candlemaking-and-soapmaking report*

read it to the class. She especially liked her lead to her soapmaking chapter (Figure 4.11) and the ending to her report (Figure 4.12).

Reassessing Karen's progress

At the end of March I had my second writing evaluation conference with Karen in preparation for her report card. She told me she had improved in everything but still wanted to get better in spelling and at putting in periods. She said she was good at using words but she hoped to get better at "using more good words."

The most interesting part of the conference for me was to read her writing evaluation form and compare it to the one she had completed at the beginning of the year and then in December. In December she was concerned with spelling. By March she felt that "knowing how to use big words, punctuation, making an interesting story" helped her become a good writer. In September she didn't know what the easiest part of writing was. Perhaps it was all difficult. By March she provided me with another clue about writing poetry by telling me, "Writing poems is easiest because you can look anywhere to get a poem and the words come." In September I imagine she had no concept of revision. By the spring she wrote, "I cut it up and add flaps with good words, details, feelings." During the first part of the year she felt her problems in writing were with spelling and "getting my ideas on paper." In the spring it appeared that getting her thoughts down was no longer a problem to her and that after attending to meaning, her main concern was with the mechanics of writing because she wanted her pieces "to be good."

Her writing evaluation conference showed me her growth over time. I saw her increased confidence as a writer and I realized her growing independence, but most of all I became aware of the pleasure she experienced as she put her own ideas on a page to share with others.

How had this happened, I wondered. I thought back to September when Karen had entered fifth grade with a poor self-image both academically and socially. At that time her social difficulties had become the focus of her school world. She did not care about academic success and was particularly aware of her deficits and weaknesses. Spelling and handwriting were stumbling blocks and she felt she had no ideas. She behaved like a very young child and took no responsibility for her actions or her learning.

However, through her writing, Karen was able to grow and change. For the first time, Karen gained a sense of control and independence. She began to make decisions for herself. Through conferences, she realized the value of response for her own revision. Once she made that discovery, she was able to participate in conferences and help others with her questions and suggestions.

More important, Karen learned about herself through the response she received. Her peers were able to disregard her baby voice during writing conferences and respond to her ideas in a supportive way. Gradually she began to realize that her ideas had value and were accepted. Over time she became aware, too, that she was receiving recognition through her efforts in writing and for her contributions to writing conferences, and she did not have to resort to her previous antics for attention. She was able to transfer what she learned about herself to other areas of the curriculum. She no longer walked around the room, chewing on things, and making inappropriate remarks. Instead she focused on discussions, experimented with and contributed ideas of greater depth, and made inferences that stimulated the thinking of the other students.

In this way, Karen was able to solve some of her learning and social problems. She was able to be accepted as a member of the classroom community of learners and school became a happier place. At the end of May she expressed her new view of school in a poem:

School

School, school
some people think
it's a place to dread.
Some people think
it's a place
to use your head,
like a scientist figuring
out an hypothesis.
Math is a swirl of numbers
waiting to be solved.
Reading is a totally different world
that sucks you in.
When you open a book
it's filled with settings, characters,
adventure, mysteries, suspense, and humor.
Stories are groups of words
in sentences, similes, metaphors,
words flowing together
forming ideas.
Communication is everything
in school.

5

Tomoko and Yasuo

Becoming literate in a second language

TOMOKO AND YASUO were two of my four ESL (English as a Second Language) students one year. It was through these two students that I learned to apply what I had discovered about youngsters with learning problems to ESL children.

Before any new students are placed in classrooms, they are tested by the skills department. However, students from other countries who do not speak English are divided equally among classrooms. Most of our ESL students come from Japan, although there are many from China and Korea. Children from South America and Europe are fewer.

Once a student is identified as ESL, he or she is tested by the ESL teacher and placed in an appropriate group, not necessarily by age but by ability to speak, write, and read in English. These students leave the regular classroom to attend ESL classes for an hour to an hour and a half each day. Students usually stay in ESL classes for at least two years. They are periodically tested and are dismissed from ESL class when they score at a certain level on a test.

From the beginning I had left the teaching of English up to the people who worked in the ESL department. Students would be gone from my room for long periods of time at different times of the day. Often they missed hands-on science activities and discussions in social studies. It became impossible to plan activities that included all of them because they were seldom in class at the same time. I had decided years ago that I would not and could not worry about them taking part in and learning all subjects and that I would not attempt to have them participate in all the activities that I planned for the class. And so I let them sit while my other students discussed. They sat while I read to the class each day. They were part of group work, if they were there, whether they spoke English or not. While my colleagues worried that these children had "nothing to do" because they couldn't understand, I went on with my teaching, expected my ESL children to participate if they were present, and assumed that they were learning something just by being in the classroom and interacting with their peers.

When I began teaching writing through the process approach, I decided that my ESL students would be part of the writing community, too. They wrote in Japanese if they did not know English. In the beginning they had conferences with other students who spoke Japanese. I always assumed they were discussing their writing pieces in these conferences, but they could easily have been discussing their weekend activities. They copied their drafts in pen and I marvelled at the beautiful Japanese figures and the artwork that went into the covers of their stories. I hung their pieces on the bulletin board with all the others.

Tomoko and Yasuo were both born in Japan but had different temperaments, abilities, and backgrounds. Tomoko, a very pretty small girl with beautiful dark eyes, had lived in Europe before she came to the United States. Both of her parents understood and spoke English, although Japanese was spoken at home. Tomoko spoke some English when she entered my school in the middle of fourth grade. She was scheduled for ESL classes at that time but in fifth grade was dismissed from these classes. She was a shy, sensitive girl who was not really accepted by the other girls. There had been some problems with her relationships with the girls in fourth grade. The girls had already formed small groups of friends when she arrived and she was not included. Her fourth-grade teacher had convinced three girls to befriend her. The girls did so reluctantly and, because the teacher thought the relationship had worked satisfactorily, Tomoko and the three girls were placed in the same class in fifth grade. From the beginning there were problems, although I wasn't aware of them until months had passed.

Tomoko followed the girls everywhere. She joined them at recess, sat next to them at lunch, asked to be seated near them in classroom, and wanted to be part of any group work that they did in class. The girls—Allison; Michiko, another Japanese girl; and Margaret—tolerated Tomoko at the beginning of the year. As the year progressed, however, the difficulties between the four girls increased, leaving Tomoko alone and very unhappy.

Yasuo entered my room a week after he arrived from Japan. His parents stood at the door with the principal on the first day of school in September. They shook my hand and bowed in respect. His father spoke some English and the mother spoke none. Yasuo, who did not understand a word that was being said, smiled at me and at the other students who sat quietly in their seats observing the proceedings. I finally led him to an empty desk and introduced him to the boys sitting near him. He continued to smile and seemed to smile for the rest of the year despite his frustrations with the language. To me he was like a ray of sunshine. He always seemed to be happy and eager to learn. He wanted to be part of everything and he wanted to be able to do anything the other children could do. In contrast to Tomoko, his friendly manner brought him many friends and he was included in all activities.

Because Yasuo spoke no English, he was scheduled for ESL classes for one hour each day on three days of the week and an hour and a half on the other two days. He was in my room for some writing periods and some reading workshops.

Both Yasuo and Tomoko were on the fringes of the writing/reading community in the fall because it was difficult for them to participate. Tomoko seemed to have nothing to write about and often sat thinking of topics. Yasuo sat, too, only he was trying to figure out what to do. He watched the other children and seemed to wriggle in anticipation. He wanted to do what they were doing. If they were writing, he wanted to write. This was a pattern that I saw from the first few days of school. He wanted desperately to communicate. He usually made contact with his smile. He smiled at everyone and at every activity he could do.

In September Yasuo wanted to speak and try out his English. In the morning he would come in, smile, and say, "Hi, Mees Feeva." At 3:00, he always came to say, "Good-bye, Mees Feeva." There was so much more that he wanted to say, but he did not have the words. Whenever he struggled to make himself understood, he seemed to quiver, shaking his wrists up and down and bouncing on his knees with impatience.

Yasuo was not always present during writing workshop because his ESL schedule changed daily. However, when he was in the classroom during writing, I wanted him to participate in the writing process.

In September I asked Takehiro, one of the other Japanese boys in the class to explain to Yasuo that he could write a story in Japanese during writing workshop. Takehiro told him to write about something that had happened to him. Yasuo seemed to understand and went straight to the paper drawer and selected some paper. He was once again excited and eager to begin. He bent over his desk and became very involved in writing. He smiled often as he wrote. His first piece was written in Japanese. This piece, when translated, showed that he had some problems with his own language (see Figure 5.1).

When he finished his story he read it to Takehiro who had become his friend. I had heard them speaking Japanese in their first writing conference which was about Yasuo's draft. He completed his story at the end of September, made a cover for it as the other children did, and decided he wanted to write his title in English. Takehiro helped him write "dog" on the cover.

All my students have the opportunity to share their finished pieces. They sit at the conference table in the chair I usually use and read their piece and show the cover. I asked Yasuo if he would like to share his piece with the class. Of course he was puzzled. I encouraged him to come and sit in my chair. I told the class that he could show us his cover. He came up shyly and then ran over to Takehiro's desk for a whispered conversation. I think Takehiro must have explained to him what he should do. Takehiro, apparently, also told him how to pronounce "dog" because when he sat down, he said the word "dog." Then he held up the cover of his writing piece which contained a picture of what seemed to be a boy being chased by a dog. He had drawn cartoon balloons which held some writing over the boy's head. When he finished showing his cover, he smiled and scurried back to his seat. He did not read his piece in Japanese although I gave him the opportunity.

My students know that when a classmate reads a piece, they must listen carefully and respond with a positive or constructive comment. When a finished piece is read, the class knows the author worked as hard as he or she could and has done his or her best. All comments on finished pieces involve telling the author what the listener liked about

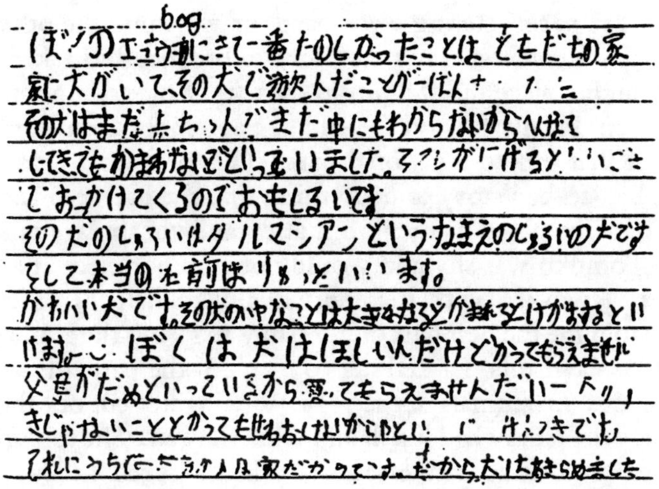

Dog

ぼくのニューヨークにきて一番たのしかったことはともだちの家
家に犬がいてその犬で遊んだことが一ばん[illegible]
その犬はまだ赤ちゃんでまだ何にもわからないからへんなて
してきてもかまわないよといっていました。そして犬がにげるとどこま
でもおっかけてくるのでおもしろいです
その犬のしゅるいはダルマシアンというなまえのしゅるいの犬です
そして本当の名前はりゅうといいます。
かわいい犬です。その犬のいやなことは大きくなるとかまれるとけがするとい
けません。ぼくは犬はほしいんだけどかってもらえません
父母がだめといっているから買ってもらえません[illegible]
きじゃないこととかってもせわをしないからだといい[illegible]けっきょくでも
それにうちは[illegible]家だかのでいます。だから犬はあきらめました

<u>Dog</u>
The most enjoyable moment I had when I came to New York was that there was a dog in my friend's house and I played with that dog was the most enjoyable moment. That dog was still a baby and did not know anything so he touched me stronge but (somebody said) not to mind. When I run, he runs after me until I stop and that is fun. The species of the dog is called Dalmation that is the name of the species. And his real name is called Ryu. He is a cute dog. The thing I don't like about that dog is I heard when he grows big and bites I may get hurt. I want to have a dog but I can't get it. My parents says no and they don't buy it for me. They say that I don't like the dog that much and I don't take a care of the dog. Besides we are not allowed to own a dog in our house. So I gave up having a dog.

FIGURE 5.1 *Yasuo's first writing piece*

the piece. The author, in the special conference table chair, calls on students who volunteer. Several children raised their hands when Yasuo shared his cover but he had rushed from the chair back to his seat. Since I felt he wasn't sure of the students' names I called on them but they directed their comments to him. They told him what they liked about his cover. Many children wanted to see the Japanese writing. I don't think Yasuo understood what the children said, but he saw their interest and their smiles and he seemed especially happy.

Tomoko remained very quiet and shy. She would not come to the conference table to share her drafts. And in the beginning I did not force her or even encourage her. I asked her if she would like to share her draft and she always shook her head. During writing periods she wrote but often spent long periods of time sitting at her desk looking at her paper, staring into space, or watching the other girls hold impromtu conferences as they wrote. Frequently I asked her to tell me about her piece and she would speak in a soft voice about a trip she had taken. Finally toward the end of September she completed a draft about that trip to a national park. This first piece was a long rambling bed-to-bed story of everything that she had seen and done on her trip. It contained many grammatical and vocabulary mistakes.

Since Tomoko was shy and would not read her piece at a group conference, I worked with her individually to help her focus her piece. She told me the best part of her trip was seeing the animals, the lions and the elephants. I asked her to pick out the parts of her piece that told about the animals in the park. We literally cut out the parts about where the family had lunch and what they ate. She told me that she wanted to include conversation. When I asked her what her family might have said during the trip, she told me what she and her sister said in response to seeing the animals. We wrote these sentences on smaller pieces of paper and included some remarks her father had made. Then we selected appropriate places in her story and taped on these flaps. She was particularly interested in a large dead elephant she had seen. "I think the people killed him because the elephant don't die like bloody," she told me. "The lion was eating that poor elephant and the blood shooted out." I asked her if she thought the part about the elephant would make her piece more interesting. She agreed it would and included it at the end. She also wrote, "I felt like I was a poor elephant and lion he bited again." When I asked her what she meant, she could not explain. I wondered what she was trying to say.

Once Tomoko had revised her piece, I worked with her individually on the correct verb tenses and the use of articles. She had great difficulty with correct usage. She then copied her piece in pen and made a cover which had little detail, showing only an animal and the sun. The cover felt closed and tight like the child herself. She did not want to read this first piece to the class.

As Tomoko finished her first story, Yasuo was completing his second. This piece, although written in Japanese, included English words, a fact first discovered by Scott. He came up to me and said in a low voice, "Yasuo's writing some American words." Nothing seems to remain a secret for very long in fifth grade and within minutes some of the other kids were looking over Yasuo's shoulder

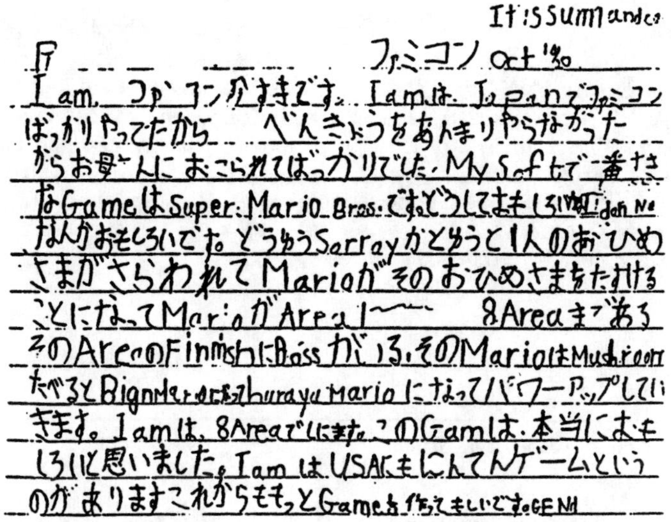

It:s Sum and[illegible]

ファミコン Oct '90

I am ファミコンがすきです。I amは Japanでファミコン
ばっかりやってたから べんきょうをあんまりやらなかった
からお母さんにおこられてばっかりでした。My Softで一番すき
なGameはSuper Mario Bros.です。どうしておもしろいかI don No
なんかおもしろいです。どうゆうSorrayかというと1人のおひめ
さまがさらわれてMarioがそのおひめさまをたすける
ことになってMarioがArea 1〜〜 8Areaまである
そのAreaのFinishにBossがいる。そのMarioはMushroom
たべるとBig Mario [illegible] hurayu Marioになってパワーアップしてい
きます。I amは、8Areaでしにます。このGamは、本当におも
しろいと思いました。I amはUSAにもにんてんゲームという
のがありますこれからももっとGameを作ってきいです。END

Fami-con(Family Computor)

I (am) like a fami-con (family computor). In Japan, I (am) played the fami-con all the time, and didn't study much so I always being scolded by my mother. Among my soft, the game I like the best is the Super Mario Bros. I don No why it is fun. Somehow it is fun. The sorroy (story) is that a princess is taken away and Mario is going to rescue the princess and Mario has area 1 to 8. There is a Boss in the finishing area. When Mario eats mushroom he becomes strong Big Mario and he can run fast. Mario usually am die at area 8. I thought this game was truly exciting. I am there is games also called NINTENDO in the USA I want to produce lots more games from now on too. END

FIGURE 5.2 *Yasuo's second writing piece*

and reading the English words. Soon Scott's discovery was announced by Dianna and the whole class was delighted with Yasuo's achievement. As usual Yasuo smiled.

This second piece seemed to be about video games (Figure 5.2). The cover showed a picture of a boy in his room playing with computer games. There was much more detail on this cover than on the first one. I am particularly interested in the covers made by ESL students because I usually find much of the story is told there. The students spend long periods of time working with care on their covers. I wondered if their limited use of the language neccessitated

American school

Iam AmericanSchol. First when I came It oK

I went to Gym, ResSese, Tatya and Hiro and Kohei are

frelnds Iam Lunches Time I with body

ESL when I went to Iam 8/25 Go USA

Halloween is My castom Lion mask and cape Sword.

a Lot costom wac haus candei eat

Mask show was fun. My first American

Friend is Scott

THE END

I am American school. First when I came, it o.k. I went to gym, recess. Tatya and Hiro and Kohei are friends. I am lunches time. I with body ESL when I went to I am 8/25 go USA. Halloween is My costume Lion mask and cape sword a lot costum walk houses candy I eat Mask show was fun. My first American friend is Scott.

The End

FIGURE 5.3 *Yasuo's piece: "American School"*

expressing themselves through detailed illustrations. The artwork seemed to fill in the gaps in their writing. The covers were always admired by the other children.

Yasuo did not try to read his piece to the class nor did he come to the round table for a group conference. His desk was near the conference table and I noticed that he watched and listened to what occurred.

In November he wrote his first piece in English. It was called "American School" (Figure 5.3). It was about the things he did in "American school" and the friends he made. It also told about Halloween which he had not celebrated before. The cover was a picture of the school gym and the Halloween parade we had. The picture had many details. His friends and teachers were there in their Halloween costumes and he had written names next to each figure with an arrow pointing to the appropriate person.

Yasuo read the draft of this piece at a group conference, struggling over the pronunciation of some of the words. The children were very pleased and excited by his progress and they told him so. While he was willing to share his cover with the whole class, he was not ready to read his piece during a whole-class sharing session. However, once again the class responded with enthusiasm to his cover and he returned to his seat smiling and bowing. The support he and others received from their peers proved to be a powerful force in encouraging risk taking. My early modeling of the importance of positive response seemed to be the beginning. My continued reinforcement of this type of response and my own delight in the growth of my students encouraged the class to behave in a similar manner. We all seemed to be part of each other's progress.

Yasuo was as motivated to learn to read in English as he was to speak and write. At the beginning of the year he primarily read picture books from the library that had no or very few words. He showed them to me and tried to describe the story when I came to him for his daily conference. During October he selected books with more words and sat with his Japanese/English dictionary on his lap during reading workshop. He wanted desperately to be able to read and he read whatever and whenever he could. He often brought books to me when he was trying to figure out meaning. In November I asked him if he would like to write letters to me about the books he was reading. He knew the other children wrote in reading journals and of course he wanted to write, too. His first letter was about a Charlie Brown book about Thanksgiving. He wrote "I am a Charlie brown Good book Thanksgiving Snoopy and boy snoopy is good bog." I wrote back to him in script and then wondered if he could read script. At my reading conference with him the next day I asked him and he smiled. I showed him the correct form for writing a letter and how to underline the title of his book. His second letter, written the next day, included the title of the book.

> Dear Miss Five,
>
> I am *"IN A DARK DARK ROOM"* Ghost Many Ghost No fearful

I wrote back to him and asked if he liked stories about ghosts. Instead of writing to me, he had a brief conference with Takehiro and then he came up and said, "Yes, I like mysteries." The next letter written five days later (see Figure 5.4) showed more of an exchange between us. He asked me a question and he answered my questions. Reading had become a very important activity for him.

Tomoko seemed to have an easier time writing to me about the books she read than she had selecting topics for her writing pieces. In the fall she read contemporary fiction and seemed to relate the experiences of the characters to real life. She wrote about *Socks* (Cleary 1972):

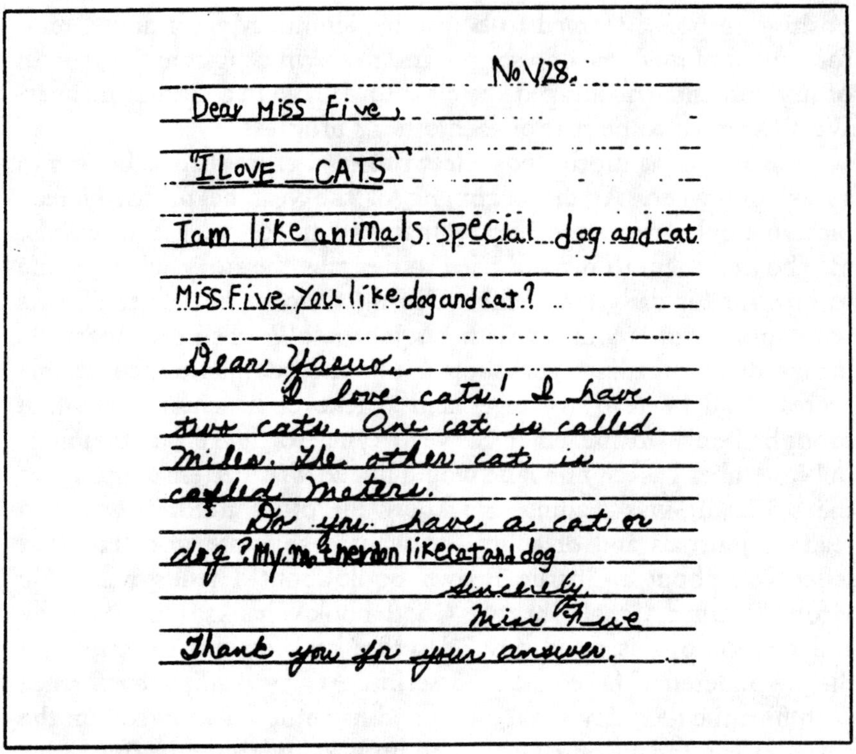

NoV28.

Dear MISS Five,

"I LovE CATS"

Iam like animals special dog and cat

MISS Five You like dog and cat?

Dear Yasuo,

I love cats! I have two cats. One cat is called Miles. The other cat is called Meters.

Do you have a cat or dog? My mother don like cat and dog

Sincerely,
Miss Five

Thank you for your answer.

FIGURE 5.4 *Correspondence with Yasuo*

> Dear Miss Five,
>
> The cat get jellous about something. I thought Socks act like a real kid who get jealous of his/her brother/sister.

When she finished *Superfudge* (Blume 1980) she wrote:

> Dear Miss Five,
>
> This was my favorite book. I like the way this author made it funny like Fudge copy the word Peter said. My sister act like that sometimes too.

Later on she began to express more of her feelings and I learned about her fears.

After I had finished reading *Bridge to Terabithia* (Paterson 1977) to the class, she wrote:

Dear Miss Five,

I liked this book because Jess's feeling changes and I can feel how Jess feel. I think this author is a good writter. I'd like to read another book of hers. I don't like the part when Leslie dies and they cremate her. when I think of the word cremate I get scared.

I do not want to be cremate if I dies.

Sincerely,
Tomoko

P.S. I like some one reading a book to me. thank you.

By November she had definite opinions about books. In response to *The Not-Just-Anybody Family* (Byars 1986), she wrote:

Dear Miss Five,

I thought Junior was silly because he wanted to fly and broke his both legs. I think this story was silly when Vern broke into jail. I wouldn't do that. Sometimes people brake out from jail but not brake in.

Tales of a Fourth Grade Nothing (Blume 1972) provoked the following:

Dear Miss Five,

I think Fudge was naughty and crazy. Nobody can swallow a turtle BUT he swallowed a turtle! I wonder how it tasted. May be it tasted like a dirty rock.

I was glad she was writing so much in her reading journal. She wrote two or three times a week and I always responded to her thoughts and feelings right away. The reading journal seemed to be the only place she could express herself easily during the first few months of fifth grade.

During writing workshop Tomoko remained at her seat for much of the time. She continued to have difficulty with selecting a topic. In October I began to encourage her to come to the conference table to listen to the ideas of others even though I suspected she was listening from her seat. Eventually she came. She would listen for awhile and then return to her desk and start to write. She experimented with different ideas and often wrote half a page. At times she returned to the conference table to read her beginning in a soft voice. The other children at the conference table were enthusiastic about her beginnings and asked questions to draw out more information. Despite the response she received, she found it difficult to put the ideas on paper.

At her November writing evaluation conference with me in preparation for her report card, she told me, "I have problems thinking of topics and writing." I wondered why. She seemed able to express herself in her reading journal. What was causing the problem in writing? I decided to wait, to give her time, time to confer with other kids, time to talk out her ideas.

I didn't have to wait as long as I expected.

After I had finished reading *Bridge to Terabithia* (Paterson 1977) to the class, Tomoko found a topic. She wanted to write about her dog, Momi, and how she had come home after school one day and found him dead. She told me that our discussions of *Bridge to Terabithia* and the death of one of the main characters made her think about her dog. The influence of books on her writing became apparent. She was so involved in *Bridge to Terabithia* that she had made a connection between the book and her own life and thoughts, one of many she would discover during the year. She wrote for the whole writing period stopping only to come up to me to ask me how to say something. She would try to describe something and say, "Isn't there a word for that?" or "I know what I want to say but I don't know how to do it." I tried to help her by having her explain to me what she wanted to describe, but she was often frustrated at her inability to express herself and would return to her desk.

During this time she began to come to the conference table more often and seemed to open up. She was more willing to discuss her ideas. Previously she had just read her piece without any additional comments. She realized the advantages of response when she began working on her lead for her story about Momi. She had started her piece with "I was scared of dogs until I had Momi." Children at the conference table asked who Momi was. Tomoko explained that Momi was her dog, her favorite dog, her only dog. Dianna suggested, "Why don't you put that in your lead?" Tomoko liked that idea and shyly accepted the suggestion.

Her second writing piece completed after a month of searching for topics flowed more easily for her:

My Dog Momi

Momi was my dog, my favorite dog, my first, my only dog. I loved him. I was scared of dogs until I had Momi.

Momi liked to splash water from the paddle. One day he was going to have a bath. He seemed to like baths because he could splash and he could break the bubbles from his body. He looked skinny when he was washed up with water. He rolled on the grass.

"It's time for dinner," my mother shouted. I poured him water and gave him food. He came running to me. I wanted to hug him but he was still wet so I patted him.

"Good night," I said to him.

There was no answer.

It was morning. I woke up at the usual time. I went downstairs. I petted Momi and gave him some dog food. I petted him again. I watched him eat as usual.

I looked at my watch. It was 8:30. I was thirty minutes late for school.

At 12 o'clock I went home. Our gardener was holding a box. I thought I saw Momi. My heart pumped quickly.

"I know it's not Momi, I saw him this morning!" I whispered to myself.

Our gardener showed me my dog. He was dead. Now he is not Momi because he is dead! I could only think of him alive. My tears were running down my cheek. I stayed with Momi a while. My gardener told me that he was bitten by two bull terriers.

I patted Momi. He lost his friendly tail. His neck was bitten too.

My family and I buried him. I couldn't think of anything else.

She read this piece in her very soft voice at a class sharing time to a smaller group of students which made it easier for her to share. The children told her the parts of her story that they especially liked. They were concerned about the death of the dog. It reminded some of the death of their own pets. The piece wrenched at my heart. I remembered the death of my own pets as a child and as an adult. And I could imagine her pain. I was also struck at the difference between her first piece in September and this second one in November. There was so much more of her in the piece about Momi, so much feeling. I wondered about the connection between her reading and her writing. In her reading she was able to identify the feelings of the characters and respond to those feelings. Did her response to her reading open up new topics for her personally? Books gave her access to her emotions and the emotions then seemed to evoke personal experiences that she was able to express in her writing.

In December Tomoko wrote "World of Windows" about a trip to New York City to look at the Christmas store windows. It was a very focused piece describing a set of windows that told a fantasy of a velvet rabbit, a boy, and a fairy. Her illustrated cover, in contrast to the previous ones, was filled with color and details. After describing the fantasy world of the windows she ended her piece by writing:

> "The fairy is going to make the rabbit real because he was real to the boy," I said.
>
> The last window was the prettiest window. Then I had to turn around. It was a whole other world. Cars were running and noisy and people were rushing. And that was the real world.

Again I began to wonder about this child. There seemed to be such depth in this quiet, sensitive girl. And it was emerging in her writing. I wondered why. I thought back to my studies of children with other kinds of problems. They had needed a supportive environment and time to develop at their own rate. Perhaps this type of environment and Tomoko's interest in reading allowed her to flourish, too.

Yasuo, as well, was flourishing within the classroom. He wanted to write about Christmas, too. This time he wanted to write it correctly so he asked Scott, his first and best American friend, for help. After conferring with Scott he showed his piece to me to make sure the sentences were right and was very proud when I said yes. I asked him if he would like to share this piece with the class. He looked at his friends Takehiro and Scott who nodded their heads in encouragement, but then he decided that he would not read it. Apparently he did not feel comfortable yet.

He was at this time very much a part of the class when he was there. He was included in social studies simulations, news teams, and science groups. All his classmates helped him and were delighted with his successes. Soon his news team was helping him report on a news article which was the first time he actually spoke at length about anything in front of the whole class.

At recess, at lunch time, and in gym he discovered the game of kick ball and the pleasure of "hitting two home runs." His fourth writing piece was about kick ball. For the first time he wrote a draft and read it at the conference table wriggling with delight at the comments he received. I helped him proofread it and then, another first, he copied it in script in pen. Up until this time, his drafts, written in pencil, had become his finished pieces. Once again he would not share the story with the whole class but was happy when I hung it on the bulletin board in the hall where he could show it to his friends in other classes. The class and I continued to marvel at his positive, sunny disposition.

This same period of time was not a happy one for Tomoko. It was the beginning of months that left her upset and socially isolated.

In the winter Tomoko's three friends from fourth grade decided that they no longer wanted her as a friend. They would not play with her at recess and would not sit with her at lunch. They wanted me to move her desk away from theirs. Tomoko did not know how to handle this situation. At first she tagged along after them despite their harsh words. She followed them everywhere. Words were exchanged and Tomoko often ended up sobbing in the girls' room. She would remain there for fifteen to twenty minutes. When I went to get her, she would not come out until she was ready. Even though I tried to mediate, the three friends would not accept her. Tomoko then began to write nasty notes to these girls and leave them in their desks. She began to provoke other incidents that eventually caused her more tears. I tried to show her how her behavior might be causing some of the pain she was experiencing. It proved to be a difficult task because both Tomoko and the girls had a different version of each incident. I also tried to encourage Tomoko to form other friendships but the girls in the class were already "grouped" as friends and were not willing to accept her.

Tomoko walked alone on the playground at recess or she stayed in the classroom with me.

It was at this time that my principal asked me if I would like the help of my favorite aide. Pam and I had worked together for many years. I was entitled to aide time if I had a child in my room who had been declared learning disabled by the Committee on Special Education. I usually hoped for Pam because we had similar philosophies and therefore could work well together. This particular year I had no CSE (Committee on Special Education) children so I had no aide. It happened that Pam had a few extra hours and my principal gave them to me. I thought perhaps Pam might work with Tomoko on vocabulary development and grammar. I remembered the times that Tomoko struggled for the right words and how to use them. Pam and I decided that she would read and discuss with Tomoko the books that she was reading to make sure that she knew and could use the new words she discovered in her reading.

I had noticed that Tomoko was having some problems in her vocabulary journal. She was selecting words from her books and writing the definitions. Her difficulty was in using the words correctly in sentences. She was often confused by the definition and the usage of the word. I had tried to work with her when I had a few minutes but I could not get to her each time she needed help. Pam began to work with her twice a week.

Pam and I became her friends during this time as well as her teachers. She stayed in at recess to be with us because at times it was better than being rejected by the girls. She told us about her life in Japan and in Europe and how she had to move so often. She mentioned that she had some friends before, that she even had a friend in another school in town. She talked about the difficulties of friendships. Even though she had us for company, of course it was not the same and she was very unhappy. She often cried in gym when she felt left out of a game or she walked out of other special classes to cry in the girls' room. Many times she went home in tears. And I went home distressed. How could I make the conditions better for her?

My talks with the other girls worked for short periods of time. I explained my philosophy of a community of learners which they had heard since the first day of school. I told them how I wanted everyone to feel comfortable in the classroom. I related my concern over Tomoko's unhappiness, how I thought and worried about the situation after school and in the evening. The girls felt uncomfortable when Tomoko tagged after them and wouldn't leave them alone. She begged and almost demanded to be included, often provoking arguments. However, they agreed to try to include her for my sake. And a few weeks would go by and Tomoko seemed relatively content. Then there would be some kind of misunderstanding and Tomoko was once again rejected. This on-again off-again pattern continued throughout the winter and spring.

Fortunately the strain of these personal relationships never carried over into the writing or reading workshops. The three girls were helpful and responsive whenever Tomoko shared her ideas and stories and she, in turn, responded well to them. I was amazed they could work so well together and that the problems with their friendships never got in the way of their writing and reading. I think that the special environment created by a community of readers and writers made it difficult for all four girls to react and respond on a very personal level. They responded to each other as writers to writers. I believe all the children were aware of the vulnerability that accompanies sharing writing and they had learned that only positive, constructive comments would be accepted. Those procedures, established early in the year, made it easier for all my students to reveal themselves on paper.

In January during a writing workshop Tomoko came to me to tell me that she had so much in her head that she wanted to say. I listened as she explained that there was "a lot in my head that can't come out." I had been reading poetry to the class in order to encourage the writing of poetry so I was not surprised when she said, "Maybe I'll write a poem." I realized again that she was influenced by her reading and the literature I read to the class.

I was surprised when she came back at the end of the period to read her poem at the conference table. She was pleased with the response and went back to her seat to decide how she wanted to arrange the words. Her final copy captured her own feelings:

Maybe It Will Explode

Your mind is a big, big
cupboard
filled with lots of things
words
numbers
time
pictures
places and
people.
If you fill your mind
with too many things
maybe
it
will
explode.

Her cover showed the inside of her mind (Figure 5.5).

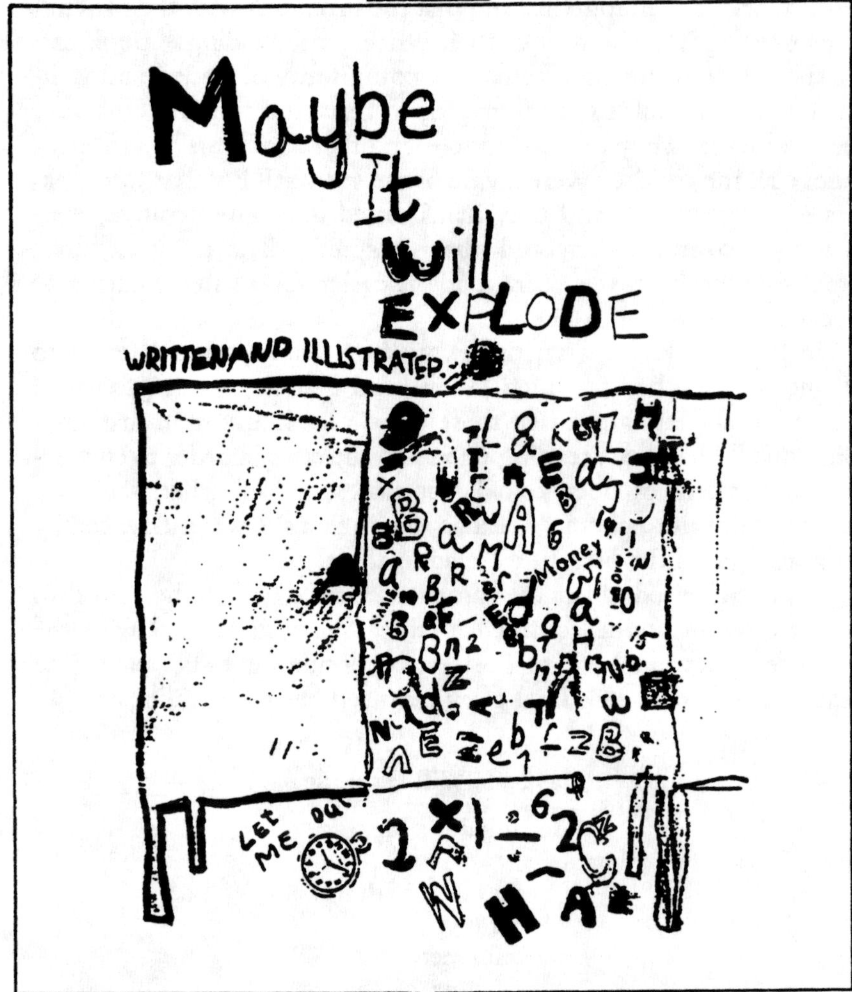

FIGURE 5.5 *Cover of Tomoko's poem "Maybe It Will Explode"*

The class liked her poem when she shared it and she was pleased with their comments. Her three desired friends were very complimentary. I marvelled not only at her poem but at the cover and the three words in the lower left corner, "Let Me Out." Were the poem and this message an expression of her former and perhaps present frustrations in writing? Did they refer to her social situation? Did she feel her ideas were still trapped in some way inside her head?

From January to March the class was involved in two important writing experiences. The first one was content writing about colonial times. After a period of reading historical fiction and nonfiction books, the students selected topics that interested them and wrote about them in a variety of ways (for an account of this experience see Five and Rosen 1985). Both Yasuo and Tomoko chose to write about the colonial farm. Yasuo's report was one and a half pages and described how the farmer made his house, what he planted, and what he ate. He explained the jobs of the blacksmith and the cooper.

Tomoko chose to write her report from the point of view of a nine-year-old colonial girl living in Pennsylvania. In three chapters she explained the work that women and girls did, the importance of animals, and the planting of crops. The report included many details and was beautifully illustrated. I noted that she seemed to have no difficulty in writing it. She had read six books on the topic. I was beginning to notice, too, that the more comfortable she felt with her writing, the more details she included in the piece and in the illustrations. The two seemed linked together.

The second writing experience that was taking place was the usual series of practice writing tests in preparation for the state writing test. Both Yasuo and Tomoko took these practice tests. I was not as concerned with Yasuo's performance because he would not have to take the real test. ESL students who have been in school in my state for less than eighteen months are excused from the test. However, Tomoko was required to take it and I worried about her ability to deal with the topics and the mechanical errors she was bound to make.

Yasuo approached the practice tests in his usual positive manner. He wrote as much as he could and didn't seem to be concerned about correct usage. He did the best he could. Tomoko, too, did her best and surprised me by focusing on each topic she was given. She did not sit thinking but started writing as soon as she understood the topic. Her first test was short and to the point. As she took more tests they were better organized and included imaginative details. She continued to have problems with verb tenses and the use of articles. Pam and I worked with her individually on these errors in addition to the special help with vocabulary.

By the March writing evaluation conference, I felt that Tomoko did not have the same problems in finding a topic. However, she told me that thinking of a subject and writing the first paragraph were still hard for her. She felt her problems in writing were "describing what people are saying and describing what it was like." She was also suddenly concerned about correct punctuation, perhaps as a result of the practice tests. I wondered whether I, under the pressure of testing, was placing too much importance on mechanics in preparing my students for the test. Tomoko told me that she thought her best piece was her poem "Maybe It Will Explode" because "I wrote what I wanted to write." Perhaps she meant she was finally able to "express" what she wanted to write in her own way.

Yasuo's conference was shorter than Tomoko's. He told me that he wanted to get better at writing. He smiled and wriggled like a puppy. He told me that he liked writing and wanted to write more stories.

In March as a result of minilessons on similes and metaphors, the class experimented with writing their own. Yasuo could not write any but I noticed Tomoko was very busy writing. She suggested "snow is a never ending carpet" and "the wind is a dancing ghost." She began to play around with what she called the beginnings of poems. She wrote lines on the inside of her writing folder.

> Wild horses running where their feelings goes
> racing with the wind in the great plains

In March the class reacted to the Alaskan oil spill. They had been concerned about the environment through our studies in science and our discussions of current events but the oil spill really got to them. They wrote about it during writing workshop in poetry and prose. It affected Tomoko in a number of ways. She responded to *Sarah, Plain and Tall* (MacLachlan 1985) in her reading journal in the following letter:

> I like the sea like Sarah but now the sea is poluted so I think the color is black and dark green. If Sarah hear this I think she would be upset.
>
> I wish the color of the sea will be blue and green. (Back to normal!)

She also began to worry about the world. She told me one day, "I think about when you are sleeping, can I wake up tomorrow? Like the oil spill, it's scary." Another time she said, "I worry when I throw plastic in my garbage because maybe I'm destroying the world."

Perhaps it was her concern for the world that inspired her to write her next piece. She came up to me and said, "I have this idea about time and how it is different in different places. You know when it's morning here it's night some place else." I told her I thought that was an interesting idea and asked how she was going to write about it. She smiled and said, "I'm going to write a poem." She went to her desk and I saw her writing quickly. She never lifted her head. She came to the conference table when she was finished and read her poem:

Night Passing

Morning in America
Pass the night to Asian children
When Asian children wake up
Pass the night to European children
When European children wake up
Pass the night to African children.

Children pass the night
because they have
dreams of the future.
They can change the world.
The night passing
is like a race
that never stops
till the end of time.

There was no need to revise it. Her thoughts had poured out of her and she was very happy. Her cover (see Figure 5.6) was a track with the numbers of a clock on the track in the appropriate places. She had drawn a child starting at 12:00 holding the night. Another child seemed to be running with it at 3:00, another at 6:00, at 9:00, and the last child was stopped just before she got to the 12. In the bottom left-hand corner she had written "relay race." The circle of the track reminded me of Babbitt's wheel analogy in *Tuck Everlasting* (Babbitt 1975), which I had just finished reading to the class. Once again Tomoko was influenced by the books I read aloud. The importance of reading became dramatic.

The class responded positively to her poem. The children were intrigued with the idea of passing the night around the world. I wondered at the ease with which she wrote poetry compared to prose. Perhaps she did not feel trapped by the conventions of grammar and usage. With poetry she was able to let her thoughts flow

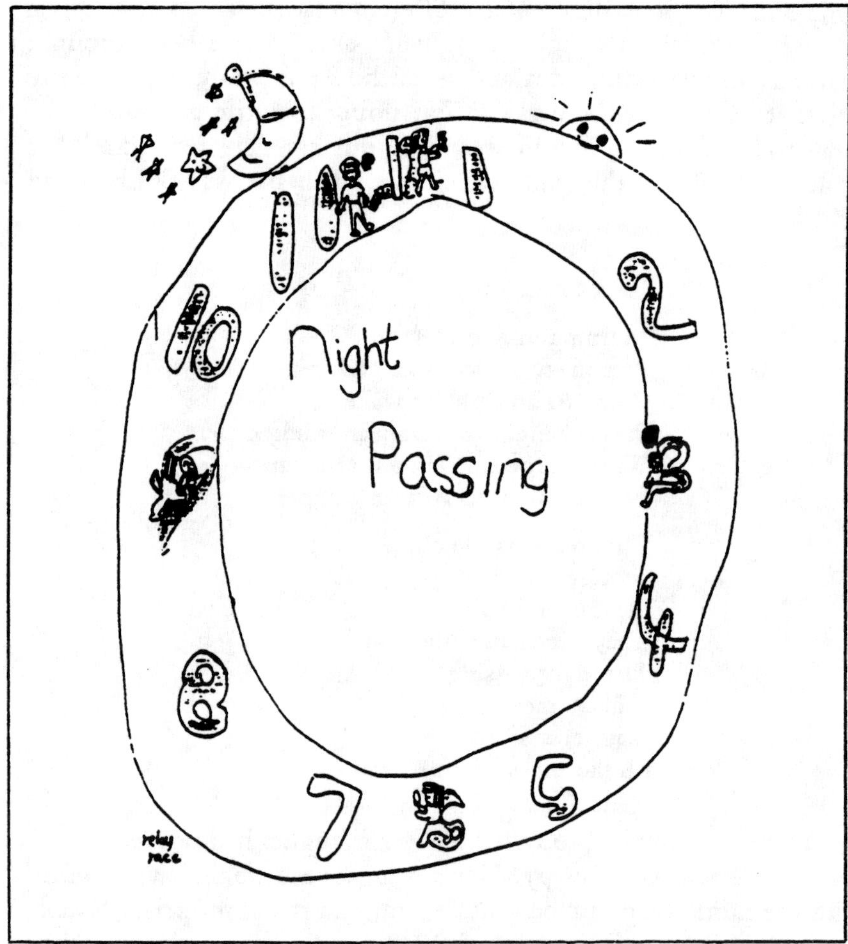

FIGURE 5.6 *Cover of Tomoko's poem "Night Passing"*

using the vocabulary she knew to express deep thoughts. Suddenly I realized that Takehiro, who also had trouble with writing because of his difficulty with vocabulary and usage, was better able to express his ideas in poetry, too. It seemed to allow him greater freedom with his thoughts and yet was more manageable because he could use fewer words. He also used poetry to express his thoughts on the environment:

An Avalanche

An avalanche is a monster of the mountain
kicking snow because we build resorts on them.

An avalanche is a giant venomous snake
trying to bite us and make us suffer.

An avalanche is a god of the wind
blowing rocks and snow, angry at us.

It is a very big wave of snow
trying to trap us for polluting the world.

An avalanche is a mad murderer
killing millions of trees, animals and humans.

What was there about poetry that freed these students to write? I wondered if poetry was part of their background in Japan but none of my students could remember. Takehiro offered his own explanation; "I think caring and writing about the world might change the world. It's easier in poetry."

I waited for Yasuo to turn to poetry, too. However, he did not. Perhaps he had not done enough reading, perhaps he did not understand all the literature I read to the class, perhaps he was not ready to take the risk. In any event, he was growing and improving in his own way. His responses to books had become longer. He was writing in complete sentences and answering my questions in sentences instead of one-word answers (see Figure 5.7).

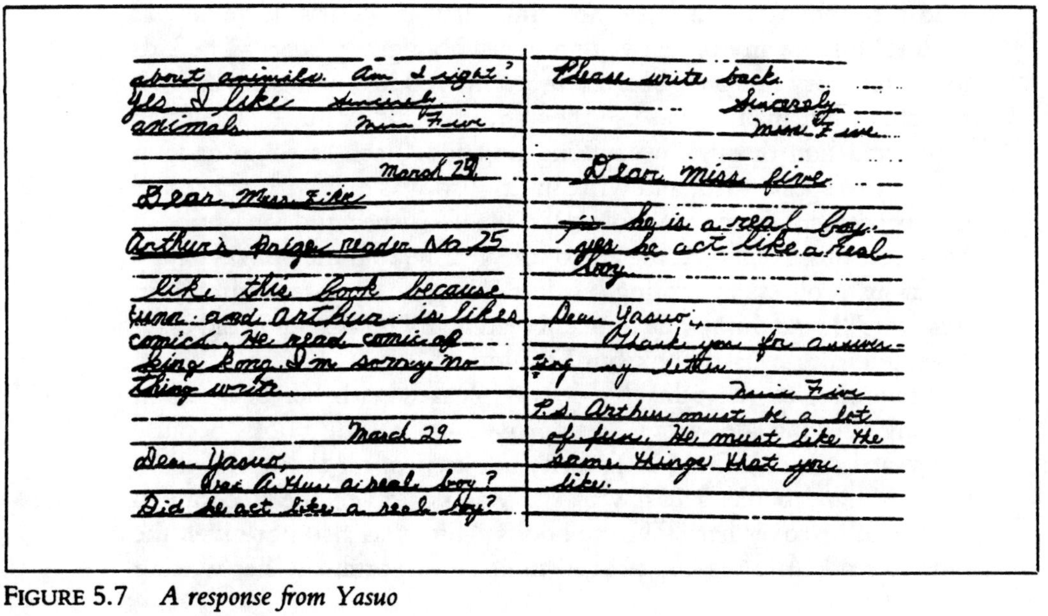

about animils. Am I right?
Yes I like
animals
Sincerely
Miss Five

March 29
Dear Miss Five
Arthur's Prize reader No. 25
like this book because
Luna and Arthur is likes
comics. He read comic of
King Kong. I'm sorry no
thing write.

March 29
Dear Yasuo,
Was Arthur a real boy?
Did he act like a real boy?
Please write back.
Sincerely
Miss Five

Dear miss five
~~yes~~ he is a real boy.
yes he act like a real
boy.

Dear Yasuo,
Thank you for answering my letter.
Miss Five
P.S. Arthur must be a lot of fun. He must like the same things that you like.

FIGURE 5.7 *A response from Yasuo*

In May he wrote a piece on dinosaurs because he had visited a dinosaur museum. Drawing on personal experience enabled him to write a longer piece. The influence of his peers was apparent when he wrote "a dinosaur is very cool." "Cool" became his favorite word for the next month. At the end of May he included it in the title to his favorite piece—"My Cool Shoes"—which celebrated his acceptance by his classmates, both American and Japanese. He felt very much a part of the classroom community. The influence of American culture was evident in his topic choice and the expressions he used.

My Cool Shoes

My shoes are Reebok. They are the best. I like Reebok shoes because of the white color and good picture on the front.

I went to a shoe store. I looked at many shoes, Nike, Adidas, Puma, and Reebok. I thought Reeboks are the best so I bought Reebok.

The first time I didn't want to take my shoes to the school but I took my Reeboks. I played kickball so my Reeboks were dirty. "Oh my gosh," I said. I thought that's o.k. I didn't care.

Now my shoes are so dirty but I think it's cool. Next time I want to buy my best shoes Reebok again.

Yasuo was so delighted with this story that he couldn't wait to read it to the class during sharing time. It was the first time he was willing to share any of his writing in a whole group share. The kids loved his story not only because they enjoyed his interest in American shoes but mainly because they admired his attitude. They had supported him through everything he tried. Each step he made in learning to speak, read, and write in English was met with praise and encouragement from the whole class. He flourished and took pride in his accomplishments. At the end of the year he told me he was happy about his progress in writing but in reading he evaluated himself in this way: "I read thirty-one books, I read many books but I read easy. I wanted to read hard book but I couldn't."

Tomoko, on the other hand, was pleased with her progress in reading. In June she wrote, "I improved on finding books because last year I couldn't find my favorite books. I never thought I could read so many books." Last year she was not given the freedom to choose or discover her "favorite books." She was also not given the time to read. And reading proved to be so important to her writing and ability to express herself. It was through her reading that she learned about writing, about the importance of expressing feelings, about the use of new vocabulary. Reading gave her opportunities to think and writing let those ideas flow. And with Pam's and my help she was able to experiment and use new words in her own writing and speaking. Perhaps this helped free her so that she could write. She was no longer trapped.

If the state writing test score is any indication of writing ability, then Tomoko had blossomed into a fine writer. Out of a possible 16, she scored 15—a very high score despite some mistakes such as "When I finished eating I hanged from the branches" and "The bird flapped the wings." She did, however, try to express her thoughts: "I thought when I come to this wood your mind cleared up like some sunshine breaking away from the clouds . . . "

In her last writing evaluation conference in June she told me that her best piece of writing was "Night Passing" because "I putted a lot of feeling." She also described her writing: "The hardest part of writing is letting my feelings free to make a story. When you let your feelings free you can write poetry, but when you tighten up, you can't." Was she telling me that poetry allowed her to "let her feelings free"?

The last day of school is always very sad for me. I hate to send my fifth graders on to the junior high. They seem so young and vulnerable. This year was no different. Before they left I asked them to write a letter to next year's fifth graders welcoming them to the room and telling them something about fifth grade. Tomoko started her letter with "Hi! You are in fifth grade! You are going to have a lot of fun in fifth grade." Perhaps she had forgotten her painful months of rejection. I hoped so. She ended the letter with "Most exciting part of fifth grade is writing because you can have conference and be free to write anything!"

This was the child who would not come for conferences, whose ideas were trapped in her head—by mechanics? by vocabulary? by her own inhibitions and lack of confidence? Did the environment of writers' workshop—the ownership of ideas, the time to develop at a student's own rate, the response at group and student/teacher conferences—allow her to take risks and give her the freedom she needed to write? I think it did.

They left one by one, saying good-bye, hugging me, promising to come back for a visit. Yasuo shook my hand, smiled, and thanked me for all he had learned. Tomoko, who had been placed in the same junior high section as two of her three "friends," hugged me and told me she would always love writing. I was grateful that despite her unhappiness socially she was still able to succeed academically and take pride in her work.

She wrote to me during the summer to share some of her writing and tell me about the books she was reading. One day I got a letter that told me she was going to Japanese school in September instead of the junior high. She said she felt good about that because she thought she would make more friends. I spoke to her two or three times the following fall. She was doing well in Japanese school. She had made friends but she was sad because she had no writing in school. She had many poems she wanted to write but she had too much homework to write on her own.

In March of that year, her sixth-grade year, she came to visit me after school to tell me she was moving back to Japan the next day. And before I knew it she was gone, this beautiful sensitive child who still seemed to have so much to express. I hoped desperately that she would find the environment that would enable her to let her feelings free so that she could and would continue to write poetry.

6

Greg

A highly creative child

ONE SEPTEMBER I returned to school after Labor Day and looked down the column of names on my class list only to discover that I did not know or recognize any of them. I hadn't even heard the names mentioned by other teachers in the teachers' room. There were no children who had been designated CSE and there were no well-known behavior problems. I was frankly disappointed. Whom would I study? This class seemed to have no special children.

The day before school started I was arranging my room and putting away supplies when I first heard about Greg. A former teacher came in and said, "Oh, you have Greg this year. He's a capable boy, very bright, but he doesn't do much work. He likes to talk to his friends and avoids doing what he doesn't like to do." Later an aide who had worked in his classroom in an earlier grade gave me a warning, one I had heard all too often in my teaching career. She told me to keep an eye on him: "He'll pretend he finished his work and say he lost it. It's usually half-finished in his desk somewhere. At times he doesn't even do it. Sometimes he looks in other kids' desks and they think he takes things. He has trouble getting along with the other kids. Just watch him."

And I decided that was exactly what I would do. I would observe and listen to him as I planned to observe and listen to the other twenty-two children in my class.

The first day of school was very quiet. The children were well behaved. We discussed the meaning of the word *philosophy*. And then I explained my philosophy of teaching to them as I do every year with each new class, emphasizing that we would be a community of learners who would learn with and from each other and that I included myself in this group. I told them that I hoped that they would learn a lot from me because I knew that I could learn from them. I also told them something that I learned from Mary Ellen Giacobbe (1985): I believed that the work they did in my room was the best they could do. They sat quietly and listened. There were few questions and responses.

The first few days of school followed that same calm pattern. I explained the program in fifth grade and spent much time describing how reading and writing workshops would operate. We began reading and writing the second week of school. The children followed my directions and listened with interest to the minilessons I presented at the beginning of each workshop. It was a good, quiet, obedient class. And I forgot everything I'd heard about Greg.

By the end of the second week, some children began to write letters to me in their reading journals about books they had completed. Usually most of the letters at the beginning of the year resemble book reports students have written in previous years. They summarize the book and make recommendations. I know it takes time for their letters to express their thoughts and interpretations; this ability develops slowly as a result of minilessons and discussions about the books I read aloud. I was, therefore, understandably jolted when I received the following letter from Greg on September 14:

> Dear Miss Five I just finished readin a book by Jhony Bellairs called The Curse of the Blue Figurine in this book Jhon Bellairs describes scary in such a way it's amazing. During some parts I was sweating heavily. he also describes how Jhony Dixon (the main character) feels after loosing his mother and father, living whith his grand parents having NO friends his age and only 1 freind that was about 40 something. This is a book that is focused on fear of lonelyness because Jhony has secrets that if his secret was told he would get into trouble but he had the WANT to tell someone but he couldn't. It was like he was liveing in a glass ball. Also this is a book where a kid would see a ghost Adults would not beleive him but then they would see a ghost.
>
> Greg

This was certainly an unusual letter for the beginning of fifth grade and I was intrigued with Greg's ideas. I wrote back and told him how much I enjoyed reading his letter because it expressed his ideas about the book. I also told him that I was curious about his sentence that described the boy as "living in a glass ball" and wondered if he could explain it. The following day he wrote back to me:

> Dear Miss Five,
>
> What I meant by "living in a glass ball" was the world was around him but yet he was cut off. he could not tell them his secrets for a few reasons. Death in one case and punishment from his grandma in another. and in my last comment the answer to your question "are the ghosts real?" well the answer is yes. and in the end—well you'll have to find out (if you read the book)

I told him how impressed I was with his letter and his thinking. He smiled and thanked me for the compliment. A few weeks later his mother stopped by to tell me how much my letter and comments had meant to Greg. She mentioned he had some problems in school in previous years but that he seemed to feel very optimistic about fifth grade.

I decided to read his earlier report cards—something I never do—to learn more about him. All reports through fourth grade indicated that he was a very bright, capable boy who did not work up to his potential. It appeared that since first grade Greg was unable to finish his work, was easily distracted, and found it difficult to concentrate. His behavior appeared to be a problem, too. His social relationships with the other children were not good because of his strong opinions and reluctance to listen to anyone else. By third grade he had become somewhat belligerent and was involved in fights. He was difficult to motivate and continued to avoid assignments that required paperwork. He fell behind in his work and again had problems with behavior. Self-control and work habits continued to be a problem in fourth grade. When I spoke with some of his former teachers they added that they thought he was a very sensitive child who did not accept constructive criticism well, often crying in response.

For the first few weeks of fifth grade I did not observe much of the negative behavior noted in the reports. Greg appeared to be a quiet boy who had a tendency to be obstinate at times. He did the assignments in which he had an interest and often had to stay in at recess to make up other work. At times his work was done carelessly and he resented making corrections. He seemed to be generally interested in class activities. I provided as much time as possible for discussions of current events, books, social studies, and science and math concepts. Greg enjoyed these discussions. He shared his ideas but often disagreed with me and other children. I had to be careful that his remarks did not hurt or inhibit others, and at the same time I worried about his own sensitivity. When I did have to explain to him that his comments might make another child feel his or her ideas were not valued, he would sit quietly at his desk, his head down, eyes tearing, and often refused to participate for the rest of the afternoon. I also noticed at this time that he was not included immediately when the children worked in groups.

Greg had not been involved in group writing conferences in third or fourth grade. He may have had conferences with another child and did share some of his written work. I am not sure whether time had been provided for response. My method of writing workshop was new to him. At first he had his own ideas about how he wanted to write and did not see the benefits of response. He wrote on his own and did not talk about his topics to the children seated near him as many of the other children did. During September and the beginning of October Greg seemed very much of a loner.

His first writing piece was about the time he caught a flounder. He started his draft by describing the family's drive down the beach in their jeep to a spot where jeeps and other vehicles could be parked. Then he told about his fishing episode. When he came for a conference and read his piece, I had already done a few minilessons on focusing on a specific topic. Still, I do not think he was prepared for the response he received at the conference table. The other children asked him questions that required more information. Greg answered their questions but when I asked him if he thought the information should be included in his draft, he said, "No!"

We had also been discussing the importance of a good lead. His lead was as follows:

> We were driving down the beach in our new used cherokee jeep. We were going out to the point. You see in Orleans (a place in Cape Cod) there is a beacon for jeeps off the road.

Children at the conference asked him if he needed the part about the jeep. I asked if there was a way he could get right to the fishing part in his lead without going through parking the jeep. He told me he liked his story the way it was. I said, "You might experiment with three or four other ways to begin your story." His eyes began to tear and he told me again that he liked it the way it was. I said, "That's fine. It is up to you. You're the writer." I then went on to other children who were at the table and wanted to share and revise leads. Greg sat and listened.

The next day we were again experimenting with leads and although he wasn't at the conference table, he seemed to be listening from his seat. The following day he came for a conference to read a new lead for his piece:

> I had always wanted to be a fisherman, a real angler. I begged my dad for a pole and he had finally bought me one.

The other children liked his new lead much better than the original. He smiled with pleasure. However, he was not interested in revising any other parts of his story. I didn't push him. He sat at his seat writing but I again suspected he was listening to the conversation at the conference table. Children were discussing how they were making their pieces clearer by adding more information or deleting certain parts. A few days later I saw him cutting parts of his draft and taping pieces together. When I wandered over to take a look I saw that he had crossed out parts and had taped on new paragraphs in various places. He had also added two thin flaps that answered questions two children had asked him when he first read his draft. I asked him if he would like to share his revised piece. "I will as soon as I finish," he told me.

"The Fabulous Flounder I Caught" was a five-page story that was revised based on the response he received specifically at the conference table and, I think, the response he heard to other students' pieces as he listened from his seat. It was focused and included humor, interesting description, good vocabulary, and sentence variety—qualities that I rarely see in a first writing piece in fifth grade. The following excerpt is taken from the beginning of his piece:

> Time dragged on. And then suddenly there I was standing knee-high in cold crisp ocean water reeling in my new "kastman"

> lure. This lure imitates spearing a type of baitfish. Spearing attracts bass, stripers, snapers, and flukes. Unfortunately that's not all it attracts.

He described the number of times he caught seaweed instead of a fish. The piece ended with Greg finally catching his fish:

> My mom gasped, "Wonderful!"
> "Let's cook him for dinner," I told my mom.
> She didn't know how but it was a first time for everybody.
> I was a fisherman but not an angler, well, not yet anyway!

Greg shared his finished piece with the whole group at the end of a writing period. He was proud of it and enjoyed the comments he received. As a result of this positive experience he began to participate in more group conferences. During September and the beginning of October he made some comments to other children about their pieces that were critical rather than constructive. I think he was aware of his own ability in writing and expected others to be able to use a variety of good words. He became impatient at their repeated use of words like "then" to begin sentences and paragraphs. I wanted him to be part of my writing community, to be accepted by the other children and included in their discussions. But I also wanted him to accept their ideas and respect them. I knew he would benefit from conferences with other children and me. I tried to show him how he could rephrase his comments so the writer would benefit from his response instead of feeling offended. Often his eyes would get teary and I realized that I had to walk a fine line between his strong opinions which could hurt others' feelings and his own sensitivity to criticism. Unfortunately at that time he could not see the connection between the two.

In October one of the girls in the class, Andrea, wrote a poem about people, their pretenses, and the way they treat each other. The class and I were very impressed with the depth of her ideas and we wondered where and how she came to them. Greg was intrigued by this poem. He told Andrea what he liked about it and I think he realized, too, that here was another good writer. The fact that Andrea wrote a poem had an impact on him. Perhaps it gave him another form of expression because the next writing piece he did was a poem about Halloween (Figure 6.1). I wondered again about poetry. Here was another child who had turned to poetry and it seemed to pour

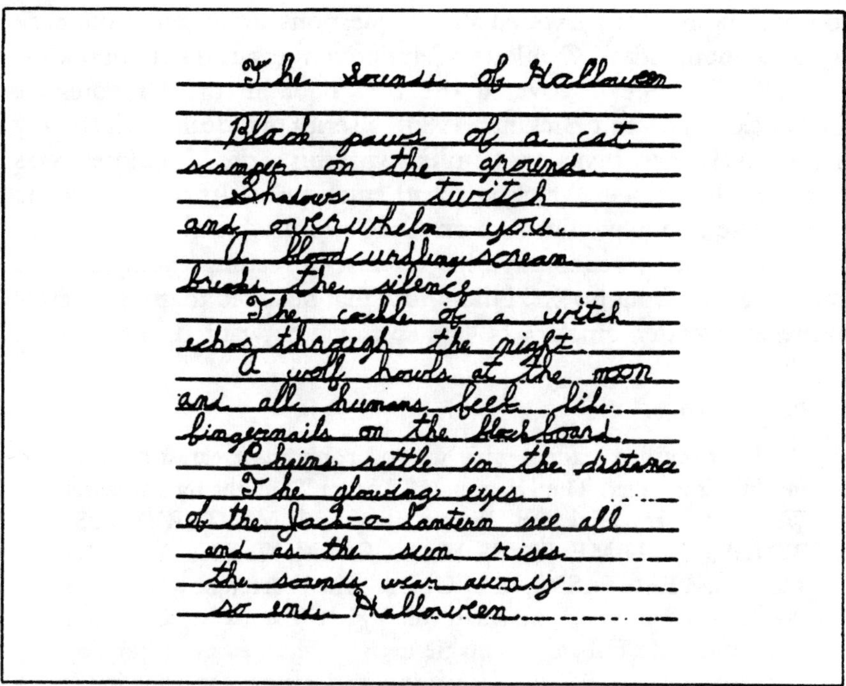

The sounds of Halloween
Black paws of a cat
scamper on the ground.
Shadows twitch
and overwhelm you.
A bloodcurdling scream
breaks the silence.
The cackle of a witch
echos through the night.
A wolf howls at the moon
and all humans feel like
fingernails on the blackboard.
Chains rattle in the distance
The glowing eyes
of the Jack-o-lanterns see all
and as the sun rises
the sounds wear away
so ends Halloween

FIGURE 6.1 *Greg's poem about Halloween*

out of him. Perhaps poetry allowed more free thought. He did very little revising. The responders to his first draft had few questions. Poetry seemed to be accepted as it flowed out of my students. Greg loved the vocabulary and the class and I loved the images.

He was very happy about this poem and even asked to read it again during sharing time during the next few weeks. I was amazed at his writing. His first story and his poem were examples of what I might see from some students in the spring or at the end of the school year. Here was a child who clearly had exceptional ability in writing. How would I deal with the challenges the gifted child presented? Like the CSE and ESL students, the needs of the talented child were often overlooked in the classroom. It was October. I wondered how his writing would grow and develop throughout the rest of the year. I hoped that time and the freedom to choose his own form of expression within a supportive environment would allow Greg to flourish as a writer. The prospects were exciting to consider.

Greg was also enjoying reading. His letters to me about the books he read continued to show depth. He wrote often and looked forward to my response. He answered all my questions and often wrote back to me about my ideas. Our letters felt like conversations about books.

In October he discovered the first book in the Dragonlance Chronicles (Weis and Hickman 1985), a series that dealt with fantasy in medieval times. I was not familiar with this series. All I knew was that these books were thick and had small print. I had no idea the effect these books would have on Greg's future writing, but fortunately I decided to encourage his interest in reading them through journal letters about books. I did know that he loved them. His letter to me was written quickly, he had so much he wanted to say:

> Dear Miss Five,
>
> I just finished reading what was probably the greatest book of my life. It is called The Dragons of Autum Twilight by Margaret Weis and Tracy Hickman. It was filled with MYSTERY, SUSPENCE, EXITEMENT, ROMANCE, EMOTION, ADVENTURE and FANTASY. All in ONE!!! The characters were Tanis (the leader) Tasselhof (the small thief) Flint (the dwarf) Goldmon (the dealer) and Fisban (the magic user or what seems to be) The first time you meet Fisban he is getting mad at a tree for being in his way. Fisban is halairious. I realy thought I was in the story. I could picture each part in my mind—two red dragons fighting, a town burning, a buetiful castle of gold, a slave caravan, and last but not least an ancient city with secret pasages all over the place. There were many more but I dare not try to mention them all for fear I might use this whole book up.
>
> Greg

Such expressions as "dare not" and "for fear" show the influence this book had on his writing.

He talked about this book for days, to me and to Alex who became interested in reading it. He told me he was sure I would like it. I told him I'd put it on my list of books to read and he seemed satisfied. He went on to read the next book in the series which he found somewhat confusing and sad. One of the main characters, he wrote, "turned evil and since she was evil she killed her own brother. VERY WIERD."

For the next few weeks he read books by Bloom, Cleary, Byars, and other authors who are popular with fifth graders. His letters, now written in cursive instead of the print that he used for the first few weeks, showed his connections to the characters in the book and often commented on an author's craft and choice of title.

During this time I had finished reading *Bridge to Terabithia* (Paterson 1977) and we had talked about the possible meanings of the word "bridge" as it related to the story. We had also discussed character development. Then I had read *Babe, the Gallant Pig* (King-Smith 1987) to the class and we had many more discussions about whether the author had a message beyond the story line. Greg was always very involved in these discussions and seemed intrigued by the idea that there might be something more to a book than just the story. He began to look for ways to interpret the books he was reading. By November he had found the third book in the Dragonlance Chronicles (Weis and Hickman 1985) and he began to wonder about its meaning:

> Dear Miss Five,
>
> I finished Dragons of Spring Dawning it was SUPER. I loved it so much!!!!!!!!!!!!!!!!!!! it has alot of meaning about feelings, about changes of people and change of the world itself and how to accept it. its about trouble and romance and traps and good and evil and darkness and hope. As fisbon once said "Good? triumph?" "NO Half Elven, the balance is restored. The evil dragons will not be banished. They remain here as do the good dragons." This story was about a war where the bad dragons ruled but then the good dragons helped the queen of darkness so that's why Tanus, Half-Elven thought good had triumphed.

In response to my letter in which I told him I was glad that goodness had triumphed over evil, he wrote:

> NO!!! good did NOT triumph over evil. They just banished the queen of Darkness. But Evil still remains.

He told me more about the book in a conference we had and sighed in exasperation at my ignorance. "Did you read the first book yet?" he asked. It was November and I had not. He asked that same question over and over again until I ran out of excuses. I usually try to read the books my students are really excited about. I read them during reading workshop and try to finish them at home. I had taken the first book home in October when Greg had given it to me, but the 451 pages and synopsis on the back cover had made me reluctant to read it. After about 50 pages I knew it was not a book I wanted to finish. But I faced a real dilemma. Should I read it anyway, violating the "don't read a book unless you love it" code I learned from Giacobbe (1985) and told my class all the time? Should I pretend I read it? Or should I just tell him honestly that I read 50 pages and found that it was not my kind of book? Would he be upset?

In the end, after much deliberation, I told him the truth, that I had started it and didn't like it. I added that I would try it again during the summer. He was disappointed that I didn't like the one book that he thought was so wonderful. In fact he looked at me in disbelief. Fortunately Alex, who sat next to Greg and had heard Greg's conferences with me, had read and finished the book, was hooked, and was then reading the second book in the series. The two boys were able to puzzle together over why I didn't like their favorite. Perhaps that incident brought them closer together. They began animated discussions about the books in the series, but their talk eventually included all the other books they read, new vocabulary words they discovered, and their writing pieces. This seemed to be Greg's first strong link to another child whose ideas he appreciated.

During November and December, Greg wrote personal narratives, about a trip to his father's office in the city and about a ride on Thunder Mountain at Disney World. These were long pieces filled with wonderful description and conversation. He read parts of his drafts to Alex and then listened to Alex's ideas. At this same time he had become very involved in writing conferences and was eager to share his drafts. He listened to the response of his peers, often using their comments to aid his revisions. He did not seem to feel as defensive as he did earlier in the year. I think once he realized that the environment was supportive and his classmates' comments were constructive, he began to relax, listen, and acknowledge the good ideas of his peers. He was also able to make positive suggestions to others. This was not the same child who, in earlier years, was unable to listen to anyone else.

At his writing evaluation conference with me at the end of November, he told me that in order to be a good writer you had to "know lots of words and have creative and funny ideas." He found revision and editing to be the easiest part of writing, and drafting and "making better endings" the hardest. He felt his poem, "The Sounds of Halloween," was the best piece he had written during the first marking period because it had "lots of description and good words."

He did not like his story about his trip to New York because he felt there was "not enough of me and my feelings." He set some goals for himself for the next three months. He wanted to improve in spelling and put more humor into his pieces. He loved having time to write every day. He told me that writing, history, and reading were his favorite subjects, and then added, "Writing and reading—they're the same thing. You can't really separate them." Once again I was jolted. Usually children don't make that connection until much later in the year, if at all. Greg was so immersed in his reading and writing, his world of ideas, that he saw reading and writing as one. For him, they were extensions of each other.

In January Greg returned to poetry. He wrote a poem about his dreams:

Dreams

Dreams are whisps of silver clouds
the gold is swirled into the mist.
The vapors they twirl
and lightly dance.
They seem to jump
and leap
and prance.
But the dream moves on
nightmares crash!
Dark and looming
deep and vast.
Treacherous screams
terrors last.
Boom!
Bang!
Blast!
"Oh no! Oh no! Help!"
"Wake up! Wake up!"
"Whew," I sighed.

"How does he think of all those good words?" asked Andrew. "How can he put them together so well?" Chris wondered. The class could identify with the poem and told him all the lines that they especially liked. He was very proud of it.

Two weeks later he was in a whimsical mood. I noticed him writing and smiling during writing workshop. When he came to the conference table he was still smiling. "I wrote a poem about ice cream," he announced. "One of my favorite topics," I told him.

The Ice Cream Cone Consumer

I wish I had an ice cream cone
It would be very high,
Its great big vanilla scoops
Would reach up to the sky.

It would taste so very sweet
A nice and yummy ice cream treat
I would eat this on a hot summer day
The coolness would drive the heat away.

When I had finished it
I'd lay down for a rest.
I'd say, "That ice cream cone
Was the very best!"

Which proves that eating ice cream
Is not a bad, bad crime
As long as the food that is eaten
Is always, always Mine!!

These poems inspired some children to start writing poetry. Just as Andrea's poem had influenced Greg's writing, his poems provided possibilities for others. They played around with rhyme and enjoyed sharing their verses with each other. Again I wondered and speculated why fifth graders turned so naturally to poetry. As I reflected I realized that poetry seemed to allow them to use fewer words to express complex ideas. It seemed to be more manageable, the volume of words was not as great, and there seemed to be less revision involved. When I asked Greg about poetry, he confirmed some of my own thoughts: "When you write a story," he told me, "you need a story around an idea. With a poem you just need an idea. And a story has so many revisions." Poems were accepted as they flowed out of my students. Peers listened to the ideas in first drafts and asked very few questions. They sat and savored.

During the next four months the poems began to grow longer and became more serious. Children wrote about saving whales, the killing of animals, the cutting of trees, the Exxon oil spill, and Pan Am Flight 103. For many of my students poetry was a way of expressing their thoughts and fears about the environment. During this time, Craig, a quiet boy in my class, emerged as a poet with a message. Greg was drawn to him. The two would often share their ideas and writing pieces together.

In January the class began reading books abut colonial America in preparation for a report. They read trade books, fiction and nonfiction. Greg, who had become very interested in history, read about colonial doctors, the Salem Witch Trials, papermakers, and the colonial farm; he finally decided to make colonial whaling his topic. He read many books and worked very hard. The introduction to his report told about whaling in general:

> Whaling was a very difficult and a very strange way to make a living. In a way, whaling was like drugs. Most people did not like it because of the dangers involved. But whaling was addictive. Once you had been whaling you wanted to go again and again.

He included a history of whaling and described the construction of larger whaling ships and processing techniques. Then he used a character, William, to tell about life as a whaler in three chapters that described whalers arriving in port, and catching and processing a whale:

> William hurried to his long boat which was being lowered. He jumped in. William was the eighth crew member. The small boat's mast was raised and it sailed toward the whale. When the boat was fifty feet away from the whale, it lowered its sail and the crew rowed (Rowing was more quiet so the whale would not notice.)
>
> The boat got very close. The harpoonist threw the harpoon into the whale. The whale went into a rage. He sped at top speed pulling the boat behind him. This was called a "Nantucket Sleigh Ride."
>
> William had heard a whale could keep going at this speed for 24 hours. By that time they would be miles away from the ship. William hoped this would not happen. He also had heard stories about whales that dove deep and took the boat with them.
>
> The whale finally got tired and stopped. Just to make sure he was dead, the harpoonist drove a spear into the whale's eye and next into its blow hole so it could not see or breathe. The whale spouted a blood and salt water mixture into the air spraying the whalers with its last breath.
>
> Disgusting, thought William on the way back to the ship. Most of the whalers in that time believed that it was the whale's life or

theirs. William, however, read the Bible and had pity on all God's creatures.

Greg made nine illustrations, which included a whale smashing a boat, a widow's walk, and whaling tools; he also compiled a glossary of whaling terms of which he was especially proud. He spent two and a half months on the report doing the research and the writing. During that time he was completely involved in whaling. This was not a boy who avoided assignments or did not work up to his potential. He researched everything, even scrimshaw, and was delighted when on a vacation he discovered a store that sold it. He brought a piece to me as a present.

During the winter the class was preparing to attend a performance, which is part of my school district's cultural arts program. Various programs from a performing arts center are brought to the schools to increase the children's appreciation of the performing arts. A teaching artist (T.A.) works with the children and with me on many activities that will enhance the program that the class eventually attends. This particular year we were preparing to see a performance based on Kipling's *Just So Stories*. The children selected animals and then did research as to how they looked, acted, and moved. Their assignment was to "become" the animal, emphasizing a particular characteristic. We had a "shy" guinea pig, a "studious" snake, and a "clumsy" cat. Greg was a "cool" mouse. Then, once students became their animals, they created appropriate masks and props. They worked in groups to make a play in which the animals encountered each other. I gave the class time to develop their animals and create their skits. I did not give directions on how to accomplish the tasks. I was much more interested in observing the development of ideas. I wondered what the children would create on their own.

Greg and three other boys wrote and produced a clever skit. Greg, wearing large sunglasses and swinging his tail, performed his part especially well—so well in fact that the T.A. mentioned to me that he had real talent. She told him this, too, adding, "Make sure you do some acting when you get into junior high because you have a lot of talent." Greg was beaming. (In sixth grade another T.A. discovered his talents again in a different setting. By the end of sixth grade he was performing in theater productions through his church and had been chosen for a countywide performing group.) I realized again the importance of providing many different opportunities for children to express themselves. Would Greg and I have discovered his creative acting abilities if time had not been devoted to these activities?

In March and April I gave practice writing tests for the state writing test. I wondered what Greg's reaction would be. He had always chosen his own topics and was never at a loss for a topic. In the beginning of the practice test period, he resisted. He disliked the topics and he questioned me over and over again for a reason why he had to write on an assigned topic. I explained to him that it wasn't only preparation for the test but that throughout his life he would have occasions where he would have to write on an assigned topic. He would engage me in discussions—more like confrontations—that would go nowhere. I would eventually stop the "discussion" and tell him that I wouldn't listen anymore and that he had to do it. And in the end, he would and usually did well—if he liked the topic.

One assigned topic turned out to be an unforgettable experience for him. The topic was to pretend to be someone else for a day. Greg decided to be Dr. Baker, our principal. In his story he was in Dr. Baker's body and Dr. Baker was in his. As Dr. Baker, he drank a lot of coffee and disciplined a child who tried to beat Greg up on a regular basis. He also suffered through all kinds of paperwork and finally hid out in the teachers' lounge where he eventually went to sleep.

I asked Greg if I could give Dr. Baker a copy of his story. Greg at first said no because he was afraid of Dr. Baker's reaction, but when I assured him that Dr. Baker had a good sense of humor, he relented. I made a copy and gave it to my principal. A week later the class and I were on our way to art when Dr. Baker walked out of the office. As Greg passed by Dr. Baker said to him, "How are you today, Dr. Baker?" Greg and the rest of the class laughed in surprise. Greg looked a little concerned when Dr. Baker added, "Why aren't you in your office at your desk?" He then invited Greg into his office and had him sit at his big desk and take a phone call from the secretary. Eventually the secretary took a picture of Greg at Dr. Baker's desk. A few days later, the class returned from gym to find Dr. Baker sitting in Greg's desk with Greg's jacket on, doing Greg's school work. Of course we took a picture. Both pictures were given to Greg and he treasured them. I think these incidents bolstered Greg's self-esteem. The class had loved his story and certainly had fun with the results. For a while Greg was a celebrity to them and I think he needed this kind of attention. When asked to write about one important incident in his elementary school career for the fifth-grade yearbook, he wrote about the experience with Dr. Baker.

Greg continued to have a very good year. None of the problems he'd had in earlier grades with peers and work habits surfaced. His social relationships were positive and he had increased his number of friends although he still thought of Alex as his special friend. He was drawn to the children who expressed their creative ideas in our discussions, in book conferences, and in their writing pieces. I noticed that he was often involved in lengthy "talks" that did not end when the bell rang for lunch or at 3:00. He would remain after class with his friends to continue sharing ideas. Often I would join them, mainly to listen but sometimes to respond to their ideas and to give my own. At times I realized it was more interesting to be part of their discussions than to be involved in conversations with my peers. Their passionate discussions about the world and their ideas for saving it gave me hope for the future. If only all fifth graders were this concerned!

Greg also felt confident as a student. His work in all areas had improved. He was even enjoying solving problems in math, a subject area that he had found tedious at the beginning of the year. He had turned into a prolific reader and writer. In May he evaluated his growth in reading and noted the importance of response to reading in one of his letters to me. He acknowledged that other children and various authors provided him with ideas:

> Dear Miss Five,
>
> I love reading. I think being able to read in class is a good idea. Last year we never read in class or anything. I used to only like mysteries and fantasy. Now I like much more topicks. Even though I always liked reading I think its fun to share with people what you read. You can get alot of ideas.
>
> I have read 2 times as many books this year although I read many books last year. This year I am reading longer books and last year I basically stuck to one series but this year not only did I read books from different series but I read from different authors altogether. They give me good ideas, too.
>
> I think that this year I have found an inner meaning to most of the books I read.

In the spring many more children were writing poems expressing their concerns about the environment. This was a topic I had not assigned but one that came from them. I think it started with their study of whales in the fall, but the Exxon oil spill also really affected this class. They worried about the animals and pollution. They discussed the situation often in class and I imagine as one or two started writing about it, the others decided to put their thoughts into words. The children conferred all the time, sharing drafts with each other and at the conference table. It was the beginning of Greg's attempt to write with greater depth. He wanted his stories to have an underlying meaning, something he had discovered in the books he read.

First he wrote a poem:

The World has Exploded, the Earth has Died . . .

Boom!! Boom!! Boom!!
The world has exploded,
the Earth has died,
all its inhabitants, too.
We crammed it up with gas and garbage
and we stuffed it to the brim.
We cut down all our trees
so we could hardly breathe.
We leaked radiation
and spilled lots of oil
all over our beautiful Earth.

My research in space has told me
Venus was once like Earth
with people and animals,
but they polluted and destroyed
the o-zone layer.
It burned away the atmosphere,
created the greenhouse affect
so they got too hot and died out.

Some clumsy oaf
at U.S.A.'s missile center
leaned against the console,
slipped and turned the key.
   KaaBoom!!
Off went the missile into Russia
so they turned all their keys
and declared war.

You can imagine what happened next
and its not a pretty thought.

The earth bombarded with many holes.
I'm lucky I got away
with this fancy new space ship I bought.

Yes, I'm Greg.
I knew this would happen sooner or later
so I got away as fast as I could.
Now I'm here all alone
the last survivor of the human race,
floating slowly in outer space,
drifting timelessly, not leaving a trace.

The class reacted to his poem with the same seriousness and concern that had typified their response to other environmental poems by classmates. I began to wonder about them. I had not had a fifth-grade class respond in this way to environmental issues although they had certainly been discussed in the past. The other fifth-grade classes were not writing about these topics. What was the difference? When I asked them they told me that it was because we spent a lot of time talking about news events. Perhaps they were right. Environmental issues were often in the news articles the children brought into school each day. Perhaps the time spent talking was an important element. The more they talked about the environment, the more they thought. Talk about ideas in the classroom allowed the children to think about topics which eventually seemed to lead to writing.

They also learned from and were influenced by each other. One or two children started writing about saving animals. The class discussed these poems and were interested to find that poetry seemed to make the message more powerful. Then others began to experiment. I think Greg's poem came as a result of a poem written by Craig called "The Sounds of Destruction," in which he described the human destruction of the planet. I knew that Greg was influenced by other writers.

I asked the class what we should do with this particular collection of poems and stories. They had two suggestions: they wanted to put all the writing on the bulletin board in the hall so "the rest of the school will be concerned and do something about the environment," and they wanted to send copies to President Bush so that he would "do something!" We put the poems on the bulletin board and, surprisingly, there was very little response. One teacher said the bulletin board was very depressing.

Greg wrote the cover letter to President Bush:

Dear President Bush

Our class is very concerned with the environment and we are also concerned with peace, arms, nuclear arms, poverty, animal experimentation, poachers, and many other world-wide problems.

So our class has written these stories and poems, and we would like you to read them carefully. Be sure not to overlook a single line. Try to help these causes to the best of your abilities. (Since you're the president.) After you finish reading, please write back and tell us what you think. We know that you are very, very busy but please find time to read them. We think these topics are very important.

Sincerely,
Miss Five's Class

Unfortunately there was very little response in this area, too. We received a form letter thanking us for writing and a picture of the White House. "I bet he didn't even read our poems," Greg remarked.

In his last writing conference of the year, Greg told me he wanted to write a "fantasy or space story with an inner meaning." In June he decided to do just that. It was called "Friends of War." He liked the title because it was such a contradiction. "You know," he explained to me, "if you're in a war, you don't exactly make friends." It was about a dwarf named Golen who is drafted by the "Royal Chieftan of Dwarves" to fight in a war against the "Elves of Samalee" to "rid the world of an unworthy race." When Golen is drafted he becomes confused about the war. "Unworthy? Who decided that? What's wrong with Elves?" he asks.

After the commander of the Dwarves issued his order to Golen to fight,

Golen closed his oak door and sat down on his chair. He stared into the fire, stunned with disbelief. He did not want to go to war, to leave his home. Golen remembered his father, Kasmar Tasem, who had gone off to war. He had come back in a casket with the dwarven symbol of a forge imprinted on it since dwarves are known for being good at blacksmithing.

Golen solemnly got up and dragged himself over to his chest. He opened it. The dwarf took out a white battered drawstring bag. He took a small book-size piece of wood with his father and mother carved into it. He held it against his heart and slipped it into the bag.

Greg continued his story as Golen takes his battle ax and is herded into a wagon with lots of other Dwarves to go to war. At night when they reach the battleground, the commander describes the battle plans and tells the Dwarves they must rid the world of Elves: " They are too tall and too slim. They have hair as long as women's. This is a disgrace." Golen decides he cannot fight and plans to escape once he gets to the battlefield. The battlefield is described, along with the commands given to the Dwarves. Golen manages to escape and runs into a forest where he meets an Elf:

> Golen sat. As he turned, he saw a tall blond bushy-haired Elf standing over him. His hair stopped at his neck. His soft green eyes stared at Golen. His soft smooth face, lightly colored, his cute nose, his teeth all looked perfect. His tattered green outfit almost blended with the forest.
>
> The Elf leaned on his staff. His long hair suddenly dropped down on his face as he bent over his staff. Golen heard a muffled sob but he dared not speak. The Elf looked up. A tear, a terrible tear, disrupted the perfection of his face. His bright soft eyes narrowed and became sharp and piercing. "Leave!" he said in a small hoarse voice.
>
> "No," said Golen, "You will have to kill me. I have deserted my fellow Dwarves. I am a disgrace. You must kill me. I have nothing to look forward to at home. They would find me and kill me anyway."
>
> "I can't," said the Elf wiping away a tear. "I have run away from my father, Chief of the Elves of Samalee. He wants me to fight. I can not. I do not want to kill, so go."
>
> Golen refused to go so Golen and the Elf sat. The Elf sheathed his sword and Golen explained his situation. Gradually they both became relaxed. After an hour they got up from the bonfire and walked off together as friends. No matter what their differences were, the look in the Elf's eyes was now soft and relaxed and the Dwarf was cheerful and happy.

Greg read the four-page story which he had typed on the computer to the class. They responded with respect. They liked the idea that he had written a story with an important message.

As I listened to him read, I realized that much of the language, characters, and theme were modeled after his much loved series of books and the ones he had been reading in the spring. His letters to me about *Westmark* (Alexander 1981) and *Dragon's Blood* (Yolen 1982) always included his attempts to discover the inner meaning, which seemed to involve conflicts between good and evil. His story of Golen and the Dwarf was, perhaps, his own attempt to resolve the issues of war that he had discovered in his books. His ending, the friendship that developed between the Elf and the Dwarf, seemed to be a plea for peace and harmony.

I was once again amazed at the influence his reading had on his writing. When I asked him about it, he explained: "I get ideas for the characters and the characters' names from the books I read. Then I change the names a little. Sometimes I get ideas for the story because I figure if the author got it published and kids love it, it must be a good idea. If I write one like it, it will be a good one, too. But I usually change the story."

During the last two weeks of school, when I was going through my usual separation anxiety, Greg often stayed in during lunch and after school to tell me about books he liked, his fears about junior high, and his plans to be a writer. One day he revealed an idea that he had been pondering for a while: "I think school takes away a child's imagination." I didn't know whether to feel hurt or intrigued. Fortunately my curiosity and interest in this sensitive child prevailed and I asked him to explain. "School fills your head with facts and numbers," he said. "Before kids go to school, their heads are filled with fairies and elves and fantasies. Then they go to school and they have no time for an imagination so it goes away sort of."

I asked him if he thought adults had imagination. He didn't think so. I told him that I thought it took imagination to write books, design buildings, conduct experiments, teach, land on the moon. "Perhaps adults have a different kind of imagination," I suggested.

He paused and thought. "I don't know," he said, "I'll have to think about it but you might be wrong, you know."

The next day he came in with a paragraph about imagination. "I'm going to make this into a story with a message. This will be the prologue."

Prologue

> You see children are the most important people on earth. In a way they are unknowing and therefore unafraid. But, more importantly, they have something people today have very little of, that is of course, imagination. Now this is a very peculiar thing. (Because) In your mind everyone is born with a special section marked

"IMAGINATION" but when you go to school your mind gets consumed by facts and numbers so the "IMAGINATION" gets pushed over until it gets pushed out your left ear. It is lost forever. And the space in your brain where those thoughts once rested now contains more facts and numbers.

Also you know, we live in a world where what you think is true, is true, but to you only. And what you think is not true is not true. So you see if you have an imagination, then you think there are fairies, and there are fairies. And if you don't believe in fairies, there aren't any.

Greg's prologue reminded me of *Tuck Everlasting* (Babbitt 1975), a book I had read to the class months before. It had a prologue with symbols representing the ideas in the fantasy that followed. Was Greg presenting his thoughts in a similar way? His reading was obviously influencing his writing.

Within days Greg wrote his story. It was about a little girl named Cindy who was five years old:

She had not gone to school yet so she still had an imagination. Therefore she was happy. At noon time, after she had done all the regular fun things, jumped rope, played hopscotch, cartwheels, sommersalts, she started to use her imagination. I'll be a pirate, she thought, digging for gold. She got a shovel and dug right by the old oak in her backyard.

Cindy and her friend, Max, discover gold dust in the hole and a fairy with a broken wing. Cindy helps the fairy find the King of the Fairies and listens in wonder as the fairy delivers the imagination census reports ("only 1 thousand people in the whole world who still have imagination.") The fairy suggests they visit more children to increase the census report. As a reward for her help, Cindy receives three wishes but with a warning; "Use them wisely or you'll regret making wishes that you can't get." Her three wishes include; "First I wish your wing gets better. Zing! Her (the fairy's) wing healed. Second I wish good health to all fairies. And third, I wish a lot more people had imagination."

Greg added an epilogue that showed a change in his thinking:

Epilogue

From that day on lots more people had imagination although never quite as many as Cindy had wished. If you ever go to the birch tree

> you'll find the fairy is still the royal messenger. And many more times she came back to the king declaring the latest imagination census reports. As before it was low but not so extreme. It was not entirely the schools' fault for the loss of imagination, but rather the organizations that take up the time after school such as camps, athletic teams, after school clubs, etc. They make it such that children never have any free time for play, real play.
>
> So if you like to play with toy cars, legos, blocks, action figures, stuffed animals, don't let your friends make you stop. If you do you will contribute to the loss of imagination. We must maintain some innocence in children. We can't let realism take over.

Where did these ideas come from? I wondered. Once again Greg had surprised me. How did this gentle, sensitive child grow from writing about catching his first fish to describing the loss of imagination? "I spend a lot of time thinking," he said. Greg's message was something I had already learned, but it had taken me years of teaching; children need time, yes, more free time to play, but certainly more time to read, to write, to talk, to listen, to think. This year Greg had had time for these things in a supportive environment, and I think he recognized and valued it. He benefited from the ideas of others, his peers and the authors of the books he loved. He needed them to give him the freedom to experiment. He explored poetry after Andrea led the way, he followed his beloved authors once he discovered them. He needed the freedom to choose his own books and his own form of expression, and he had many different opportunities to take risks and discover himself as he struggled to interpret not only the books he read but his own world as well. The result was that there was, indeed, a "special" child in my class that year, one who provided a different kind of challenge. Greg was a boy who, "despite or because of school," but definitely through reading and writing, was able to reclaim his imagination and emerge as a gifted writer.

7

Andrew

A child at risk

"YOU'RE HIS LAST hope, Cora," my principal said shaking his head, referring to Andrew, a student in my class. It was the second day of school. I had met with my principal to discuss a letter I had received from Andrew's mother describing Andrew's problems and particular needs. She noted that Andrew had had a very bad year in fourth grade and she explained why. Because he was not on grade level in various subjects, he had been given different books which the other children noticed were much easier. He did not know easy math facts when called on to recite. He had difficulties in reading and writing. As a result he felt "dumb," and it seemed as though his learning problems were beginning to cause emotional problems at home.

My principal read the letter and we discussed its contents. He told me that Andrew had been classified learning disabled by the Committee on Special Education. Dr. Baker explained that since I would already have an aide in my room to work with another child who had been designated learning disabled, the aide might give extra help to Andrew, too. My principal went on to explain more about Andrew, telling me that he had been a severe discipline problem in fourth grade. "He was in trouble all the time and he always denied doing anything," he said, shaking his head again. Andrew had had difficulties in the classroom, in the lunch room, at recess, and after school. He had often picked on younger children and had made friends with a group of boys who were known for being "tough." The boys would saunter down the halls together scaring and threatening not only younger children, but their peers, fifth graders, and some teachers as well. "I'm counting on you. It's his last chance," Dr. Baker said, as he put an arm around my shoulder and walked with me through the office and into the hall. I smiled at him. I was immediately interested in this child because I couldn't believe the situation could be so bad, so hopeless.

Andrew had been in my class for three hours on the first day of school. During those three hours, the psychologist, a reading skills teacher, and the speech therapist had beckoned me to the doorway to tell me, "We'll have to talk about Andrew and set up his schedule." I had responded that I wanted to get to know him and find out what he could do before I met with them. "Well, he goes to skills four times a week," said the skills teacher. "He has speech twice a week," said the speech therapist. "We'll have to have a meeting about him," said the psychologist. STOP! I screamed to myself. I nodded at them and gently closed the door.

Andrew sat in the back row with the boys. On the first day of school I greet my class at the door and tell them to take any seat. The boys usually end up sitting on one side of the room and the girls on the other. This year the boys had taken the back row of the semicircle of desks and girls were in the front.

Even though Andrew sat in the back with the boys, he did very little talking during the first short week of school. He didn't talk to the boys, he didn't talk during class discussions, and he didn't talk to me. He came and went with his head down and did not smile. If I stopped to talk to him privately, he scowled at me and said in annoyance, "What?" All attempts at conversation with him were disappointing because he only responded with yes or no or short sentences: "I don't know" or "Can I go now?" He met his former friends from fourth grade who had been split up into the other fifth-grade classes. Together they moved as a pack to lunch, to recess, and to go to their homes after school. The only time I saw him talk was when he was with this group.

Dr. Baker checked with me after the first week of school and I told him things were fine. I had had no problems with Andrew. During that first week of school I gave reading inventories and some sheets to assess computation skills. I noticed that Andrew worked very slowly. He kept an eye on the children sitting near him, I think, to see if they were watching him or looking at his paper. He handed his papers in when most of the other children did whether he was finished or not. The act of writing the answers to questions seemed to be extremely difficult. As a result he did not answer many questions and completed only the first few examples on the math sheets.

In the afternoons of that first week the children worked on a bulletin board that I had given them. They each had a section which they decorated with pictures or souvenirs that showed their interests, hobbies, and pets. They wrote down their favorite movie, book, and author. I took pictures of each student to put on their section of the board. The purpose of this activity was to get to know each other. I had a section for myself because I was building on the idea that we would all be a community of learners.

The children eventually selected partners and interviewed each other. The results of the interviews were stapled on the board next to their pictures. Andrew ended up with no partner for the interview. I told him I would be his partner; little did I know that it would become a strong partnership that would last ten months and benefit both of us. At the time, however, Andrew sighed in exasperation and sat solemnly down at the conference table next to me. I learned from him that he had a cat and that he liked bikes. He asked me questions and slowly printed the answers, frequently asking me how to spell words. I noticed that he printed his interview, that he included lower- and uppercase letters randomly, and that he left little space between many of the words:

> MsFIVE HAS 2 CAts anDSHELiVEsin tHe City. SHe LiKESto run anD pLAY tennis AnD SKi. SHE LiKE FiSH. Her FAVOrite color is BLUE.

When I questioned him, he added to his interview that he did not like school and had no favorite subjects except recess. He did not want me to include those answers in my paragraph on him so I didn't. When I took his picture, he did not smile. His was the only picture on the board that showed a sad face. Even though I knew more about Andrew the student after the first week of school, I knew very little about Andrew the boy.

By the middle of the second week, Dr. Baker checked with me again. This was quite unusual because he didn't ordinarily go out of his way to find out how things were going. He assumed that if he didn't hear from me, all was well. Apparently, even though all was well in the classroom, all was not well in the lunch room. Andrew was in trouble for throwing food and talking back to lunch-room personnel. When I asked him about it, he said in a low voice, "I didn't do anything," and headed for his desk.

By the beginning of the third week, Andrew was in more trouble. He had been involved in some destructive behavior over the weekend. He had also terrorized some younger children and had spit on them. My principal called me and the school psychologist to the office to tell us that based on Andrew's previous behavior and these latest incidents he was planning to recommend placing Andrew in a special school. I was horrified. "You can't do that!" I blurted out. He looked at me. "He hasn't had a chance," I said. I wonder now if what I really meant was that "we," Andrew and I, hadn't had a chance. All I remember thinking in Dr. Baker's office was, they can't take him away from me yet. The psychologist suggested a meeting with the parents.

The meeting was arranged for the following week. However, before the meeting, Dr. Baker met with Andrew and me together. Andrew denied the latest incidents, saying that he had been blamed for everything since he was in first grade. Now, he felt, everyone just naturally blamed him for everything bad that happened. This year, he said, he was trying to be good to get rid of his poor reputation. Dr. Baker gave Andrew time to think and opportunities to take responsibility for his actions. But Andrew continued to deny his role in the series of unfortunate incidents. And I continued to ask for more time with him.

When the parents finally met with us, it was the last week of September. Dr. Baker explained the seriousness of Andrew's actions and how he could no longer take the risk of having a smaller child hurt in school because of Andrew's actions. He suggested that if Andrew's behavior got worse, he'd have to go to a special school. The parents were at a loss as to what to do. Apparently Andrew was as uncontrollable at home, often hitting and kicking family members and causing damage in the neighborhood. I made plans with them to communicate on a regular basis concerning Andrew's progress.

Dr. Baker decided to keep Andrew in school but to remove him from the lunch room and playground for most of the month of October. He arranged with me that Andrew would spend the first half of the lunch hour with me in my room and the second half in the office. If Andrew behaved during this arrangement, he would be allowed to spend more time in the lunch room by the middle of the month and during the last week in October he would be allowed to go out on the playground for ten minutes.

One of the problems Andrew had at home concerned homework. He wouldn't or couldn't do it. Conflicts occurred when his mother tried to help. It had been suggested that the parents not help Andrew with his work in order to avoid and minimize the nightly fights. I told them that if Andrew couldn't do the work, I would help him in the morning before school. I wanted him to do all he could do by himself at home and bring the rest to me. At this time Andrew was also having trouble during the hour before school started. His parents went to work early and he went to child care, where he continued to have difficulties with younger children. I suggested that instead of going to child care, he come to me and I would help him with his class and homework. The parents agreed to this plan and were very grateful.

October 1 was both the beginning and the end: the beginning of hope and trust and a more positive image and the end of much of the turbulence that seemed to be part of Andrew's school world. I worked with Andrew for forty-five minutes before school each day, for a half hour at lunch time, and whenever I saw he was struggling in the classroom.

Andrew's background

Andrew was the only boy in his family. Both parents were professional people who worked full time. He had two sweet older sisters who did well in school. They caused the parents little concern, while Andrew always seemed to be in trouble. By the end of fourth grade the parents felt desperate. They were not only concerned about his behavior, but his learning ability as well.

Andrew's academic history was one of frustration. He had received skills help in reading, writing, and math since first grade. He had also received special help in speech for many years. This special help in skills and speech made it necessary for him to leave the classroom for many periods each week.

At the end of fourth grade Andrew's learning problems were discussed extensively and a plan for fifth grade was established. His program was to be in a regular classroom with skills help outside the classroom from three to five times per week. He was to have speech and language therapy at least once a week. A modified currriculum and modified assignments were recommended. Andrew's reading score on a standardized test was below grade level. It was noted that he did very little independent reading. His math skills were also below grade level. It was recommended that he memorize the math facts. Written expression was difficult for him. He had, in the past, dictated stories, but had written few stories during fourth grade. His relationships with peers and adults needed improvement. He did not participate in class discussions. Handwriting was a problem for him because of his poor eye/hand coordination. He practiced cursive writing and was learning keyboarding three times a week with little success. It was felt that Andrew needed to be monitored and given a great deal of individual attention. He could not complete written assignments independently. The picture of Andrew as a fourth grader was one of a boy who was not motivated, was easily distracted, and who would not initiate and complete his work.

The beginning

Andrew usually arrived each morning at 7:50, a few minutes after I opened the door to the classroom. However, sometimes I found him sitting on the step waiting for me. I always greeted him and told him I was happy to see him. In the beginning he would mumble something and head for his desk. Then he would take out his homework assignment notebook where I had written his homework the previous afternoon. I decided to write his homework assignments for him for two reasons: first, I knew how long it would take him to copy the work because of his difficulties with the act of writing; and second, because I was modifying assignments based on what he could do, I did not want the other children to know he was doing less.

Every day Andrew brought his homework assignment book to me at the conference table. We would check off the items he had done at home. I would check them and we would make corrections if necessary. Finally we would tackle the work that he didn't do at home, which was usually math. We worked together on the examples and at 8:25 I gave him a break and he went outside to play with his friends for ten minutes before the bell rang. If we finished his homework before 8:25, I would try to talk to him about school or about books. A few times during that first week we went to the library to select a book for reading workshop. Andrew did not seem to resent coming in early each morning. He was cooperative and willing to work.

However, he did resent the lunch time he spent with me. He asked me over and over again why he had to stay with me, and I would explain over and over again that Dr. Baker had decided that he could not participate in the lunch program at this time because of his actions. Andrew told me that he'd prefer to sit in the office for the whole lunch period rather than stay with me. We spent the time going over his homework for the following night and reviewing math examples that had been done in class so he would remember how to do them. During this time I also tried to get to know Andrew, but he only wanted to express his anger at Dr. Baker.

Andrew was part of reading and writing workshops from the beginning. The first book he chose was *The Love Bug* (Walt Disney Productions 1979). I don't know if he read it. I do know that it was a thick book, one that Andrew felt was respectable to read. His first letter in his reading journal (which eventually became decorated with guns, skulls and bones, spider webs, the initials I.R.A., and Guns & Roses) was brief:

> DEAr miss FiVE, I AmrEADing tHE LoveBug. I tHink tHAtit isA good BookILiKE in.
>
> from Andrew

Unfortunately I wrote back in script. He did not tell me that he couldn't read script until after I had written my second letter to him. I had wondered why he hadn't answered my question and he admitted that he couldn't read my letter. From then on, I printed my response.

After *The Love Bug,* Andrew was stuck for a book. He wandered around the classroom looking at the books I had and couldn't seem to find one he liked. Finally I suggested he try *Pickle Puss* (Giff 1986), which he read and wrote about in a longer letter to me (see Figure 7.1).

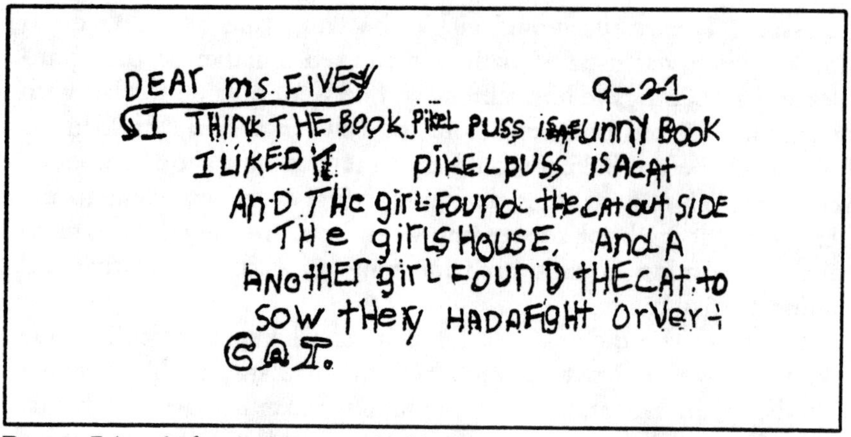

DEAR ms. FIVEY 9-21
I THINK THE BOOK PiKEL PUSS iS A FUNNY BOOK
I LIKED IT. PiKELPUSS iS A CAT
AND THE girl FOUND THE CAT OUT SIDE
THE girls HOUSE. And A
ANOTHER girl FOUND THE CAT to
SOW THEY HAD A FIGHT OrVer the
CAT.

FIGURE 7.1 *Andrew's response to Pickle Puss*

He had clearly read the book. I realized that he felt more comfortable reading shorter books. However, he did not want the other children to see him reading thin books, so he kept these books hidden, open inside his desk and read them in that manner for a number of weeks. The next book he read was one I read at home first called *Camp Ghost Away* (Delton 1988). It included some adventure and was a short, easy book to read. He really became interested in it and finished it in two days. After that he went to the library during one of our early morning sessions looking for another Giff book. By chance, he discovered another in the Pee Wee Scouts series among the Giff books and decided to read it. He liked the characters and felt a sense of accomplishment that he could finish a book so quickly. I decided to read all the books he read so we could talk about them in the morning. Every time he found a Pee Wee book that he wanted to read, he took out a second copy for me. I would read them at home and usually each morning he would ask me, "Where are you up to?" We'd discuss the characters and make predictions about the endings.

Writing workshop proved to be more difficult for him. It took him a long time to decide on a topic. I had rearranged the students' desks after the first week of school, placing him in the front row near the conference table. I wanted to be near enough so I could help him as soon as I saw he was having trouble and I also wanted him to be able to hear the conferences at the table. I think he selected his first topic as a result of the discussion at the table. His first piece was about a ride he had taken at an amusement park—a common first-piece topic. He started to print his draft. I saw how slowly he wrote and asked him if he would like to write it on the computer. He looked around quickly at the other children to see if they had heard and said, "No!" He did not want to be different in any way. I knew that but had hoped that he might have realized that all the children in the class did not have the same abilities. He struggled on printing his draft. He would not read it at the conference table but read it to me the next day. I noticed he started his piece with conversation. I thought he must have been listening to children trying out leads during minilessons and in conferences. I helped him correct the spelling and put in punctuation marks and paragraphs. I asked him if he would like to do the final copy on the computer, but again he said, "No!" He began to copy the piece in pen on September 25, carefully using white-out on his mistakes. By the end of writing workshop he had copied only five sentences.

The next day, when Andrew was sent back to the room from a special class for misbehaving, I went over to the computer and turned it on. "Let's try your story on the computer," I said. He protested but eventually came over and sat next to me. I began to type the first part of his draft. As I typed, he began to add words and make changes. He changed "The rain stopped" to "It finally stopped." I also asked him questions to see if he would add more to the story. When he answered, I asked him if he thought we should put the information into the story. He usually added it. After I had typed half of his story, I asked him if he would like to finish it. He shrugged and changed seats with me. He typed the remainder of his draft using two fingers and searching for some of the letters. His method of typing was still faster than his printing. I noticed that he left out some sentences and added others. When I asked him about it, he shrugged again. I wondered if he left out the last two sentences because he got tired of typing or because he didn't want to admit that the man who ran the ride had scared him. When he finished I came over to read his piece and helped him make corrections. We agreed that it was easier to make corrections on the computer than on white paper. He seemed to be pleased that he had completed his piece.

The Sky Flyer

"Let's go on the Sky Flyer," I said to my friend. We walked towards the Sky Flyer. It started to rain. Half the people left Playland because it was raining. It finally stopped. About eighteen people were there including us.

> There was no line. We asked the man if the ride was open. He said, "yes." We gave him the tickets. We got on the ride. We pulled the bar over our legs and it locked tight. Good, we could start now. I said to myself, "This is crazy." I took a deep breath.
>
> We started to move. We went around six times and stopped. It was fun. We went on the Sky Flyer five times and the sand was pouring out of my shoes.

He made a cover for it but refused to read it or share it with anyone. He was even reluctant to have me put it on the writing bulletin board. However, after a few days, he agreed to put it up.

At the beginning of October I was approached again by the skills teacher and the speech therapist. They wanted to set up Andrew's schedule. He saw them come into the room, looked at me, and began to shake his head. During our lunch time together, he told me he did not want to go to skills. "I hate it," he said. I explained to him that it was part of his program. "I don't want to leave the room," he responded and added, "I won't go."

I had a meeting with Dr. Baker and asked him if Andrew had to go to skills and speech. I explained that he was making progress in the classroom and seemed to be developing some confidence. I told him I thought he would feel worse about himself if he had to leave to go to skills three to five times a week. Dr. Baker told me that Andrew was required to have skills a certain number of times each week. I told him I thought being pulled out for skills might have more of a negative effect than a positive one. He asked me what Andrew and I worked on each morning. I told him math and reading, and that we did some writing. Dr. Baker determined that the forty minutes I worked with Andrew in the morning could substitute for the amount of skills time he required. He decided that Andrew would go to skills only once a week. When I discussed the issue of speech, he told me we would hold off on scheduling speech.

Both specialists were not happy with the decision and neither was Andrew. He was furious that he had to go even once a week. "I hate her," he fumed. I explained to him that I had spoken to Dr. Baker on his behalf and I think he eventually realized that I had intervened for him, that I was on his side. I was the only one who was happy about Dr. Baker's decision. At least Andrew would not be pulled out of the classroom at various times six periods a week. Perhaps he'd be able to become part of the classroom community instead of feeling so isolated and different.

By the middle of October, Andrew came to school feeling happier. He started talking to me right away about his weekend, his parents, his friends, and his cat. One morning he came in and started telling me about his trip to Maryland. He sat at the computer and said, "I think I have a topic to write about for my next piece." Then he talked about his cat. He finally decided Maryland would be a better topic. He set up the program and started to write. After he had written two or three sentences, he had nothing else to write. He became restless and wanted to go out. I told him he could work on his story again during writing workshop in the afternoon.

Afternoons, however, were not the best time for Andrew. He seemed to have trouble concentrating on his work and sometimes laughed and made noises while the class was working. At times he appeared angry and was often fresh. He mumbled words under his breath and talked back to me when I set limits. He did not work on his writing piece for the next three days and would not go near the computer.

The following Monday Andrew came in early and the first thing he said was, "I have a good idea for writing. I caught twenty fish over the weekend when I was in Maryland. I have another topic, too, about skin boarding and when they stole my board." He set up the computer and started to write. I came over and he talked to me about his weekend and continued to write. Then he stopped and talked again and then wrote some more. While he wrote I moved some furniture around near the computer, making the computer, the desk near it, and two chairs a private little area of the room. When he asked what I was doing, I told him I wanted to make a special computer area. I wondered if this might make him feel more comfortable working at the computer during writing workshop. The other children would not be so aware of him working in a different way. The problem for me was that the computer was not near the conference table and I wondered how he was going to benefit from conferences sitting across the room. I would have to wait to see what happened.

In the afternoon when we had writing, he got his folder and told me in a low voice that he was going to work on the computer. I smiled at him. It worked, I thought to myself.

Andrew came in smiling the next morning. "Can I work on my story?" he asked. He got right to work and wrote for twenty minutes straight without any talking. I wandered over now and then but I didn't want to interrupt him. At 8:25 he stopped and said, "I can't write anymore. I have nothing left in me."

That afternoon he continued his story. During the next few days he revised it as a result of conferences with me. He was not willing to read his draft at the conference table. I helped him edit it. This second piece, "What a Day," was twice the length of the first piece. He described how he caught twenty-two fish, told how much they weighed, and how he threw some back in the water. This piece had longer sentences and more interesting vocabulary than his first story. There was more of Andrew in it. His last paragraph described his attempts to get rid of the smell of the fish:

> Once I got into the house I washed off the sandy dead fish that smelled like they were rotting in my hands. I couldn't take the smell because it was so strong. I felt like putting the smelly fish in the dishwasher but instead I put them in the sink and I washed them off. My dad put them in tin foil for another night. I ran upstairs and took a one and a half hour shower and I still smelled like fish so I picked up the shampoo and poured it all over myself. I used up the whole bottle and the smell finally came off. I was relieved. I dried myself off, changed my clothes, went downstairs, and plopped down on the couch. My energy was all worn out from casting my line and catching the fish. I fell asleep.
>
> I don't like to eat fish but my parents love fish. WHAT A DAY!

Andrew made an elaborate cover. I realized he was quite artistic and really enjoyed drawing.

During October I was reading *Bridge to Terabithia* (Paterson 1977) to the class. In our early morning sessions I would sometimes read chapters to Andrew because I had discovered he loved to listen to books read aloud. He discussed the anger that Jess felt after Leslie's death when he hurled the paints that Leslie had given him into the water. Andrew seemed to relate to that. He talked about his own anger and how he would throw things that his parents had given him and they would break. "Then the next day I want it and I'm very sorry I did it." He also talked about the death of a friend's brother, the death of a friend's father, and his own grandfather's death. One morning he told me that he knew he was learning disabled and then blurted out his concerns over junior high, his fear of being put in a special class: "My friends will make fun of me." A few minutes later, he looked at me and told me something that frightened me: "It's better to be bad than to be dumb." Did this philosophy explain his previous behavior, I wondered

By November Andrew came in talking when he arrived in the morning. He had a lot he wanted to discuss: arguments at home, the books he was reading, and ideas for writing pieces. He continued to make progress in all areas, but I realized that he did very little work without me next to him. I always made sure that I was near him when he started his work so he knew what to do and had a chance at success. He would not work with Pam, the aide assigned to my room. She helped the other children and corrected papers while I worked with Andrew.

Andrew continued to read the Pee Wee books while I frantically looked for another series for him to read when he finished with these. His letters to me about the books he read were still short, I think because of his difficulty with the physical act of writing. I suggested writing to me on the computer but he wanted to have his letters in his reading journal "the way the other kids do." His letters now had pictures drawn under them, not necessarily related to the books. He read books from other series that were on a second- or third-grade level. He read them in class and, when he remembered, at home. He liked them and began to compare the characters in the different series. In November I went to an NCTE conference and found the Julian books (Cameron 1986, 1987, 1988). I bought four or five in the series for the classroom and had the author autograph them. I bought one book especially for Andrew and the author wrote a dedication to him. He was very pleased with this book.

One book in the Julian series, *Julian, Secret Agent* (Cameron 1988), got him very excited. He came in one morning to tell me he had read for one and a half hours the previous night. "I thought the cook did it, too," he said and he began to tell me all the clues. "The scar above his lips, he liked traveling, he used different names. What did you think?" he wanted to know. This book prompted him to write a letter to me that very day (see Figure 7.2). I was surprised that he wrote much of it in cursive, something we had been working on in our sessions together.

Andrew really liked all of the books in this series and would read parts aloud to me. I realized that despite his problems with decoding, he figured out, if not the correct word, an appropriate word, from the text.

Andrew had had trouble with phonics since he had entered school and I did not think he was going to learn to sound out words in fifth grade. It did not seem to affect his comprehension although he had a

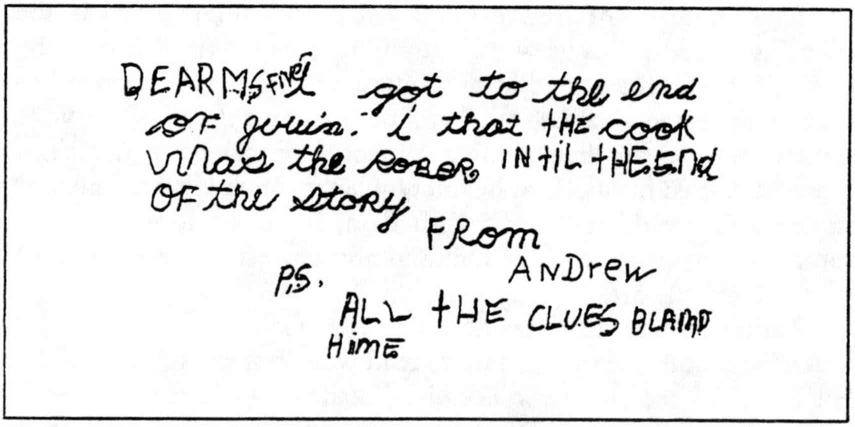

DEAR MS FINE I got to the end
OF JULIA. I that THE cook
Was the ROBER INTIL THE END
OF the Story
FROM
ANDrew
P.S.
ALL THE CLUES BLAMD
HIME

FIGURE 7.2 *Andrew's response to Julian, Secret Agent*

terrible time with spelling. When I gave him a form of the Silvaroli reading inventory, he tested above grade level. However, he had taken so many forms of this test throughout his schooling, I had a feeling he knew the selections well. And since the test offers very short passages, I decided to use other means to determine his reading ability. I selected whole short stories or fables for him to read and then asked him to retell what he had read. We also talked about the characters and discussed the themes of these longer selections. I saw that despite his inability to pronounce every word correctly, he was able to retell stories and to state the theme.

Often we talked about reading and he told me how bad he felt because he read so slowly and how he tended to give up on longer books. He had very little confidence in his reading and spelling ability and still felt he was "dumb." I began to work with him on strategies that might increase his speed, although my main objective was still getting him hooked on books.

I had more time to work with Andrew by the end of November. After a dispute with the instrumental music teacher, he quit band which meant he would be in my room for the hour when the band rehearsed. I had only one other child who did not go to band. We used the time to write, to work on math concepts, and to complete assignments in history. One day during band time Andrew said to me, "Can't I just read? I haven't had a chance to read all day." He spent most of the hour reading his Julian book. I was delighted.

It was during this extra hour that I had with Andrew that I discovered more about him. I had given the class a three-page history test. I did not expect Andrew to do all of the test because it involved so much writing. But since I had the time, I decided to ask him the questions and have him discuss them orally. I was curious as to how much he was learning from class activities and discussions because at times he had seemed so removed from what the class was doing. I was amazed that he knew all the answers and that he had ideas of his own about the topic. His passivity was misleading. He was really listening and learning. I suggested to him that he might want to share some of his good ideas with the class during our discussions, but he shook his head and said, "No, I don't want to." I hoped that with time and increased confidence, he eventually would.

During that gift of the extra hour with Andrew I also learned that he was very good mechanically. He began fixing things in the classroom that the custodians hadn't touched for five years. He fixed the emergency door and the overhead projector. He gave me ideas about the pencil sharpener and helped me find a better place for file cabinets. I think he was very pleased that he could do these things that I could not do. From then on, whenever he noticed something in the classroom that needed repair, he would tell me quietly that he was going to fix it and he usually did.

Andrew's third writing piece was written quickly on the computer. He was very excited about the topic. His parents had promised him a motorcycle for Christmas and his lead on his draft told much of the story:

> my dream since I was two was to have a motorcycle. Now I am gonna get one for Ericmas this year for my hobby. my Dad wants me to have a hobby to keep out of trouble. I think that is a good idea becase I get in to much trbule after school. so my Dads geting me a mine bike so I will kepe out of troubal.

The rest of the piece described the bike, the cost, and possible problems with riding the bike and the police. His next writing piece was about the Honda bike he received (see Figure 7.3). He wrote it on the computer and made revisions in pencil on the printed draft. This kind of revision was new for him. I had told him about how I revised my own writing by reading my printed draft and adding or deleting in pen. I wondered if my writing strategies had influenced his. I began to wish he had more contact with the rest of the class during writing. I felt he needed to learn from them, too. When he wrote on

My Honda XL 75

I got a honda last night at a
store called motor fixx in
Chester, / It is a red small motor
cycle.I am go to paint it black. It is
off road dirt bike. wen I ride my
Honda it kicks up grass. It is
clutch. and it is kick sart. And its
fast.The top speed is 45 miles per
hour, I think. But it feels like it
can go 75 miles per hour, and thats
fast for a off road dirt bike. It cost
350 dollars. It is used. It is illegal
on road. So my Dad and me have to put
it in my Dad's new Jeep cherokee.—I
have to load it in to the back of the
Jeep and lie it down on its side to
bring it some where. My Dad got it for
me because I do not have a hoby./ I
ride it in front of my house. And on
tracks. I am go to go to a motor cross
camp. Motor cross is an motor cycleing
off road sport. Becase ther are not to
meney tracks arond hear. At the motor
cross team. Thay made tracks ther and
jumps. At the camp I will race my bike
thar.It is for kids from 10 yeards old
to 14 yeards olds.

At THE stor
it took ME 3
HOURS to LEAr
to DrivE cLutc

it wighight 150.

I WAS HAPPY

I REALLE want to go to CAMP BECASE i Doi
wont to gEt CAUght BY tHE COPS
At CAMP I Dont HAVE to tAKE A RICKS

Figure 7.3 *Andrew's fourth writing piece*

the computer he was away from the conference table and I knew from previous studies the importance of being near or at the conference table in order to learn from other children. Andrew was really working in isolation when he wrote at the computer during writing workshop. I had to do something.

Finally I told him I wanted him to come to the conference table to listen to other children's drafts. I told him we needed his good ideas. He looked at me with a strange expression but he came to the table and sat near me. I heard him make a comment in a low voice. Instead of asking him to repeat it, I told the group about Andrew's suggestion. They listened and responded to it. The conversation went on until Andrew made another quiet remark which I repeated in the same way. He didn't say any more that day but I think he felt included. I made sure to invite him to the conference table at least twice a week. Soon he began to speak in a louder voice and took part in the conferences. He still would not share his own drafts although he did read a finished piece during band time when there was one other student present. Fortunately she told him all the things she liked about his story.

In my first writing evaluation conference with Andrew he told me his piece about the Honda was his best piece because he really liked it. He had drawn a detailed cover and on the bottom had pasted a picture of himself on the bike. He thought his worst piece was his first piece, "The Sky Flyer." When I asked him what kind of changes he made when he revised, he answered: "It depends. I change a word. I stop and think for a minute for a better word. Instead of 'bought' I could use 'purchased.' I add details. I take leads and stick them together and see which is the best one. I do that in my brain, not on the computer."

Andrew's comment on revising in his brain reminded me of his explanation of a math example. I had been curious about his math. He seemed to know how to do examples and often he would get many right. At other times, he made lots of mistakes. I soon realized that the mistakes were due to his difficulties with the number facts. He just did not know them. He could solve difficult problems, but it took him longer than other children. One day I asked him how he solved a particular set of problems without writing the examples on paper and he said, "My head is a sheet of paper. The problem is going through your head. It takes less time than writing it on paper." And for him that was true. Paper-and-pencil tasks took time for Andrew. He much preferred doing as much as he could in his head. I wondered if the use of the computer would change things.

Before Christmas Andrew gave me a small running shoe he had made out of clay and had fired. His parents wrote a very warm note thanking me for my efforts. They also sent a note to my principal and the superintendent. The shoe and the notes made me very happy as did comments by some of the special teachers who noticed a big difference in Andrew's attitude and behavior between fourth grade and fifth grade.

Changes

In the winter four exciting things happened. First Andrew came in early and announced that he had finished all his homework, even the math. This was the first time for him. He told me he had done most of it by himself and he seemed pleased with this accomplishment. I told him that he was taking much more responsibility for completing his work independently and that I noticed how well he was doing. He tried very hard to finish all his homework assignments for the next few weeks. There were occasional lapses when he would do all his work except the math. He still felt that math was an area that he could not do well. Rather than attempt any of the work and possibly fail, he just didn't do it and waited for me. For the remainder of the year, however, he was much more conscientious about doing his work.

The second event should not have been a surprise to me because it had happened before with other children. Andrew wrote a poem. I had been introducing similes and metaphors in my reading minilessons and the class had experimented with writing their own. I noticed Andrew was bent over his paper and seemed to be writing faster than usual. When we stopped to share some metaphors, he was still writing. When the class took out their books for reading workshop, he came up to me to ask if he could finish his metaphor. I told him he could. I watched him as he wrote, looked out the window, and wrote some more. At the end of reading workshop when the bell was about to ring for lunch, Andrew waited to show me what he had written. It was a metaphor about a window (see Figure 7.4).

I said, "You know, this could be a poem." He was curious. During writing workshop I showed him how his words could be put into poetic form. The next day when he was once again thrown out

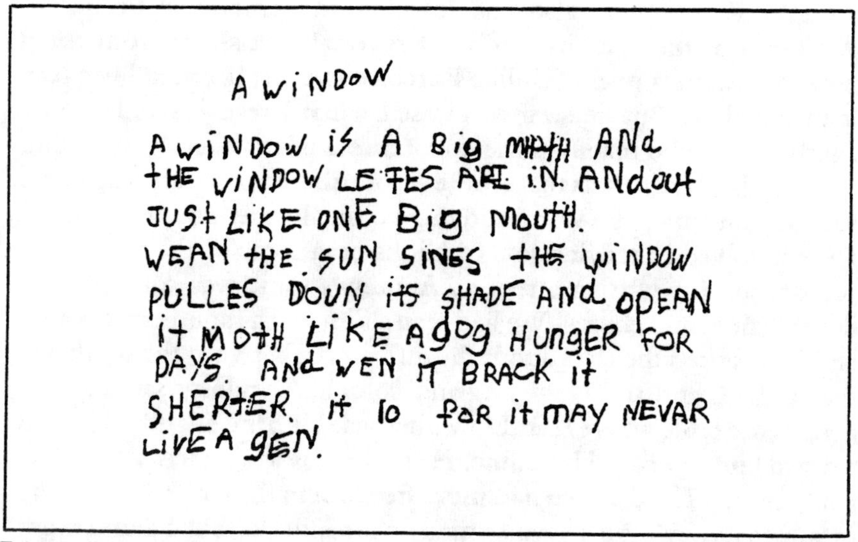

A WINDOW

A WINDOW IS A BIG MAUTH AND
THE WINDOW LETES ARE IN ANDOUT
JUST LIKE ONE BIG MOUTH.
WEAN THE SUN SINES THE WINDOW
PULLES DOUN ITS SHADE AND OPEAN
IT MOTH LIKE A DOG HUNGER FOR
DAYS. AND WEN IT BRACK IT
SHERTER. IT IO FOR IT MAY NEVAR
LIVE A GEN.

FIGURE 7.4 *Andrew's metaphor: "A Window"*

of a special class for bad behavior and was sent back in my room, he wanted to add onto his metaphor. I helped him correct the spelling and he typed his poem on the computer:

A Window

A window is a big mouth.
It lets air in and out
Just like one huge mouth.
When the sun shines
the window drops its blinds
and opens its mouth
like a dog starving for days.

A window is a watchdog
howling at the moon.
When it breaks
it shatters into ten.
For it may never
live again.

Another window has to
take its place.
But only a younger one
with a stronger face.

Like Karen, who also had learning and emotional problems, Andrew was the first child in his class to take a risk, try something new, and write a poem. Unlike Karen, however, he would not read it to the class. But he seemed pleased when I read his and one by another boy who made his metaphor into a poem after Andrew did.

The third event was that Andrew contributed to a class discussion for the first time. We were studying colonial times and the children were involved in reading lots of books on a topic of their choice in preparation for writing a report. Andrew's topic was colonial children's games and chores. We had seen a film on the southern colonies and I had asked the class about the differences between the southern, the middle, and the New England colonies. Andrew sat near the conference table where I sat. I saw him raise his hand slightly. I leaned toward him as I called his name. He said in his low voice, which few could hear, "The children had more freedom in the south." I think he meant that they didn't have as many chores to do, but I didn't want to push him for an explanation for fear he might not volunteer again. I repeated what he said and went on to another child. I think it was easier for him to respond because he sat close to the conference table and could make himself heard to me despite his soft voice. He continued to participate in discussions from that time on following the same pattern—a slight raising of his hand, his response in a low voice, and my repetition of his response for the class to hear. By February and March when we were involved in heated debates on the Constitution and especially the First Amendment, he had lots to say and he did not need me any more to repeat his words.

The fourth important event was that Andrew became friendly with two boys in the class, Brian and Eric, who were involved in class activities and were not part of the "tough" group. He seemed to move away from his previous set of friends and began to play organized games with the boys from my class on the playground. Up until this time he had spent his recess walking around with his "tough" friends. Now he was involved in basketball.

Through his friendship with Brian and Eric, Andrew became a more active member of the classroom community. He must have developed greater self-confidence and also must have trusted these two boys because he allowed himself to become involved in conferences with them. The boys shared the books they were reading and parts of their history reports. Andrew worked on math examples with Brian who sat next to him. Brian seemed to be more accurate in computation but Andrew was better at problem solving. I was amazed at the way they built on each other's strengths. They also read parts of writing pieces to each other. Both Eric and Brian recommended books to Andrew. That is how he discovered Betsy Byars and *The Not-Just-Anybody Family* (Byars 1986). He was very happy with this book because his friends were reading it or had just finished it, and it was thicker than the books he had been reading. He liked the characters and enjoyed discussing the book with his friends.

Andrew liked the book so much he read it during class while we were correcting spelling and he even took it home and finished it over a weekend! He had never read during a weekend before. When he finished the book, he tried other books that his friends recommended. However, because he read slowly he would often put those books aside and substitute a Giff book instead. At this time he didn't have to hide the book in his desk.

By the end of February Andrew was participating in more writing conferences. He would come to the table without being asked and take a seat. He still spoke in a low voice but he made many good suggestions. He offered ideas and good words and phrases for the poems children were writing. He contributed his information on colonial children's chores when another child was confused about whether children in colonial times made candles or not. Brian became involved in this discussion because he was doing a report on the same topic. Andrew and Brian began to work together to share their information.

This was the opportunity I was waiting for. I wondered if Andrew would have a conference about his draft with Brian at the computer. I suggested it. At first I could see that Andrew was reluctant. I imagined he still worried about his spelling mistakes. However, he agreed and the two boys went to the computer area where I heard Andrew reading his draft from the computer to Brian. I saw Brian leaning over pointing to places where Andrew could add information. Brian also helped Andrew with punctuation and spelling. Andrew discussed ideas for illustrations and a report cover with Brian. When Andrew finished his report at the beginning of March, he included his feelings at the end of his two chapters:

> I think chores would be boring and they take too long because back then they did not have machines to cut the hay. Now we have electric razors to shave the sheep. For boys and girls it was a rule to do chores. Now many girls and boys don't have to do chores.

> I think games today are better because we have more games like Nintendo and more sports like snow boarding. I would rather live today than in colonial times.

As Andrew became more involved with other children in writing and reading conferences, he became better able to work in groups. He now took responsibility for bringing in news for his news team. He participated to a greater extent in science activities. And he observed with interest the behavior of a few other boys in the class who were clearly the "behavior problems" of my class and my reactions to them. In fact, in our early morning sessions he would often comment on their actions, the motivation behind their behavior, and how he thought I should handle it.

However, despite the fact that Andrew was cooperative and willing to work with me, he did not show the same attitude in music class or in chorus. He was often sent back to my room during these special classes and for most of the year he denied doing anything wrong. He was finally removed permanently from chorus by Dr. Baker. This meant, of course, that I had forty minutes more to work with Andrew alone. It gave us added time to work on math computation and to catch up on history and science activities. Often though, Andrew worked on his writing pieces.

As the year progressed, my fondness for Andrew increased. At times I felt we were buddies pulling for each other, at times I felt we learned from each other, at times I was too protective, and at times I became frustrated when I gave him too much independence and he wasn't ready for it. One thing that remained constant, however, was my belief in him. I felt he had ability and that he would be able to succeed. I always emphasized the positive. I looked forward to seeing him each morning even though it meant that I had to get up a half hour earlier to get to school in time. I would not give up that morning time. Even if I had a curriculum meeting or workshop and didn't have to be at work until 9:00, I was there at 7:50. I looked forward to the times he spent in my room alone during the day even though he took away my only prep period. I worried often about what would happen to him when he went to junior high. He must have felt ambivalent too, because one morning when we were working on math, he stopped and said, "I don't want to leave and go to the junior high. I mean I want to go to the junior high but I don't want to leave my teacher." I wished I could have him for one more year because then I felt he would be more confident of his abilities and would be ready for the next grade. And I overlooked reports from other teachers about his behavior at recess and during art and music classes.

I'm sure Dr. Baker was aware of my feelings and was reluctant to tell me about Andrew's misdeeds. When he did, he would call me into his office first and tell me about the problem. Then he would ask me what I thought he should do. Usually I pleaded Andrew's case, telling him that Andrew was doing so well in class that I didn't think he should be punished severely for throwing food in the lunch room, tossing paper through the girls' room window, or breaking a spotlight. Dr. Baker would then call Andrew and the three of us would have a conference. The result was that Dr. Baker would have a long talk with Andrew but he did not deprive him of any privileges. During the spring, instead of denying his actions as he had done in the past, Andrew began to admit his part in various incidents and took responsibility for his actions, which I saw as another sign of his growth and progress. He even accepted the consequences without his usual anger and blame.

Andrew's greater independence in writing was evident when I began to give my usual series of practice tests in preparation for the state writing test. I wondered how Andrew would deal with assigned topics. He had trouble with the first practice test. He sat at the computer and told me he could not think of anything. The topic was to write about something the writer had lost. Andrew and I brainstormed for a long time. I wanted to show him how he could write about a topic even though he didn't like the topic and thought he had no ideas. We talked about combining experiences to write for a test. We talked about exaggerating details and creating an interesting beginning or ending that might not have actually happened. Finally he remembered he had lost a tape once. He was able to write a short piece about the loss of this tape but he needed constant help and prodding from me in order to finish.

The second test was surprisingly different. For this test, the writer had to imagine that he or she had found a magic carpet on the floor one morning and then describe an adventure with the carpet. It was exciting to observe Andrew. He had an idea right away and he sat at the computer and wrote all morning. He seemed to have no trouble creating his story and he included many details. I wondered if it was easier for him to write an imaginary story rather than one based on personal experience. Andrew's story started in a carpet store where his father bought a new carpet to put next to Andrew's bed. Andrew discovered the carpet had magical powers the next morning. He wrote most of the test in small letters with capital letters at the beginning of sentences. Toward the end of the piece he switched to capital letters because "those parts are important."

> The carpet took off with me on it. I was in a place 175 years from now. Stop sines were in the air by magnets. Cars were floating in the air. And I was floating on my carpet. Boys had hover boards for skate bords. For gas cars used water.
>
> A cop chased me on his hover bord because I was going slower than the speed limet. NICE LAW!
>
> I had to go back to 1990 because the cop was still chasing me. My carpet said, "I AM GETTING OUT OF HERE!. AND WE TOOK OFF!
>
> When I got home MOM GROUNDED ME FOR COMING IN LATE. THE CARPET was LAUGHING AT ME AND SAID, "I AM ALODE TO GO OUTSIDE."
>
> I SAID, "WHAT A LIFE!"

The third test, however, posed a problem for Andrew. He did not want to do it on the computer. He had done all his writing pieces on the computer since the beginning of the year. I had already made a special request to the director of student personnel to allow him to take the test on the computer. After checking with the CSE report, the director had granted my request. However, Andrew decided in March that he was going to take the test on regular paper "like all the other kids." I told him it would take too long to finish it if he wrote it by hand. He sat in his seat angrily staring at me. When I asked him what the matter was he blurted out, "What am I going to do—write everything on the computer in junior high and high school, too? Why can't I do it on paper?" When I repeated that it would be much faster on the computer than writing, revising, and copying over on paper, he said, "I don't care. I hate the computer! I can do it on paper!"

I realized again how much he wanted to be able to do what all the other students could do. Or perhaps he had developed enough confidence in himself to try to write on paper again. I knew I had to give him the chance even though I wasn't optimistic. "O.K.," I said, "Let's try it. Work on it in the morning on paper and let's see how you do." He agreed to this arrangement and spent the morning

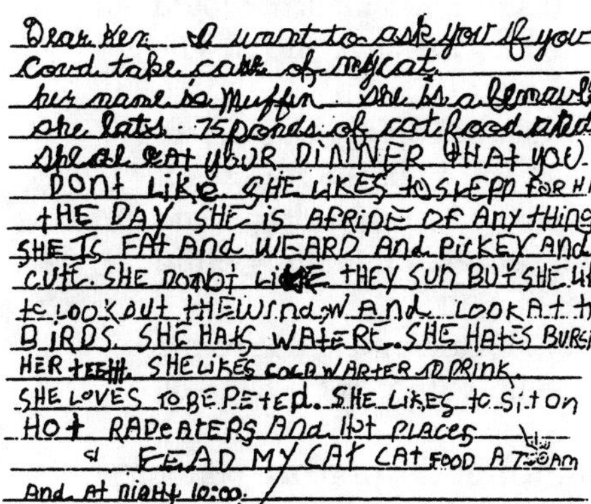

Dear ken I want to ask you if you coud take care of my cat. her name is Muffin. she is a femaull. she eats 75 ponds of cat food and sheal eat your dinner that you dont like. She likes to slepp for hf the day she is afride of any thing. She is fat and weard and pickey and cute. She do not like the they sun but she like to look out the window and look at the birds. She hats watere. She hates bursh her teeth. She like cold warter to drink. She loves to be peted. She likes to sit on hot radeaters and hot places
Fead my cat cat food a 7:00 AM and at night 10:00

Figure 7.5 *Andrew's attempt to move away from the computer*

writing and stopping to think. At noon he brought me his draft (see Figure 7.5). It was interesting to me that he wrote the first part in script but then reverted to print because "I had trouble remembering the letters in script."

In the afternoon when Andrew faced the prospect of copying the piece in pen, he returned to the computer. It was his choice. He did the remaining practice tests on the computer without any complaints. Each time he took a practice test I gave him less and less assistance. I knew he would have to take the state test with no help from me. The last practice test was one that Andrew wrote and edited by himself. When he finished it I put checks near the lines that had errors in them and he worked hard to correct the mistakes. The topic was another imaginary one about pretending to be someone else. Andrew decided to be his friend Brian:

> I was at Brian's house. I was sleeping over. When I woke up I looked in the mirror and I saw Brian's face not mine. I thought I was dreaming but I wasn't. I was as tall as Brian and I sounded like Brian.
>
> I went into Brian's room. He wasn't there. I got dressed and I went down stairs thinking what had happened. I was puzzled. I didn't know who I was. Then Brian's mom came running down the hall. When she saw me she called me Brian. She told me I was going to get my hair cut. I must be Brian I thought.

Brian's Mom and I got in the car pulled out of the driveway and left. We finally got there. I thought that I, I mean Brian, would like a mohawk because Brian saw a kid with a mohawk and said he liked it.

The barber took an electric razor and shaved off my hair except for a streak in the middle. Brian's mom sreamed but she got over it and when I got to Brian's house I was tired so I went to sleep. And in the morning I thought it was a dream because I found myself in my room and I was myself again.

It was a school day and I went to school. Brian walked in to the school with a mohawk and said he woke up with it and I fainted!

Andrew had included details and humor in the practice test and I hoped he would be able to do the same on the real test which would follow two weeks later.

May was a difficult month for me and my class. Three or four boys began acting out. They knew they had two months left in elementary school and it seemed they were prepared to stop working. They had difficulty completing assignments and didn't appear to care. They talked, threw things, destroyed property, and were cruel to each other. They caused problems in other classes and on the playground, as well. Soon the number of discipline problems grew to five or six boys. I couldn't remember if and when this had happened with previous classes.

At times the class seemed to disintegrate into chaos. I could not teach according to my philosophy but instead had to be very firm and deal with constant disruptions. Teaching was not enjoyable or rewarding but seemed a continuous struggle. I worried constantly about what I could do to restore peace and preserve the sense of community for the remainder of my class. I did not look forward to going to work. My only motivation for coming to school was my commitment to Andrew. He became my reason to teach. If it hadn't been for him I think I would have given up. He didn't know it but his presence helped me survive the last two months of school that year. I took such pleasure from his steady progress and his increasing interest and intellectual curiosity. Once again I became aware of the reciprocal nature of teaching.

May was also difficult because I had the pressure of three weeks of testing. The state writing test was given during one week, and the Stanford Achievement Tests were spread out over the following two weeks. I had to keep the class motivated to do their best on these tests. It was not an easy task.

The week before the writing test Andrew was in trouble again. This time he and another child in my class had hurled wads of wet toilet paper through the doors and windows of the rooms of teachers they didn't like. It took three days before the first child was caught. He then implicated Andrew who admitted his part in the crime. Gone were the days of denial, I hoped. When I asked him why he did it, he answered, "For revenge. Those teachers always hated me." His answer bothered me because I felt there was no sense of remorse, no feeling that what he did was wrong. In fact he firmly believed that what he had done was fair.

Fortunately something good came out of the incident. He was able to use it on the writing test the following week. When he addressed the topic of a remembered day in school, Andrew wrote about "A Bad Day." He told of being thrown out of a special class because he was talking "to ask a question." He described his visit to the boys' room and his plan to throw wet toilet paper. "I thout I shoud to get reveng for kicking me out. So I did. I threw two wet pieces of toilet paper." He went on to explain how he spent time in the office. He also combined some other incidents that had happened during the year into his piece to make the day an especially bad one.

He wrote by himself and seemed absorbed for a long time. I paced around the room hoping all my students would do well but my concern was for Andrew. I wanted him to do well so he would know he could do it. I needn't have worried. He scored a 12 out of a possible 16 points with 8 as the passing grade.

Andrew told me that he wanted to do well on the achievement tests because he knew the scores went to the junior high. He was not required to take all thirteen parts of the test and the parts he did take were to be untimed. He wanted to take all of the test and was angry when I told him he was only going to take four sections. I did not want him to struggle through reading pages and pages of questions in social studies and science. I thought he would do the first few pages and then tire. And I certainly did not want to inflict the spelling section on him. Spelling caused him enough frustration in his daily life. I gave him parts of the math test during our early morning sessions and he started the reading, vocabulary, and listening comprehension with the class. Although I don't pay much attention to standardized test scores because I'm not sure what they really indicate,

I was pleased to see that Andrew had tested above grade level on all of the tests that he took (seventh-grade level in reading comprehension and listening comprehension, eighth-grade level in vocabulary, and ninth-grade level in math). I hoped the test results would relieve his worried parents who, although very pleased with his progress in fifth grade, still showed great concern about their son's future in junior high.

In June Andrew wrote his last writing piece. It was a story about his first-grade partner whom he had worked with throughout the year. This had been a good experience for Andrew, because he began to care about this younger child. When I saw them working together, I thought back to the beginning of the year when Andrew used to threaten little children. How different he was now. Would his new attitude last? I wondered.

His story was written on the computer and after we printed it, we enlarged the type so Andrew could paste it into the book he had made. Andrew illustrated the text with care. He worked on this book for many days making sure everything was done neatly. When it was time to read the stories to the first-grade class, I wondered what Andrew would do. He had not read any of his writing pieces to my class. Would he be able to read this story to a combined group of fifth and first graders? I remembered Angela. She, too, had not read anything to her peers and yet, when it was time to read the first-grade stories, she had read hers. Would Andrew do the same?

He asked me if he had to read his story. "You could read it to the whole group or you could read it to your first grader alone," I answered. He decided to read it to his first grader alone and we arranged a time when he would read it. The next day when the class went down to the first-grade classroom to listen to three or four fifth graders read their stories, he told me that he would read his story to the whole group. Once again I realized how important it was for him to be part of the class, to be the same, to be able to do the same things. Was it that he did not want to be different even if it meant overcoming his embarrassment and lack of confidence in his reading ability? Or was it, instead, that he had developed enough confidence in his reading and writing abilities and now wanted to share his accomplishment? He certainly was very proud of the finished product. He read his story, quickly and in a low voice. I imagine his first grader who sat next to him was the only one who heard it. Fortunately the other children seemed to know not to ask him to slow down and read in a louder voice. They listened and they clapped as they had for the other readers. When he finished he solemnly gave me his book to put in the pile which would become part of the library's picture-book collection. I had a feeling he was trying hard not to smile.

During the last week of school Andrew evaluated his writing and his reading. He explained how to be a good writer: "I write on the topic. I try not to go off it. You should be more open, be more willing to try new things like different topics." He told me that he liked a piece he wrote on learning how to drive a bike that had a clutch the best. "It was my topic," he said, "I liked writing about it. I couldn't really stop writing because there were lots of details. I like riding my motorcycle. It was my topic." He had discovered the importance of a good topic and realized that writing was easier when he was familiar with that topic. When he described his progress in reading, Andrew wrote, "I like reading alot better in five grade because it is longer and funner and there are better books."

Two days before school ended Andrew gave me a Siamese cat that he and his father had made out of clay, painted, and fired. It was the size of a real kitten and it even looked like a real kitten, so real in fact that my two Siamese cats were puzzled and unnerved by its presence in my apartment. I told him how much I loved it. I placed it next to the running shoe he had made for me earlier.

The last day of school was an emotional one for me. Andrew and his parents came in early in the morning. The parents thanked me for making fifth grade such a positive experience for Andrew. When they left Andrew helped me fold the end-of-the-year letters I had written to each child. We continued our usual early morning chatter. I wondered what it would be like next year when I faced my empty classroom instead of finding Andrew waiting for me on the steps.

How could I say good-bye to this child? How could I let him go to the impersonal world of the junior high? Was he ready? When I assessed his progress I knew he was better able to work independently. He had developed greater self-confidence through the success he experienced academically. He could work well with his peers and he had formed positive relationships. He took responsibility for his behavior and realized the consequences of his actions. Was this enough for him to make it? Or would the threat of that special school hover over him once again?

I could deal with saying good-bye only by believing that Andrew and I would continue our partnership in some way, that we'd stay in touch if only through memories. He described his most important memory of elementary school for the fifth-grade yearbook:

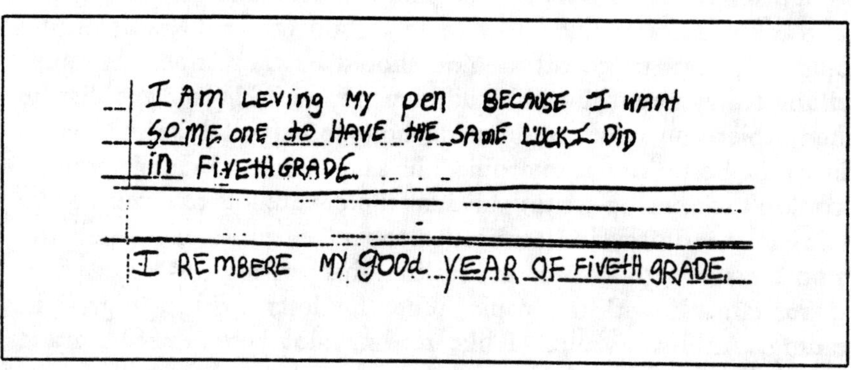

I Am LEVing MY pen BECAUSE I WANT
SOME ONE to HAVE THE SAME LUCK I DID
in FIVETH GRADE.

I REMBERE MY good YEAR OF FIVETH GRADE.

I would remember Andrew's good year in fifth grade, too, and be grateful that we turned that last chance into a new beginning.

8

Conclusion

Implications for teaching special needs children in the classroom

THROUGH MY READINGS, instruction I had received, and my role as a teacher researcher I developed theories about teaching children with special needs. My subsequent study of these children confirmed my theories. My study of Angela provided me with a background that I could use in my work with other students. Each study extended my knowledge. I realized from my case studies that special students—whether they were labeled ESL, gifted, behavioral problems, learning disabled, emotionally disabled, or a combination of these—could be worked with in much the same way and could achieve success beyond expectations. Despite their varying degrees of language deficits, these students became writers. The self-confidence they developed from their writing spread to other areas of the curriculum, enabling them to become more fully involved in class activities.

Certain elements were necessary to insure these writers' success: a literate, supportive classroom environment, one that immersed students in oral and written language; the development of communities of writers, readers, and learners; response from peers and the teacher; alternate communication systems; time; expectations; and ownership of ideas.

All of the special students I studied came into fifth grade with poor self-images, both academically and socially. They did not take their academic work and learning seriously. None felt comfortable with peers. For years Karen, Peter, Andrew, and Greg, to some extent, had been disruptive, establishing reputations for themselves among teachers and peers as behavior problems, children to be avoided. Angela, Mark, Tomoko, and Yasuo started the year as quiet, passive students who might easily have remained unnoticed. However, the stories of all these children show they were all able to grow and change, develop greater self-esteem, and achieve academic success and some measure of social acceptance. The first step in this development occurred through the process approach to writing.

In the beginning all of the children (with the exception of Greg) had difficulty with writing. They did not take writing workshop seriously. Unsure of themselves and unsure of what they could do in the workshop setting, they viewed it as a block of unstructured time in which not much was expected, a time to fulfill their own needs. Most felt they had no ideas. They were unable to focus on a topic or to participate in writing conferences. However, because their desks were near the conference table, I believe that they listened and observed and sensed the respect for ideas that was part of the classroom environment. This respect and enthusiasm for everyone's ideas eventually enabled these special students to become involved, to take risks, and to enter the community of writers. Through conferences, they realized the value of response for their own revision. Once they had made that discovery, they were able to participate in conferences and even help others with their questions and suggestions.

I also think that through this immersion in reading, writing, speaking, and listening, the children slowly became aware of the importance and power of language for themselves.

Classroom environment

In the classroom environment, students' ideas were valued and they were treated with respect. This type of environment was especially crucial for these learners. Rhodes and Dudley-Marling also stress the importance of environment: "The environments within which students learn will affect what they learn, how they learn, and how they feel about learning" (1988, 95). As my students began to trust in the reliability of the classroom environment, they started to take risks with me, with their peers, and, most important, with their own minds. It was in this environment that I was able to discover Greg. He made me aware that gifted learners are special, too, because they are often not challenged. He needed the freedom to make his own choices and create his own challenges—challenges that may not have been part of a traditional teacher-directed environment.

All of the students felt free to experiment in this environment with topics, genres, leads, and vocabulary, despite problems they had with mechanics. Eventually they were able to recognize the importance of expressing their ideas and were able to put their concerns about skills such as spelling, punctuation, and handwriting in the background.

In this environment many of the students explored different genres, often leading the way for the rest of the class. Karen, Andrew, Tomoko, and Greg drew their peers into the realm of poetry, which proved to be a powerful form of expression for these special ten-year-olds. Poetry allowed all of my students freer thought, but especially my ESL children and those with learning disabilities. The more flexible rules for grammar and usage enabled these students to express themselves in a more manageable form. Words didn't have to fill every line and poems were not as lengthy as stories. As Andrew explained to me, "A poem is shorter. It just comes into your mind. A story takes longer. You have to write a lot on the topic." Poetry also seemed to require much less revision. For many of my students poetry enabled them to express deep emotion and complex ideas in relatively few words.

As these students felt the freedom to write and began to take more control over their writing, their interest in reading increased. They selected their own books and began to wonder about authors. They tried to imitate authors' techniques in their own writing. They shared recommendations for books and talked about those they had read. They looked for feelings, for believable characters, and for interesting words, and they were delighted with effective dialogue. Their enthusiasm was infectious: I was constantly drawn into their discussions and especially their thinking, as I became more and more involved in their reading and their responses to books.

Reading, in turn, had a dramatic effect on their writing. Karen began writing poetry as a result of reading and listening to poetry.

Andrew, too, wrote poems that stemmed from recognizing similes and metaphors in familiar books. Tomoko's connections to characters in books freed her to write, to find topics, to discover her own wonderful ideas. And Greg's search for meaning in his own writing came from his immersion in the books and authors he loved.

I began to see the strong influence of reading. Again my journey as a teacher paralleled my students' progress. Reading and writing became part of everything I taught. And as a result I saw that each of my special children achieved greater independence as learners. They read and wrote in all areas. They experimented and took risks with new concepts in science and social studies and were motivated to do more of their work on their own in all areas.

Response

Response to writing is necessary for all writers but seems to be especially important for children with special needs. Becoming part of writing conferences was critical for these children. Despite the children's individual personality problems (Mark, Angela, Tomoko, and Andrew's insecurity and shyness; Peter and Karen's disruptiveness; Greg's critical nature and sensitivity), they were all accepted as part of the writing community. This happened as a result of participating in conferences. The social problems they had with their peers on the playground never intruded on or entered the writing community. The other children supported and encouraged them as they did with all their classmates with positive comments in response to their writing pieces. And they respected and listened to the comments the special needs children made in response to the writing of their peers. All of the children became aware that they could learn and benefit from the response they received from each other.

Karen realized her own need for response in order to revise and improve her piece. She told me: "Conferences help you get out of a stuck situation and into a good lead and a good ending. By listening to someone else's good lead, it gives you ideas for your own. I learned to start my leads with conversation." She came to the conference table almost daily and gradually began to shift her dependence on me to her group of peers.

Conferences generated and extended ideas for Greg and he learned to accept and respect the ideas of others. Mark, Peter, and Angela also benefited from the response they received from peers. Mark was pleased when collaboration helped him come up with a lead and a title that he liked. Peter's involvement in the writing process was only through conferences at first. A conference every day seemed to insure his attention to his writing. Listening to and discussing the writing pieces of other students gave him ideas and helped him understand how to focus his own work. Angela, through the response she received about her first attempts at fiction, was able to write in another genre. Andrew was pleased when he realized he could contribute and help others with his ideas. For Tomoko and Yasuo, conferences were places where they could feel safe and included as they experimented with expressing themselves in English. For Tomoko, writing conferences were especially important, because it was the one time where she felt accepted by the girls in the class.

Stires (1983) also found that supportive response was a key factor in helping disabled writers. She observed in her studies that this type of writer needed the positive involvement of peers or the teacher to solve writing problems. Once confident of supportive response, these writers then were particularly aware of the benefits of peer feedback.

The sharing of published or completed pieces is another vital part of the writing process. For some children who felt particularly vulnerable and inadequate, sharing their works did not come until the end of the year. For others, group sharing was at first another way to command attention but, as the year progressed, it became a time to communicate in a more positive, rewarding way.

Eventually all of the children enjoyed sharing their writing pieces and were especially happy with the comments they received. For Karen, Greg, and Peter, the kinds of comments made to them taught them in turn how to respond to other students' pieces. Although Angela, Andrew, Mark, and Yasuo did not share their writing until the end of the year, they, too, learned how to respond by listening to other students responding to each other.

Another benefit of sharing for these special students was that as they listened to classmates' pieces, they began to form ideas about the qualities of good writing. They realized what they liked and what was effective. Through our sharing times they began to learn how to evaluate their own writing and establish goals for themselves.

The special students in particular began to depend on the conference for their involvement in writing. It was their way of becoming part of the community of writers. This was a new experience for all of them and they began to learn not only about writing but also about group interaction. They were able to transfer what they learned at the conference table and during sharing time to other collaborative learning settings.

Talk

Many of these children needed exposure to alternative communication systems. They used various other strategies to make meaning: art work, discussions in small groups, simulations, and mapping. However, at first, talking proved to be the most effective way they could express their ideas. It became necessary for each of these children to discuss their ideas before they could write. This seemed to confirm Jagger's (quoted in Marino 1988) idea that talking is the bridge between reading and writing. Talking may have been Karen's strategy for solving her sequencing problems. Talking was effective in helping her figure out the sequence for her fiction story and her content writing about colonial times. Although I gave her little help, I did give her reassurance. It seemed to be what she needed to make small steps from dependence on adults to greater independence.

Talk was also significant for Mark and Peter. Once I turned their desire to talk into a collaborative learning effort, their "kid" talk became "learning" talk. Pairing them up with other students proved to be effective. These pairs helped and taught each other.

Greg realized the value of talk early in the year not only in regard to writing but reading as well.

Angela and Andrew had to talk first before they could write. Talking was a starting point for interacting with and learning from other children. They, Tomoko, and Yasuo continued to learn from classmates when they gathered information for their colonial report. Talking with and listening to peers who had read extensively about colonial schools provided these students with information that they were not able to get themselves from reading but could include in their reports. Talking and working with other students gave all of these students greater self-confidence and helped bring them into my community of learners.

Time

Time is another important ingredient for the special student. Often this type of learner has not thought of himself or herself as an achiever. He or she has not been able to perform to the same extent at the same rate as other learners. Special students, like all other students, need time to value themselves as writers and readers and time to become part of the writing/reading community. They need time to think, to wonder, to reflect, and to try out ideas and discover themselves. This process does not involve a fast lesson or two. It takes time and progress can be slow. Mark, Angela, and Andrew, in particular, needed the freedom and much time to experiment and take risks and it had to happen at their own pace. Not only was time important but timing as well. Through my studies as a teacher researcher, I became aware that children do not change quickly and that their changes are often very subtle. It is necessary to look for growth over time. Support for this type of learner can come from the time given to grow and develop at his or her own rate.

Expectations

Atwell (1988) found in her study of a special education student that expectations on the part of the teacher and classmates were important. Expectations can provide the child with a new self-image. I found that to be true with my studies. When these students had worked on a one-to-one basis with an aide, there had been few or low expectations set for them. They worked on isolated skills in an isolated setting. Their specialized program was based on what they didn't know and what they couldn't do. They didn't expect much of themselves and neither did anyone else. I found when these children were in the classroom context working on meaningful activities with their peers, they set the same expectations for themselves as the other children set. I also had positive expectations for them, expectations based on their strengths. I never felt that they couldn't succeed so I never excluded them from any assignments, activities, or projects. I always believed they could achieve and I respected their ideas and early attempts and built on them. I think they sensed my confidence in them and my expectations became theirs.

In the beginning Karen's and Mark's response to most academic endeavors was "I don't know," "I don't know how," or "I can't." But gradually they began to see that they could. School reports indicated all the things these special learners couldn't do and recommended an abbreviated curriculum. However, I found in the right environment with positive expectations from me and the class, they were able to accomplish what the other students did.

For example, contrary to reports, Karen could listen, focus, and organize her oral communication, which turned out to be her greatest strength. She was able to recognize relationships and make inferences. She did not have to dictate her responses to an aide, although it was necessary for her to rehearse her ideas before she could write. And assignments in writing did not have to be shortened. Her writing evaluation conferences demonstrated that she could evaluate her progress and set expectations for herself. She knew that once she was able to attend to meaning, her new goals were to improve in mechanics, specifically spelling and punctuation. To spell and punctuate correctly had special meaning for her now. She wanted to learn so that her writing could be read and understood by others. And despite her poor motor ability, her handwriting began to improve, perhaps through the amount and kind of writing she was doing. Graves (1983) says, "If children have enough writing time, and are in control of their topics, their handwriting improves" (178). Karen was also motivated by her peers. She wanted her handwriting to look like the handwriting of the other fifth graders. Her progress is just one example of what happened with all these children.

Ownership

Ownership of ideas is one of the most exciting parts of the writing-process approach. And while this concept is very important to every student writer, it seems to be crucial for children with special needs. At the beginning these students had great difficulty with selecting a topic and making decisions about revision. They had not been encouraged or allowed to make decisions before this time. Angela's aide decided what she could and would learn. Because of Karen's behavior, the adults surrounding her had made decisions for her in and out of school.

As these special writers developed a sense of ownership of their ideas, they began to take responsibility for their writing and learning. They learned skills in a holistic, meaningful way. They created the text and, because there was a personal investment, they were ready to learn skills when needed. They made choices about their learning and wrote and read in many contexts. From this sense of control or authority over their work came greater independence. They became proud of their efforts and enjoyed sharing their writing with the class. Through the response they received, they began to gain confidence not only as writers but as learners. They realized they had ideas and opinions that were valued which enhanced their self esteem. Being part of a community of writers and receiving peer response and support were important aspects of this development. They were included and no longer felt different.

In the past these special students had worked separately with an aide on specific skills through meaningless drill. The aide did not build on prior experience or allow time for the child to think and verbalize ideas. Often the aide provided the ideas—the answers—taking the ownership away from the student and fostering increased dependence on the adult. All of the students let the aides do much of the work when they worked with them during the first part of the year. I began to see that once the aide gave the child the answers, the child gave up or did not take risks with his or her own ideas.

These special students discovered that they had ideas, that they could gain respect through their ideas, that they could be taken seriously. It happened first through writing. As they experimented with their ideas on paper during writing workshop, their self-confidence increased. Gradually they began to explore their ideas in reading, history, and science. They began to realize that no longer was there one right answer. Different ideas for reading and writing were acceptable. Through the process approach to writing, which fosters interaction with other writers and readers, all of the special students were able to solve many of their learning and social problems.

How special students affected me

My own story was filled with highs and lows. I was excited and rejuvenated as I began to learn with and from my students. The classroom became a special and challenging place to be. I "felt" the environment each morning as I took out my key and opened the door to what seemed like an empty room. Despite my students' absence early in the morning, the room was filled with them—their writing, their reading, their notes to each other and to me, the messiness that made the room creative and "theirs." And to my satisfaction my special students were very much a part of that room. Suddenly "special" didn't seem to be applicable anymore, because at some point all children had become special children to me; they all thrived under similar conditions.

The studies of these particular children taught me much but my studies were not without difficulties. When I tried to involve the school specialists in these students' progress, I was not always successful. Often I felt lonely and isolated. I needed someone with whom I could discuss my students' progress. For Mark there were specific skills help and suggestions, but I was still left to my own resources to provide an environment that was conducive to his learning. When I had difficulties with Mark's aide, I was on my own to figure out solutions until finally, in desperation, I turned to my principal. With Peter, I felt entirely alone. True, the skills teachers scheduled him and tried to fill in the academic gaps, but help, advice, and support were unavailable when it came to my attempts to have him become an integral part of the community of learners that had formed in my room. I learned through readings I found, different approaches I tried, and through my network of friends who were also involved in teacher research. Fortunately when I had Karen and Andrew, I was able to apply what I learned from working with Peter.

My story also includes tremendous personal involvement with all of my students, although I do not think this kind of commitment is necessary for special students to succeed. A language-rich environment demands a lot of work but it does not always require devoting the extra time I did to individual children. My additional commitment and dedication came from my own interest and involvement in teacher research. Bissex says, "Problems can become questions to investigate, occasions for learning rather than lamenting" (1987, 4). Instead of lamenting and viewing these children as problems, I began to look closely at what each student was able to do and I worked hard to insure success.

Mark, Angela, Greg, and Yasuo were able to flourish in the environment I provided. Peter, Karen, Andrew, and Tomoko were different stories. As I struggled to help them learn and become part of my community of learners, they became part of my life. I thought about ways to support them during school, on the weekends, and always on my daily run. I needed the time I set aside to jog for reflection, to take stock of what was actually happening in my classroom. Like my students I needed time to think. It was only then that I could reflect back to previous studies of children, plan solutions to problems, and assess progress. All of these children had become special to me. Their successes became mine too, and I suffered with their failures. But like my special needs children, I realized that these feelings of frustration and defeat were limited in time and manageable, and that success would eventually follow.

The stories of these fifth graders are finished. Mine is not. It continues. Each year brings new students, new revelations, new ideas to examine, because each year there are questions to ponder, special voices to hear, and so much to learn.

Postscript

I think the importance of these studies lies in the implication for the teaching of children with special needs. What I have found is that despite learning and emotional problems, these students are able to grow and develop as writers, make continued progress as learners and solve some of their emotional and social problems within the classroom. Think of the possibilities! However, is one year in this type of classroom enough?

Lisa, a learning disabled girl, whose story is not presented here, told me at the beginning of fifth grade that she wanted to be a hairdresser when she grew up. She could then leave school when she was sixteen. "You don't have to finish high school or go to college," she explained. By the middle of fifth grade when she had discovered herself as a writer and reader, a confident person with ideas, she told me she had decided to become a writer and looked forward to college. She left fifth grade feeling secure and happy. In November she returned from sixth grade at the junior high for a visit. Her happy buoyant self had disappeared. She had decided she would become a hairdresser again. I couldn't help but wonder if Lisa's aspirations and newfound confidence in herself as a writer and learner could have been maintained if her new classroom environment had included the ingredients that allowed her to emerge as a person who experienced success and joy in learning.

Works Cited

ALEXANDER, L. 1981. *Westmark*. New York: Dutton.

ATWELL, NANCIE. 1988. "A Special Writer at Work." In *Understanding Writing: Ways of Observing, Learning, and Teaching,* ed. Thomas Newkirk and Nancie Atwell, 114–29. Portsmouth, N.H.: Heinemann.

———. 1987. *In the Middle*. Portsmouth, N.H.: Boynton/Cook.

———. 1984. "Writing and Reading Literature from the Inside Out." *Language Arts* 61:240–52.

———. 1982. "Class-based Writing Research: Teachers Learn from Students." *English Journal* 71:81–87.

BABBITT, NATALIE. 1975. *Tuck Everlasting*. New York: Farrar, Straus & Giroux.

BISSEX, GLENDA, and RICHARD BULLOCK, eds. 1987. *Seeing for Ourselves: Case-Study Research by Teachers of Writing*. Portsmouth, N.H.: Heinemann.

BLUME, JUDY. 1980. *Superfudge*. New York: Dutton.

———. 1972. *Tales of a Fourth Grade Nothing*. New York: Dutton.

BRUNER, JEROME. 1960. *The Process of Education*. Cambridge, Mass.: Harvard University Press.

BYARS, BETSY. 1986. *The Not-Just-Anybody Family*. New York: Delacorte.

CAMERON, A. 1988. *Julian, Secret Agent*. New York: Random House.

———. 1987. *More Stories Julian Tells*. New York: Random House.

———. 1986. *The Stories Julian Tells*. New York: Random House.

CLEARY, BEVERLY. 1972. *Socks*. New York: Morrow.

DAHL, ROALD. 1961. *James and the Giant Peach*. New York: Knopf.

DELTON, J. 1988. *Camp Ghost Away*. Pee Wee Scouts Series. New York: Dell.

FIVE, CORA. 1989. "A Garden of Poets." In *Workshop I,* ed. Nancie Atwell. 61–71 Portsmouth, N.H.: Heinemann.

———. 1986. "Fifth Graders Respond to a Changed Reading Program." *Harvard Educational Review* 56:395–405.

FIVE, CORA, and MARTHA ROSEN. 1985. "Children Recreate History in Their Own Voices." *Breaking Ground: Teachers Relate Reading and Writing in the Elementary School,* ed. Jane Hansen, Thomas Newkirk, and Donald Graves, 91–96. Portsmouth, N.H.: Heinemann.

GIACOBBE, M. E. 1986. "Learning to Write and Writing to Learn in the Elementary School." *The Teaching of Writing: 85th Yearbook of the National Society for the Study of Education*. 85.2. Ed. Anthony R. Petrosky and David Bartholomae. Chicago: Univ. of Chicago Press. 131–147.

GIACOBBE, M. E. 1985. "Reading, Writing, Thinking, Learning." Course offered through the Institute on Writing and Teaching, sponsored by Northeastern University. Martha's Vineyard, Mass., July.

GIFF, P. 1986. *Pickle Puss*. New York: Dell.

GRAVES, DONALD. 1983. *Writing: Teachers and Children at Work*. Portsmouth, N.H.: Heinemann.

HARSTE, JEROME C. 1985. *Creativity and Intentionality*. Course offered through the Institute on Writing and Teaching, sponsored by Northeastern University. Martha's Vineyard, Mass. July.

HARSTE, JEROME C., Virginia A. Woodward, and Carolyn L. Burke. 1984. *Language Stories and Literacy Lessons*. Portsmouth, N.H.: Heinemann.

KING-SMITH, D. 1987. *Babe, the Gallant Pig*. New York: Dell.

MACLACHLAN, PATRICIA. 1985. *Sarah, Plain and Tall*. New York: Harper & Row.

MARINO, MARIANNE. 1988. "Pursuing Knowledge by Making Yourself an Expert in One Topic at a Time." Paper presented at NCTE Spring Conference, Boston, Mass.

NEWKIRK, THOMAS, and NANCIE ATWELL, eds. 1988. *Understanding Writing: Ways of Observing, Learning, and Teaching*. Portsmouth, N.H.: Heinemann.

PATERSON, KATHERINE. 1977. *Bridge to Terabithia*. New York: Crowell.

RHODES, LYNN K., and CURT DUDLEY-MARLING. 1988. *Readers and Writers with a Difference*. Portsmouth, N.H.: Heinemann.

STIRES, SUSAN. 1988. "Reading and Talking: 'Special' Readers Show They Know." *Understanding Writing: Ways of Observing, Learning, and Teaching,* ed. Thomas Newkirk and Nancie Atwell, 207–15. Portsmouth, N.H.: Heinemann.

———1983. "Disabled Writers: A Positive Approach." *Teaching All the Children to Write,* ed. James L. Collins, 29–37. New York State English Council.

WALT DISNEY PRODUCTIONS, 1979. *The Love Bug*. New York: Random House.

WEIS, M., and T. HICKMAN. 1985. *Dragonlance Chronicles*. New York: Random.

YOLEN, J. 1982. *Dragon's Blood*. New York: Delacorte.